282
Woo

17310

The Consolations of

Catholicism

282
Woo

17310

The Consolations of
Catholicism

DEMCO

Editor Ralph Woods explains that the purpose of this unusual treasury is to spell out:

how and why the actual *living out* of Catholic beliefs gives one serenity and spiritual poise that nothing else can.

Woods, a noted Catholic anthologist of the 1940s and '50s, does this by collecting into one volume some of the most overlooked, yet uplifting writings from saints and other inspired Catholic authors.

"Animating, sustaining...express the glory of God's love as reflected in the teachings of holy men, those who have felt what the Psalmist meant when he said, 'Taste and see what the Lord is sweet.'" — *Ave Maria*

THE CONSOLATIONS OF CATHOLICISM

By the Editor of

A TREASURY OF CATHOLIC THINKING

A TREASURY OF THE FAMILIAR

A TREASURY OF INSPIRATION

The
Consolations
of Catholicism

Compiled and Edited by

RALPH L. WOODS

ROMAN CATHOLIC BOOKS
P.O. Box 2286
Ft. Collins, CO 80522-2286

NIHIL OBSTAT:
Carolus E. Diviney
Censor Librorum

IMPRIMATUR:
✠ Thomas Edmundus Molloy, S.T.D.
Archiepiscopus–
Episcopus Brooklyniensis

BROOKLYNII
Die xxix Iunii, 1954

ACKNOWLEDGMENTS

The editor and the publisher thank the following copyright owners, publishers and authors for their fine cooperation in granting permission to include in this book passages from the following works:

GEORGE ALLEN AND UNWIN LTD: Hilaire Belloc's *The Path to Rome.*

BENEDICTINE CONVENT OF PERPETUAL ADORATION, Clyde, Mo.: *Treasures of the Mass,* published 1936. BENZIGER BROTHERS, INC.: Edward F.

publishers, Charles Scribner's Sons. SHEED AND WARD, INC.: Ronald A. Knox's *A Retreat for Priests,* copyright, 1946, Sheed and Ward, Inc., New York; P. R. Regamey's *Poverty,* translated by Rosemary Sheed, copyright, 1949, Sheed and Ward, Inc., New York; William Lawson's *For Goodness Sake,* copyright, 1951, Sheed and Ward, Inc., New York; Caryll Houselander's *Guilt,* copyright, 1951, Sheed and Ward, Inc., New York; Caryll Houselander's *The Reed of God,* copyright, 1944, Sheed and Ward, Inc., New York; St. Teresa of Avila's *The Interior Castle,* translated by Allison Peers, published by Sheed and Ward, Inc., New York; Alfred Wilson's *Pardon and Peace,* copyright, 1947, Sheed and Ward, Inc., New York; Maisie Ward's *The Splendor of the Rosary,* copyright, 1945, Sheed and Ward, Inc., New York; Maurice Zundel's *The Splendour of the Liturgy,* published by Sheed and Ward, Inc., New York; Gerald Vann's *The Divine Pity,* copyright, 1946, Sheed and Ward, Inc., New York; Ronald A. Knox's *God and the Atom,* copyright, 1945, Sheed and Ward, Inc., New York; M. C. D'Arcy's *The Nature of Belief,* published by Sheed and Ward, Inc., New York; Henry Perrin's *Priest-Workmen in Germany,* copyright, 1948, Sheed and Ward, Inc., New York; Russell Wilbur's *Essays and Verses,* copyright, 1940, Sheed and Ward, Inc., New York; Dom Hubert Van Zeller's *We Live With Our Eyes Open,* copyright, 1949, Sheed and Ward, Inc., New York; Romano Guardini's *The Church and the Catholic* and *The Spirit of the Liturgy* (two vols. published as one), published by Sheed and Ward, Inc., New York; Dom John Chapman's *Spiritual Letters,* edited by Roger Huddleston, published by Sheed and Ward, Inc., New York. THE SODALITY OF OUR LADY, *The Queen's Work,* St. Louis, Mo.: Richard L. Rooney's *Our Gifted Selves,* copyright, 1947, *The Queen's Work.* THE STRATFORD COMPANY: James J. Walsh's *A Catholic Looks at Life,* copyright, 1928, The Stratford Company.

It is also a pleasure to acknowledge valuable suggestions from Patricia Joan Woods, and from Rita Keckeissen and Joan O'Callaghan of the excellent St. Peter's Catholic Lending Library, New York, N.Y. and from Dorothy Sorg of the equally fine St. John's Library Forum, New York, N.Y. Patricia Schartle of the publisher's editorial staff pointed out several omissions which would have been glaring had they remained undetected. Lillias Watt Woods helped check manuscript and the Index.

R. L. W.

Port Washington, N.Y.

To
Paul R. Lightfoot

Come to me all you that labour and are burdened; and I will refresh you.

St. Matthew 11:28

He Who has His House very high in a secret place, hath also on earth a tabernacle. His tabernacle on earth is the Church. It is here that He is to be sought.

St. Augustine, *Ennaration on Psalm XLI*

Catholicism . . . is a life to be lived and a means—the only means—to live that life.

Rev. Philip Hughes, *The Faith in Practice*

PREFACE

THE GENESIS of a book is, no doubt, of greater interest to its author or editor than to its readers.

However, I believe I can more effectively indicate the objective I have had in mind for this volume by briefly relating how it came about.

It all began several years ago when my merely casual interest in Catholic thinking on contemporary questions gradually became so intense that I felt impelled—although with considerable trepidation—to turn from strictly secular books to the compiling of *A Treasury of Catholic Thinking*.

At about midway in my work on the *Thinking* book I knew I must follow it with this companion volume of equally meritorious writings that tell what Catholicism means to the *individual*—how it influences, affects and enriches the *individual's spiritual life*.

This book, therefore, developed quite naturally from the previous volume. The *Catholic Thinking* book sets forth the Church's position on such vital problems of the day as Capitalism, War, Marriage, Education, Democracy, Labor, the State, Secularism, Free Will, Freedom, Science, etc. It is primarily concerned with Catholic truths, philosophy and theories as they apply to contemporary life. Consequently, the Church's solutions of the individual's problems and needs were inevitably and necessarily left to another book; specifically to this book.

I was further stimulated to get moving on the present book while reading the fifth-century Roman philosopher Boethius' *Consolations of Philosophy,* one of the hardiest of literary perennials. It occurred to me that the book then beginning to germinate in my mind should tell of all the greater, deeper and more enduring *Consolations of Catholicism.* This gave me the direction— the prescription, if you will—which I was seeking for the new book I had decided to do.

This is not to ignore or dismiss the uncounted hundreds of truly fine and often great books of consolation written during the past nineteen hundred years by Catholics of great learning and even greater saintliness. As a matter of obvious fact, but for these treasures of spiritual reading I could not even have begun to compile the present volume. It just seemed to me desirable that a single book should attempt—however rashly—to tell of all or most of the *consolations* the Catholic Church offers to the individual, and to do so with an absence of theological abstractions and a minimum of apologetics.

Perhaps I can make myself still clearer by saying that I have been most concerned to show how Catholic beliefs and teachings, the Church's principles and practices, can and do penetrate and activate a man's very soul and thereby persuade and guide it to that eternal happiness which each of us instinctively yearns for.

Consequently, I have not been concerned to have this book state what Catholics believe, but rather how and why the actual living of these beliefs gives one serenity and spiritual poise that the world cannot give.

In pursuing my objective I came to the pleasant realization that the material in this book at the same time emphasizes a seldom-recognized aspect of Catholicism, *i.e.,* its affirmative nature. This, many readers may very well find themselves saying, is a positive religion—productive and creative as a religion of sterile negation can never be.

Moreover, I believe this volume helpfully reminds us that Catholicism is—as Father Philip Hughes so well puts it—"a life to be lived and a means—the only means —to live that life."

Someone with more cleverness than knowledge has said that the Catholic Faith is a tough one to live in but a good one to die in. The contents of this book effectively refute this shallow saying by detailing both the *here and now* rewards of Catholicism and the inestimable eternal rewards. Thus, the so often stressed demands and commands of the Church—for which crocodile tears are shed by some of our so compassionate friends—are here abundantly counterbalanced by the rewards the Catholic Faith showers on those who are true to it.

From what I have thus far said some readers may fear that this is a sternly forbidding spiritual book, and therefore back away from it under the mistaken impression that it explores the upper reaches of mysticism. It is not at all that kind of a book.

It is, of course, a spiritual book in that it demonstrates how and why the Catholic Church unites one's soul with God and tells—to the extent words can—what this means to one in terms of interior peace and consolation.

The degree or the quality of the book's spirituality, however, may safely be left to other and better-qualified minds to decide. I will content myself with the hope and belief that the volume will at least serve as an introduction—or perhaps an invitation—to readers to venture farther into the world of spiritual reading and thus discover ever newer and greater riches for their minds and souls. As B. W. Maturin says of Catholicism, "It is scarcely possible for long to rest in a cold intellectual study of it, for here the heart sets the brain on fire, and the more he knows the more he loves, and every new throb of his heart opens some hitherto unseen door into a deeper knowledge."

I anticipate it may be said that many of the passages in this volume are too brief. However, this is not a manual, textbook or handbook. It is intended to give the spirit—the flavor—of Catholic beliefs and practices rather than their theological content. Finally, let me take refuge in these words of Bishop John Lancaster Spalding: "In literature, as in all things spiritual, quality is everything, quantity goes for nothing. A phrase outweighs whole volumes."

R. L. W.

CONTENTS

xvii

xviii

I

Our God is our refuge and strength; a helper in troubles, which have found us exceedingly.

Psalm 45:2

INFINITE GOD AND
FINITE MAN

THE REV. BEDE JARRETT, O.P.

WHENEVER I come in contact with God, I come into contact with something that is utterly above me. God is infinite and I am finite, so that truths about Him can never be packed into my limited intelligence. If I could understand God, I should be at least His equal. . . . It is impossible for me to understand God's being or His acts. There must be in everything He does a great deal that I can never comprehend nor ever hope to comprehend. Let me begin by realizing that I must expect when I come in contact with God to find very much that is above my understanding. . . . I have, therefore, to repeat to myself that if all the ways of God were capable of explanation, then I should know for certain that He did not

1

exist, but was the creation of man's mind. It is just because He is so difficult to comprehend that I know He is, indeed, a revealer of truth. . . .

I am content to go through life in trust—conscious and, indeed, proclaiming as part of my belief, that the ways of God ought to be mysteries to me, yet not thereby depressed or losing confidence, but rather keeping tighter hold of the little knowledge of God that has come to me through revelation. It is good for me that when I go out at night I do not bump my head against the stars.

IT FREQUENTLY happens that a man of the people who does not know how to read, will speak more learnedly of God and divine things than a celebrated doctor of theology who spends all his time among books. This is due to the fact that experience excels speculation, and love surpasses knowledge. We are united to God more intimately by the affections of the heart than by the meditations of the mind.

GIOVANNI CARDINAL BONA

"THE OMNIPRESENT GOD"

THE REV. FREDERICK WILLIAM FABER

WE ARE never really outside God nor He outside us. He is more with us than we are ourselves. The soul is less intrinsically in the body, than He is both in our bodies and our souls. He as it were flows into us, or we are in Him as the fish is in the sea. We use God, if we may dare say so, whenever we make an act of our will, and when we proceed to execute a purpose. He has not merely given us clearness of head, tenderness of heart, and strength of limb, as gifts which we may use independently of Him when once He has conferred them upon us. But He distinctly permits and actually concurs with every exercise of them in thinking, loving, or acting. . . . Everything is penetrated with God, while His inexpressible purity is all untainted, and His adorable simplicity unmingled with that which He so intimately pervades, enlightens, animates, and sustains. Our commonest actions, our lightest recreations, the freedoms in which we most unbend—all these things take place and are transacted, not so much on the earth and in the air, as in the bosom of the omnipresent God.

THE glory of God is the beauty of heaven and earth, of stars and angels, of human acts worthy of the doer, of human suffering nobly borne, beauty of character and aspect, material and spiritual beauty. God relucent everywhere. The glory of God reaches from the past through the present hour into the ages to come, a permanent streamer and pillar of light. It is what St. Thomas calls "the beauty of the universe." God and His glory are the everlasting joy of the saints, and the advancement of that glory is the saint's occupation on earth.

THE REV. JOSEPH RICKABY, S.J.

3

THE KINGDOM OF GOD
WITHIN US

THE MOST REV. FRANÇOIS FÉNELON

THE chief resource of our perfection is enclosed in that word which God said long ago to Abraham, "Walk in my presence, and you will be perfect." The presence of God calms the mind, gives peaceful sleep and rest, even during the day in the midst of all our work; but we must be God's without any reservation. When we have found God, there is nothing more to look for in men. We must sacrifice our best friends. The good friend is within our heart. He is the bridegroom who is jealous and who does away with all the rest.

It does not take much time to love God, in order to renew ourselves in his presence, to raise our heart to him or to worship him in the depths of our heart, to offer him what we do and what we suffer. That is the true kingdom of God within us, which nothing can disturb. . . .

If anyone can be happy, even in this life, it is he who loves God. If the love of God can be the principle of something good, it ought to carry us to the point of giving up all else, in order to be wholly God's. When his love is alone in a soul, it enjoys the peace of a good conscience. It is content and happy. It needs neither grandeur nor riches, nor reputation, nor indeed anything of all those things which time carries away without leaving any traces. It wishes only for the fulfilment of the will of the well-beloved. It is enough that it knows that that will is being accomplished. It watches constantly while awaiting the bridegroom. Prosperity cannot inflate it, nor adversity bow it down. It is this detachment from its own will in which all Christian perfection consists. . . .

Happy the man who gives himself to God! He is delivered from his passions, from the judgments of men, from their malice, from the tyranny of their sayings, from their cold and wretched mocking, from the misfortunes which the world distributes to wealth, from the unfaithfulness and inconstancy of friends, from the wiles and snares of enemies, from our own weakness, from the misery and brevity of life, from the horrors of a profane death, from the cruel remorse attached to wicked pleasures, and in the end from the eternal condemnation of God. He is delivered from this countless mass of evils, because, placing his will entirely in the hands of God, he wants only what God wants, and thus he finds his consolation in faith, and consequently hope in the midst of all his sufferings. . . .

It is not a question of knowing much, of having great talent, nor even of doing great things. We only need to have a heart and to desire the good. Outer works are the fruits and the inseparable consequences by which we recognize true devotion. But true devotion, the source of these works, is all in the depths of the heart. There are some virtues which are for some conditions, and not for others. Some are suitable at one time, and some at another, but the good intention is for all times and all places. To want all that God wants, always to want it, for all occasions and without reservations, this is the kingdom of God which is all within.

THE God of the Christians is a God who makes the soul feel that He is her only good, that her only rest is in Him, that her only delight is in loving Him; and who makes her at the same time abhor the obstacles which keep her back, and prevent her from loving God with all her strength. Self-love and lust, which hinder us, are unbearable to her. Thus God makes her feel that she has this root of self-love which destroys her, and which He alone can cure.

BLAISE PASCAL

"RICH IN MERCY"

ST. ALPHONSUS RODRIGUEZ, S.J.

FATHERS, says St. Ambrose, behold the falls of their children rather with compassion than anger; God does the same to us. He loves us as His children; He knows our frailty, and our falls and weaknesses excite Him rather to tender compassion, than to any indignation towards us. . . . One of the great consolations those have who serve God with the fervor they ought is, to know that, though they correspond not to His Goodness as they should, yet He ceases not to bear with them and to love them, because He is "rich in mercy" (Eph. ii.4); so that all our sins disappear before His infinite mercy, and become like wax that melts before the fire. What sentiments of zeal, gratitude, and cheerfulness, ought not to be excited in us by the thought that the many faults we daily fall into through weakness, do not hinder God from loving us according to His wonted goodness, and not at all diminish His grace in us!

6

THAT great student of the spiritual life, Father Mateo Crawley-Boevey, tells of a scrupulous person who was forever returning to her spiritual father confessing the same sin over and over again, and with apparent concern that it had never been forgiven. Wishing to teach her a much needed lesson, the confessor asked:

"What other sin have you committed?"

"None," she replied.

"Oh, yes," he said. "You have failed to mention the greatest of all."

"What is that?" she asked in horror.

"You doubted the mercy of God. That is the *capital* sin."

THE REV. JOHN A. O'BRIEN

GOD'S ETERNAL LOVE
FOR MAN

ST. ALPHONSUS DE' LIGUORI

GOD deserves your love because He has loved you before you loved Him, and because He has been the first of all to love you. *I have loved thee with an everlasting love.* (Jer. xxxi.3) Your parents have been the first to love you on this earth; but they have loved you only after they have known you. Before your father or your mother came into this world, God loved you: even before the world was created, He loved you. And how longer before the creation of the world did God love you? Perhaps a thousand years, or a thousand ages? It is useless to count years or ages; God has loved you from eternity. In a word, as long as He has been God, He has loved you; as long as He has loved Himself, He has loved you. . . .

God has loved you from eternity, and through pure love has taken you from among so many men whom He could create; He has given you existence, and has placed you in the world. For the love of you, God has created so many other beautiful creatures, that they might serve you, and remind you of the love which He has borne to you, and of the love which you owe Him. "Heaven and earth," says St. Augustine, "tell me to love Thee." When the saint looked at the sun, the moon, the stars, the mountains, the rivers, they appeared to him to speak, and say: "Augustine, love your God; for He has created us for you, that you might love Him." The Abbot de Rancé, founder of La Trappe, when he saw a hill, a fountain, or a flower, would say that all these creatures upbraided him with ingratitude to God.

THE Goodness of God means that God gives us what we *need* for our perfection, not what we *want* for our pleasure and sometimes for our destruction. As a sculptor, He sometimes applies the chisel to the marble of our imperfect selves and knocks off huge chunks of selfishness that His image may better stand revealed. Like a musician, whenever He finds the strings too loose on the violin of our personality, He tightens them even though it hurts, that we may better reveal our hidden harmonies.

THE MOST REV. FULTON J. SHEEN

GOD'S KNOWLEDGE OF EACH
INDIVIDUAL

JOHN HENRY CARDINAL NEWMAN

GOD beholds thee individually, whoever thou art. He "calls thee by thy name." He sees thee, and understands thee, as He made thee. He knows what is in thee, all thy own peculiar feelings and thoughts, thy dispositions and likings, thy strength and thy weakness. He views thee in thy day of rejoicing, and thy day of sorrow. He sympathizes in thy hopes and thy temptations. He interests Himself in all thy anxieties and remembrances, all the risings and fallings of thy spirit. He has numbered the very hairs of thy head and the cubits of thy stature. He compasses thee round and bears thee in His arms; He takes thee up and sets thee down. He notes thy very countenance, whether smiling or in tears, whether healthful or sickly. He looks tenderly upon thy hands and thy feet; He hears thy voice, the beating of thy heart, and thy very breathing. Thou dost not love thyself better than He loves thee. Thou canst not shrink from pain more than He dislikes thy bearing it; and if He puts it on thee, it is as thou wilt put it on thyself; if thou art wise, for a greater good afterwards. Thou are not only His creature (though for the very sparrows He has a care, and pitied the "much cattle" of Nineveh), thou art man redeemed and sanctified, His adopted son, favoured with a portion of that glory and blessedness which flows from Him everlastingly unto the Only-begotten. Thou art chosen to be His, even above thy fellows who dwell in the East and South. Thou wast one of those for whom

Christ offered up His last prayer, and sealed it with His precious blood. What a thought is this, a thought almost too great for our faith!

THE PATIENCE OF GOD

DOM ANSCAR VONIER, O.S.B.

MANY a sermon has been preached from Christian pulpits on the patience of God towards man. The more often we speak of that divine attribute, patience, the greater will be our service to the cause of religion. No doubt it requires a faith that is sure of itself to make of the patience of God one of its commonplaces; for at first sight it would seem that nothing could do less to further the interests of religion than belief in God's patience. Such a confidence, the detractor would say, must, of necessity, breed spiritual indolence; man will bank on God's patience with him and in the meantime offend in every possible way in the conviction that God's patience is inexhaustible. The dogma of the divine patience is indeed essentially Christian: a human-made religion could not afford a Godhead that has patience. . . .

The patience of God has, of course, for its object the sins of the people; God bears with our infirmities, God puts His hand under our head in our very falls; the Christian people have every right to appropriate to themselves all those magnificent scriptural expressions. If Peter is ordered to forgive his brother til seventy times seven a hint is given to him as to the spirit of the New Law. The only return God expects for His forebearance is this: that the Christian also should bear with his brother.

It is evident that this faith in God's patience with His people creates a temperament in the Catholic mind, in the Catholic judgement of ecclesiastical events. To expect the course of Church history to be such that there is no call for God's patience is truly absurd from the Christian point of view. All we know of God's intentions through the Incarnation makes it clear that from the very start God has put at the disposal of His Church an inexhaustible treasure of patience on His part; it is the Church's supernatural capital, on it the people can safely bank. There is no sin so big, there is no disorder so prolonged as to exhaust God's patience with us. We ought never in our zeal for sanctity to dream of an order of things in which there would no longer be room for the longanimity of God; God has not promised any such order of things, but He has made a definite pact with His Son that He will forgive His people all their sins.

THE NEARNESS OF GOD

ST. AUGUSTINE

BEHOLD, when thou art in trouble, that which thou seekest is not before thee, but He whom thou seekest is near thee. Seek thou Him who never can be wanting. Suppose those things which He gave withdrawn; is He who gave them therefore withdrawn? Let those things which He gave be restored; is it true wealth when these things are restored; is this not He who withdrew them to prove thee and restored them to console thee? For He consoleth us when those things are not wanting to us. He consoleth us in the way, but only if we understand the way. For the whole of this life, and all things which thou usest in this life, ought to be to thee as an inn to a traveller, not as a house to dwell in. Remember though thou hast accomplished somewhat, that somewhat remaineth, that thou hast been tarrying for refection not for defection.

THE EYES OF GOD

THE REV. VINCENT MC NABB, O.P.

I CAN hardly tear myself away from the first sentence [of John ix]: "And Jesus, passing by, saw a man who was blind from his birth." Jesus wasn't blind. What a terrible thing if God was blind! What an awful day for us! Jesus saw the one who didn't see Him. That is enough for us to go to bed with! God sees us when we didn't see Him. God loves us when we don't love Him. Jesus, passing by, saw the man who couldn't see Him; He saw the sightless eyes. God sees more in us than we see in ourselves. God's magnificent view of us is a great compliment. He sees the poor sightless eyes and thinks it's possible for them to see. He sees the poor withered spiritual limbs and sees it is possible for them to walk. He sees us content with earth and knows it is possible for us to have Divine desires. One of our prayers to God should be that we may see ourselves as He sees us.

"FAITH'S SIGHT OF HIM"

THE REV. FREDERICK WILLIAM FABER

WHAT is religiousness but the sensible presence of God, and religion the worship of Him? In religion, the presence of God is our atmosphere. Sacraments, and prayer, and mortification, and all the exercises of the spiritual life are so many appointments not only for realizing it, but for substantially introducing it both into the body and soul. The respiration of our soul depends upon it. It produces a certain kind of character, a type of its own sort and easily recognized, a supernatural character which inspires other men with awe, love, hatred, or contempt, according to the different points of view from which they look at it. To the pure-minded, it is the greatest possible amount of happiness on earth; for it infuses into us a certain marvelous unreasoning instinct for another world, as being faith's sight of Him who is invisible. Yet it is hardly conscious of what it is it sees.

IF GOD is man's supreme good . . . it clearly follows, since to seek the supreme good is to live well, that to live well is nothing else but to love God with all the heart, with all the soul, with all the mind; and, as arising from this, that this love be kept entire and incorrupt, which is the part of temperance; that it give way before no troubles, which is the part of fortitude; that it serve no other, which is the part of justice; that it be watchful in its discernment of things lest deception or fraud steal

13

in, in which is the part of prudence. This is man's one perfection, by which alone he can succeed in attaining to the purity of truth.

ST. AUGUSTINE

THE HAND OF GOD

ST. AUGUSTINE

LET my enemies rage. What can they do? They can take my money, strip, proscribe, banish me; they can rack me with sorrows and tortures; and at last, if they be allowed, even kill me. Can they do aught more? But thou, O Lord, "hast stretched forth Thy hand against the wrath of my enemies" (Ps. cxxxvii, 7), against what my enemies can do, Thou hast stretched forth Thy hand. For my enemies cannot separate me from Thee; but Thou repayest me the more, because Thou dost still delay: "Thou hast stretched forth Thy hand against the wrath of my enemies."

Let my enemy rage as much as he can, he cannot separate me from God. But Thou, O Lord, hast not as yet received me; and still Thou weariest me in wandering; as yet Thou dost not give me Thy joy and sweetness; as yet Thou hast not "inebriated me with the plenty of Thy house," as yet Thou hast not made me "drink of the torrents of Thy pleasure. For with Thee is the fountain of life; and in Thy light we shall see light" (Ps. xxxv, 9, 10). But behold! I have given Thee the first-fruits of my spirit, and have believed in Thee, and "with the mind serve the law of God" (Rom. vii, 25); yet still "we

14

ourselves groan within ourselves waiting for the adoption, the redemption of our body" (id. viii, 23). This life hath God given to us sinners, wherein also it is needful that Adam be wearied in the sweat and toil of his face, since the earth brought forth to him thorns and thistles (Gen. iii, 18 sq.). Can any enemy lay more on him? "Thou hast stretched forth Thy hand against the wrath of my enemies"; yet not to make me despair, for there follow the words, "and Thy right hand hath saved me."

THE thought of God, and nothing short of it, is the happiness of man; for though there is much besides to serve as subject of knowledge, or motive for action, or means of excitement, yet the affections require a something more vast and more enduring than anything created. What is novel and sudden excites, but does not influence; what is pleasurable and useful raises no awe; self moves no reverence, and mere knowledge kindles no love. He alone is sufficient for the heart Who made it.

JOHN HENRY CARDINAL NEWMAN

DIVINE JUSTICE

THE REV. EDWARD F. GARESCHÉ, S.J.

GOD gives to each of us our plot of ground to till and work on, and to some He gives exceedingly stony ground. Their characters are hard, unyielding, unresponsive to spiritual motives. They are a barren plot and need to be dug and fertilized and watered and walled about, before they will produce even a few blades of spiritual growth. On the other hand, God gives to others deep, rich and fertile souls full of natural goodness. . . . Yet the merits of each one depends not directly upon what sort of soil God has given him to cultivate, but on what use he makes of what God has given. Many a one will shine in glory before the angels and the saints because out of a stony, harsh and barren soil he has with huge labor and many tears and much sweat brought forth fruit worthy of the Kingdom of Heaven.

These reflections should be a great consolation to us, because they show that our merit does not depend altogether on the outward results of all our efforts and trials, but rather on the endeavor we make and on the energy we develop. One need never repine at having been given by God's providence a harsh and difficult nature, troublesome to till and hard to cultivate, because the reward that we shall receive and the credit that we shall have in the eyes of God and His saints for all eternity, will not depend upon the soil, but upon the tillage; not upon what we have received from God, but upon the proportionate return we have made Him for His gifts.

BECAUSE God is eternal, because He spares the wicked in this life, bringing them to repentance, and chastises the good, making them wise for the kingdom of heaven, therefore *there is no inquity in Him*. Fear not.

ST. AUGUSTINE

DIVINE INSPIRATION

HENRY EDWARD CARDINAL MANNING

IT IS certain, by the voice of all mankind, that God speaks to us through His works—that He whispers to us through our natural conscience—that He attracts us to Him by instincts, and desires, and aspirations offer a happiness higher than sense, and more enduring, more changeless, than this natural life. God speaks to me articulately, in the stirring life of nature and the silence of our own being. What is all this but a spiritual action of the intelligence, and the will of God upon the intelligence, and will of man? and what is this but a Divine inspiration? . . . It is God speaking to man, God illuminating man to know Him, and drawing man to love Him. He created us as objects whereon to exercise His benevolence. His love and His goodness are the fountains of the light of nature. His image, in which He has created us, by its own instincts turns to Him with the rational and moral confidence that if we feel after Him, we shall find Him. And His love and His goodness are such, that our yearning for a knowledge of Him are satisfied not only by the light of nature, but through His grace by the supernatural revelation of Himself.

THE POWER OF THE
HOLY SPIRIT

THE REV. M. JOSEPH SCHEEBEN

OUR Lord sent the Holy Ghost twice: the first time, when after His resurrection, whilst yet sojourning on earth, He breathed upon His Apostles and said: "Receive ye the Holy Ghost"—and again after His ascension into Heaven on the day of Pentecost at Jerusalem. . . . The Holy Ghost inspires us with the love of God, when He gives us the power and inclination for this love, and gives us Himself as the pledge, that God will eternally love us, and with all that He possesses, will be ours. The love of our neighbor He works in us, by making him also His temple, by giving Himself also to our neighbor and dwelling in him, that we may henceforth love in our neighbor, not a man, but God Himself, who lives in him. Oh, how few remember that they must honor and love their fellow-man as a sacred and venerable temple of the Holy Ghost! . . . Were we as enlightened as the Saints, we should kneel down before the sick and helpless, and with the greatest reverence render them the meanest services, knowing well that about the temple of God even the lowest service is infinitely great and holy.

THIS is our highest reward that we should fully enjoy God, and that all who enjoy Him should enjoy one another in Him. . . . But when you have joy of a man in God, it is God rather than the man whom you enjoy.

For you enjoy Him by whom you are made happy, and you rejoice to have come to Him in whom you place your hope that you may come to Him.

ST. AUGUSTINE

THE VOICE OF GOD
WITHIN US

DÉSIRÉ JOSEPH CARDINAL MERCIER

THE fatherly solicitude of God extends to each and every one of us. Where is there a soul in this wide world over which God does not brood with love ineffable? Did He not liken Himself to the hen gathering her little ones under her wings? The very concept of the supernatural life communicated to us, a life the focus of which dwells within ourselves, presupposes the formation of a permanent disposition to welcome the diffusion of Divine grace within our intellects and wills, and sustained in their efforts. The experience of souls who are attentive to what goes on within them bears witness to the living reality of this action from above.

How is it, then, that the voice of God is not more distinctly heard by men?

The answer to this question is: To be heard it must be listened for.

THE UNSEEN GOD
WITHIN US

THE REV. F. P. LE BUFFE, S.J.

PHYSICAL childhood is done for all who read these lines, yet there is another childhood none of us must outgrow, the childhood of the Saints of God. If our faith is real and live and strong, all our days are fairy-filled and we have an "inner sight" that is as piercing as ever a child's sight was, and yet all real. "Out beyond the shining of the farthest star," and yet intimately present within us, is the unseen God in whose fairy-land we dwell. Round Him we know His myriad Angels kneel in courtly adoration, or speed upon His high commands or guard with tenderest care our waking and our sleeping hours. God hides Himself behind the veils of bread and wine and yet faith tears away the wrapping of our hidden King, and we kneel in prayerful adoration within His home or hasten with joy to the altar-rail that we may bring Him back within the temple of our frail and failing bodies. As children we were wont to dream of being rich and thought of coffers heaped with gold and jewels and now we know we carry stamped within our souls the likeness of the King and own imperishable riches in the graces He gives us so plentifully. A prince or a princess we would be and a queen would be our mother, and now, never did prince or princess have a mother like Mother Mary who watches us and wins from her kingly Son all the help we need to be true children of our royal home of Heaven. "Turn but a stone and start an Angel's wing," indeed is true of the matters of our soul. Everywhere we stumble on the things of God—the kindly illuminations of our minds by holy thoughts, the drawing of our wills by His sweetly compelling grace, the buoyancy brought into our lives by the companionship with His holy folks. And beneath and within and around the plain, everyday facts of life we catch the sight of Him in whom "we live and move and are."

THE SOUL YEARNS FOR GOD

ANONYMOUS

IT IS at once our duty and our privilege to keep in touch with Almighty God. We live always in His presence, and He is speaking to us at all hours. Our souls are made to His image and likeness, and they must be in sympathy and contact with their Origin. They naturally yearn for God and tend towards Him; they are not filled or satisfied with sights and sounds of earth; their desires stretch far wider, and are not laid to rest save only in the full vision and enjoyment of the "good things of the Lord in the land of the living." God, then, is ever speaking to us; the works of His hands proclaim His power and resources and His tender care for our needs; the works of His redeeming love proclaim to us the value of our souls and His sense of their value. The Crucifix, the Tabernacle, the Sacraments, these, O my God, are chosen instruments by which Thou deignest day by day to speak to my soul. And "My sheep hear My voice," says our Lord.

THE striving after God is therefore the desire of beatitude, the attainment of God is beatitude itself. We seek to attain God by loving Him; we attain to Him, not by becoming entirely what He is, but in nearness to Him, and in wonderful and sensible contact with Him, and in being inwardly illuminated and occupied by His truth and holiness. He is light itself; it is given to us to be illuminated by that light.

ST. AUGUSTINE

DEFEAT TURNS US TO GOD

THE REV. ANTONIN SERTILLANGES, O.P.

DEFEAT is never anything but an invitation to have recourse to God. A humiliation is the prelude to the honor which is found again in God. A fall is the preliminary to falling into the arms of God. Can this be called defeat in the true sense of the word?

It makes no difference that you say: "It is my fault." Every fault is effaced by regretting it. What remains, then, is only the bare facts or Providence; but facts are subservient to the spirit, and Providence is all ours. Of things as they are, even by our own fault, we shall make, with God, whatever we will; perhaps not in the form we desire, but in an equivalent form which will be even superior.

Thou hast created us for Thyself, and our heart knows
no rest, until it may repose in Thee.

ST. AUGUSTINE

LOVE FINDS GOD

THE REV. JEAN BAPTISTE LACORDAIRE

Love being the supreme act of the soul, and the master-
piece of man, what we owe God is to love Him. The love
of God is a virtue which we have not yet named, which
crowns all other virtues, and opens to us, by means of
the transformation it effects, the shortest way to our end.
For it is peculiar to love that it unites those who love
one another, that it blends their thoughts, their desires,
their sentiments, every outcome and possession of their
lives. Even the love for finite beings acquires an energy
which exalts man above himself; how much more the
love of God! In Him it finds and imparts to us all that is
wanting to our feeble nature. It finds God, and it gives
us to God.

RELIGION LEADS US TO GOD

THE MOST REV. JOHN LANCASTER SPAULDING

The conscious communion of man with God and with
nature, as it is transformed by the soul, is the vital source

of religion. We perceive the limitations of our being, because we are immersed in God; we understand that our thought is partial, because we know that its true object is the Infinite; that our love is incomplete because we dimly discern the love that is perfect. We are related to God as the child is related to the parent, and our existence, therefore, involves His Being. All things are ours to know and to love and to use, because He is with us and for us; because He is our Father, the Father not merely of our physical nature, but of whatever our endowments make us capable of, as truth, love, and goodness. Thus religion is necessary, not because it is useful or consoling, but because it is involved in the nature of man and in the nature of things. It is not a form in which we live and act, but spirit of our spirit, and life of our life. It is enrooted in the necessity which constrains whoever thinks or loves to transcend the limited and apparent, and to rise to the absolute and infinite. It is more than a doctrine and a cult—it is life, life manifesting itself not in worship alone, but in science, art, morality, and civilization also. God is in all truth, love, and sympathy, in all the beauty and power, which are the spiritual bonds of men and the gladness of the world.

Religion is as deep as God and as wide as the sphere of human activity. . . . It is the ruling power in the lives of individuals and of peoples; the gradual and increasing penetration of the world by the Divine Spirit of wisdom, sympathy and truth. To morality it gives warmth and vigor, and it nourishes the faculty of admiration and awe. It inspires the faith and hope which mold character, and it confers the capacity to take the high views of life which foster right feeling, without which little that is great or worthy can be accomplished; for the heart of man is controlled by feeling rather than by thought, by emotions more than by ideas. To be drawn to what is noble and great is a better fortune than to have merely an intellectual perception of truth and beauty, for attraction leads to union while the beholder stands aloof. We become part of all we love and sincerely strive for, and religion makes us capable of the self-surrender to the Infinite Being which is the purpose and end of our life, and in which alone we may find peace.

GOD is the only being that is never sought in vain, even though He cannot perfectly be found.

ST. BERNARD OF CLAIRVAUX

OUR GIFTS TO GOD

THE REV. ANTONIN SERTILLANGES, O.P.

NOTHING in our existence is indifferent, for God loves us in our entirety in the unity of His Christ. There is nothing small in our offerings and consecrations motivated and made in the spirit of love uniting us with Christ. God sees them all and in all He sees Christ, since love, the soul of all works, is as the soul in the body: all in the whole and in the least part of it.

Love likes little things, because nothing in them impedes it, and it can reign without interference from self-assertive values which often hamper it, but by no means take its place. The love of God delights especially in things which are of no importance so that God alone may be important, together with the heart that rises to Him, and with that mysterious bond for the cementing of which any pretext suffices because He is Himself its real motive.

Like La Boétie Montaigne, I love God on account of God; I love God on account of me. The least object may contain this self-sufficing sentiment. The slightest gesture satisfies it. There is no need of marvelous gifts or heroic actions.

How consoling for little lives! What a lesson for great ones! Nothing is of any worth but the sentiment behind it. Nothing counts in the gift but the giver himself.

Little lives, recognize what you are. If you so will it, you are the greatest of all. Learn then, true greatness, and vivify by love what without love is nothing.

"THE GIFT GIVING HIMSELF"

THE REV. VALENTIN-M. BRETON, O.F.M.

THE Mystery of the Blessed Trinity is, at once, the basis, the centre and the sublime summit of the whole Christian life. The existence in Three Persons of the one Godhead is the foundation of the supernatural order, that is, of the communication by God to His free and intelligent creatures of His own life and happiness. It is the justification of their faith, the pledge of their hope, the consolation of their charity. Upon it depend the possibility of the Incarnation and the reality of our Redemption and adoption. . . . One day it will cease to be a mystery to us, and His Revelation of Himself, here begun in in faith, and made perfect in the beatific vision, will constitute what we know as Heaven. . . .

In revealing the mystery of the Trinity, God declared Himself as the living God, taught us that He is our Father, and that He looks on us as sons and friends, and offers us a share in His own life and happiness. . . .

God, as known by reason, almighty, eternal, infinitely removed from creatures, is a Master before whom all tremble. . . . In Aristotle's eyes He is shut up in his own perfection, too far above His creatures to care about them. . . .

Can His pure perfection have a heart, and can there be any mercy in Him? If we look only at the miseries of the world, where all things are in continual struggle and revolt, we might well doubt. The real meaning of the unabated strife, which is, in reality, nothing but a call to a higher life, would be always hidden from us.

But God reveals Himself as the Father with a Son. Therefore His creatures can be His children, and His works can be seen by them as educative, kind and beneficent, despite their want of understanding and their resistance.

And so God loves and is love; He is the Gift, giving Himself. A gift passes from giver to receiver as a sign of affection, and is valued more for what it means than for what it is. But God's love is such that He Himself becomes its sign and gauge.

IN THE bosom of the Most High God, amid the astounding marvels of the Most Holy Trinity, amid the boundless silences and the uncreated fires of the illimitable majesty of God—there is our home—there is to be our life—there are our interests, our tastes, and our occupation for all eternity! What an incredible faith, incredible even from the very exceedingness of its simplicity. What grave, broad thoughts it suggests to us, and yet such homely, plain, practical truths! The grandeur of the Mystery of the Most Holy Trinity makes us all children at once.

THE REV. FREDERICK WILLIAM FABER

GOD'S SAVING PITY

FATHER CUTHBERT, O.S.F.C.

IN THE world drama of history the Catholic sees the saving pity of God brooding over a fallen world, permitting man in his rebellious self-will to learn by bitter experience that misery of sin, but at the same time meeting this growing "conviction of sin" with the promise of an eventual redemption, planted in the heart of man. Further, as history proceeds the dawn of that redemption appears in the gradual revelation of the Christ to come to the people of Israel. . . . Under the divine influence of that revelation Israel awakens to a concept of the diviner life of man as founded in obedience to the law of divine holiness; it realizes sin not merely as a world-evil pitiless in its judgments, but as a rebellion against this holiness of God, the true law of man's life; further, it recognizes that only in a return to holiness can the world get free from sin and its consequences. But this revelation in its gradual development is given not merely as an intellectual concept but as a life to be lived, as a law set in the midst of the nation for its acceptance or rejection; and in its stages of development accommodated to the growing spiritual capacity of the nation to receive it; until at length "in the fulness of time" it is finally made manifest in the person of the Redeemer Himself.

BY LOOKING upon God as the end of her life and upon Jesus as her guide, the soul becomes enamoured of the divine sweetness and perfections; she unites herself to her Saviour in such wise that the divine will becomes the moving principle of her life. Fear has passed away; hope, so far as self is concerned, becomes dormant, love triumphs and dominates all. The soul then ceases to belong to herself, in order to belong wholly to God whom she loves.

THE REV. Y. E. MASSON, O.P.

II

Jesus saith to him: I am the way, and the truth, and the life. No man cometh to the Father, but by me.

St. John 14:6

CHRIST TURNS US TOWARD THE FUTURE

THE REV. JOSEPH MC SORLEY, C.S.P.

CHRIST came in human form chiefly for the purpose of awakening man to a sense of divine possibilities. He rose visibly from the dead in order to bear witness to the truth of His message. He vanished into the unseen world again to emphasize the fact that the battle is still unwon and human perfection is still unattained, to show that only in the life beyond do we arrive at the real goal of our existence.

Belief in Christ implies a facing toward the future, a confession of the inadequacy of the present. Only in another state of existence at a distant time, shall the reward of the disciple be given, and the wage of the laborer be paid; there and then only shall the weary be at rest, and the soldier free to lay down his arms. The immediate purpose of Christ's earthly existence was fulfilled when once He had flashed this vision of a perfect life before humanity's wondering eyes. Forever after, His figure and His story would be seen to break in upon the dreams of a slumbering world and trouble its self-contentment. The risen Christ could never be wholly forgotten. So long as that lesson haunted human memory, the present, the visible, the merely natural, could never suffice to quench the thirst in the soul of man.

Christ, then, willed to bestow upon us a new conception of life, to erect a new scale of values. He gave to men's eyes a fresh perception of spiritual beauty. He stirred men's souls with a new discontent; He made it forever impossible that His disciples should be satisfied with the things produced by earth. Into their hearts He flung the dart of a divine ambition; before their sight He flashed the image of Godlike possibilities. To the meanest of human creatures was granted the opportunity of one day sharing in this life of God. . . .

Sometimes doubt afflicts a man. Then the vision of the risen Christ appears. It is as if a whisper from heaven had been uttered and the voice of God had commanded us to put away hesitation, to cast out fear, to trust in the goodness of the Father, who sent us Christ and who promises to give Him to us again forever.

THE grace of God could never be more gracefully displayed than when the only-begotten Son of God remaining immutably Himself took on man's nature, and by becoming man gave the Spirit of His love to men, by which they might come to Him who was so far removed from men, immortal while they are mortal, immutable while they are mutable, just while they are sinful, blessed while they are wretched. And because He has implanted in us the natural desire to be eternally blessed, He remaining blessed, and putting on our mortal nature to give us what we desired, taught us by His patience in suffering to despise what we feared.

ST. AUGUSTINE

CHRIST, THE CENTER AND SOURCE OF OUR SUPER-NATURAL LIFE

FATHER CUTHBERT, O.S.F.C.

THE conception of Christianity as directly of supernatural origin and character is fundamental to the Catholic position. The Christian revelation is not and never could be derived from the operation of man's own reason. The most complete content of human reason left to itself is circumscribed by the created finite world in which our natural existence lies, and the Christian revelation carries us beyond that into the higher life of conscious union with God Himself. In this supernatural life, there is a transformation of values both as regards ourselves and the world in which we live, a transformation brought about by the direct operation of the Divine Spirit through Jesus Christ. Christ as the Divine Word is the giver of this new life to us; we are and ever shall be merely recipients. The centre and source of this new life is always outside ourselves in Christ the manifested Word of God to man. If, then, we seek for the sufficient reason and guide to this higher life, we find it not in ourselves but in Christ alone, and our ultimate salvation lies not in the fuller or fullest realization of our natural self but in the apprehension of the life which is in Christ.

JUST as our Heavenly Father is ever near to us by that undimmed look with which He follows in mercy and compassion all our interior and exterior life, so Jesus Christ Whom He has sent, with sympathetic emotion and answering Heart, has his ministering and healing Hand upon us all in our steps and all our fortunes. There is no aspect of the Incarnation more fertile in courage and confidence to men than the thought of the fellow-feeling of Him Who came to seek us and to save us.

THE MOST REV. JOHN CUTHBERT
HEDLEY, O.S.B.

CHRIST, THE BRIDGE BETWEEN TIME AND ETERNITY

DOM AELRED GRAHAM, O.S.B.

CHRISTIANITY's saving truths partake of the everlasting quality of the God Who reveals them. We cannot say, for example, that man fell from grace, was restored, and there is an end of the matter. Day by day he lapses into sin, day by day he is reclaimed; the great drama of the first chapters of Genesis is continually being re-enacted. The Atonement wrought on Calvary, all-sufficient in itself, did not finally close the scene, leaving the rest as a sort of epilogue. Through the centuries we are being won to grace, until Christ comes to gather the final fruits of the redemption. In the hidden depths of the soul we rise from the dead to enjoy the only immortality that is of value, though the glory of the first resurrection be for a time withheld. . . .

The intersection of time and eternity represented by the Incarnation offers much food for thought. Be it noted that only in Christ are humanity and divinity wholly at one. Here is the absolute harmony; elsewhere there is tension, even in those who would willingly reproduce the Christ-life in themselves. Where there is no such desire the impact of the divine upon the human is a source of hostility and confusion. "Behold this child is set for the fall and the resurrection of many in Israel and for a sign which shall be contradicted." (Luke ii, 34) Jesus is indeed "our peace" (Ephesians ii, 14), breaking down the dividing wall between Jew and Gentile, and abolishing man's enmity with God; but there is much evidence to show that His role of peacemaker must be conceived as something very different from that of an amiable settler of differences between human disputants. The warfare of which He puts an end is that between man and God; between man and man also—but only in so far as each surrenders his heart to God and accepts the mediatorship of Christ.

34

HE WHO was God was made man, by taking what He was not, not by losing what He was: thus was God made man. . . . Let Christ, therefore, lift thee up by that which is man, let Him lead thee by that which is God-man, let Him guide thee through to that which is God.

ST. AUGUSTINE

"PREPARE THY HEART TO CHRIST"

THOMAS À KEMPIS

THE kingdom of God is within you, saith Christ our Saviour. . . . The kingdom of God is peace and joy in the Holy Ghost, that is not given to wicked people. Our Lord Jesus Christ will come to thee and will show to thee His consolation. If thou wilt make ready for Him in thy heart a dwelling-place, that is all He desireth to have in thee, and there it is His pleasure to be. Betwixt Almighty God and a devout soul there are many ghostly visitings, sweet inward speaking, great gifts of grace, many consolations, much heavenly peace and wondrous familiarity of the blessed presence of God.

Therefore, thou faithful soul, prepare thy heart to Christ thy Spouse, that He may come to thee and dwell in thee: for He saith Himself: If a man love me, he will keep my words: and my Father will love him, and we will come unto him, and make our abode with him. Give, therefore, to Christ free entry into thy heart, and keep out all things that may hinder His entry; and when thou hast Him thou art rich enough, and He only shall suffice

35

to thee. He shall be thy provider and defender, and thy faithful helper in every necessity; so that thou shalt not need to put thy trust in any other without Him. Man is soon changed, and light falleth away, but Christ abideth for ever, and standeth strongly with His lover unto the end.

OUR Lord often looks on us; indeed He is always doing so, but we may feel it more at one time than at another. He looks at us with eyes of welcome in Holy Communion, with eyes of joy and compassion at Confession, with eyes of hope as He offers us our daily graces, with eyes of congratulation when we have done well, with eyes of friendship when we have sinned; and by His sick and suffering children our Lord is ever standing, watching their pain and need, and the look of His eyes seems to say: "I am with you in tribulation; I see it all; it is all noted down in the books of life." This thought may help you, especially towards evening, after a long day, as you raise your eyes to heaven and meet our Lord's cheering look, to tell you all is well, that He is satisfied; and tears may come to your eyes, but they will be tears of joy and peace.

ANONYMOUS

LO, THOU art far from God, O man, and God is far above man. Between them the God-man placed Himself. Acknowledge Christ, and through Him as Man ascend to God.

ST. AUGUSTINE

"LORD, REMEMBER ME"

ANONYMOUS

THERE is nothing more superb in the history of our Lord's dealings with souls than the conversion of the good thief—St. Dismas, as he is sometimes called. . . .

From his bed of death, now become his pulpit, amid all his pain, before the soldiers and rabble of priests and people, he [the good thief] makes a glorious confession of his sins, and proclaims in simple but immortal words, the praises of his Redeemer. "We indeed suffer justly: but this Man hath done no evil: we receive the due reward of our deeds." And then he turned to our Lord, with beautiful modesty, yet with intense faith and hope: "Lord, remember me when Thou shalt come into Thy kingdom." And the answer comes with lightning-speed: "Amen, I say to thee, this day thou shalt be with Me in paradise." All is forgiven; every sin is blotted out; the first trophy of the precious Blood is secured.

Learn from this how our Lord is generous beyond hope or thought to those who suffer with Him. He leaves them on their cross, perchance, but He is at their side, and His reward comes a hundredfold. Next, let the sick and desolate adopt and make their own the prayer of the good thief. When in pain, when a darkness of soul as that of Calvary seems to enshroud you and hide all light and joy from your eyes, cry out to our Lord who is very near, "Lord, remember me!" There is such pathos and simple humility in that word "Remember." "Remember me!" And the answer will swiftly come and sink deep into your heart! "One day thou shalt be with Me in paradise," for "if we suffer with Christ, we shall also reign with Him."

CHRIST is rich, who will maintain you; He is a king, who will provide you; He is a sumptuous entertainer, who will feast you; He is beautiful, who will give in abundance all that can make you happy. Enrol yourselves in His service, that with Him you may gain triumphs, and show yourselves men truly most learned, truly most illustrious.

BLESSED EDMUND CAMPION, S.J.

OUR KINSHIP WITH CHRIST

THE REV. JOHN BERNARD KELLY

THE Sign of the Cross is to the true Christian something more than a symbol commemorating the death of a figure of history who passed from the realm of time nineteen hundred years ago, leaving as his bequest to posterity only a record of a beautiful life. Every time the Catholic gazes upon the crucified Figure nailed to the gibbet of torture he sees there the replica of One with Whom he has a Flesh and Blood kinship—One of a Holy Family of which he has been made a member. He sees in the symbol of the Crucified a memorial of the love unto death in the heart of One Who has dwelt within his own body as He did within Mary's womb. It is the replica of the agonized One Who gave Himself, Body and Blood, Soul and Divinity into the keeping of His creature to

38

have and to hold eternally. To the Roman Catholic, Christ is not a figure of ancient history still influencing civilization. He is a divine Contemporary of the current century's year and hour.

Christ emptied Himself of His glory upon Calvary's hill that mankind might be filled with the splendor of divine endowments when called to the heights of the Ascension. Adam lost Paradise in time and eternity. Christ bought back with His precious blood, spilt upon the Cross, the inheritance of the prodigal race disowned. Christ rewarded the faith of the good thief who found eternal happiness after gazing upon the woes of the Author of Life approaching His death. God's helplessness is the source of man's power. Both priest and layman can stand at Calvary's altar and speak with the prophetic assurance of Christ the words of eternity's Lord and God. "This day thou shalt be with me here in Paradise!", the priest can say, and with the speaking of the words of Consecration in the Mass his prophecy is fulfilled. The layman can make the same prophecy as he approaches the altar rail to receive the Author of Life in Holy Communion.

So it is that Christ is given to us by the Father to live and die and rise again within us that we may have life, and have it more abundantly.

The death of Christ symbolized in the Cross is to the true Christian the guarantee of divine glory inherited in time and assured for eternity to those who suffer themselves to be lifted up with the Crucified.

CHRISTIANITY is not so much the pursuit of an ideal as an Ideal that pursues humanity, stooping down in an

Incarnation to take up dwelling in the hearts of men. By becoming man Christ wished not only to indicate how each one might lead a life divine, but actively to help in the transformation of human nature. Just as the human nature of Christ was not destroyed by its proximity to Godhead in the Person of Jesus Christ, so the Christian does not cease to be by contact with Christ. On the contrary, humanity will reach the true ideal of personality only when it surrenders to the active influence of God in Christ.

FATHER JAMES, O.F.M. CAP.

THE PEACE OF CHRIST

THE REV. BEDE JARRETT, O.P.

IT IS sometimes said that those who live away from God can have no peace in their hearts: but a far more terrible punishment befalls them—namely, the exact reverse. The horror of their position is just this, that they can acquire a definite peace which lulls them into so firm a sense of security that nothing on earth, short of a startling miracle of grace, can ever awaken them. . . . The peace, then, that the world can give; it brings with it real happiness and security, and, while it lasts, cannot be distinguished from the peace of Christ, except in that it rests upon a quite different foundation. In its effects it is as powerful as the other; in its causes it is less lasting. For the peace that the world has to give rests entirely upon external things; it depends upon certain conditions which are not conditions of soul, but conditions of environment or possession. I am at peace, in the world's meaning of the phrase, when I have all that I desire—health and wealth and friends, work that is congenial or even no work at all, the pleasure of art and the distractions of amusement. I am at peace in this way just so long as these things accompany me, just so long also as I am able to appreciate them. But if they are taken away, or if my senses fail to register their delights, then I have no peace.

Our Lord's gift of peace was to be different: "Not as the world giveth do I give unto you." The peace He came to bring was dependent entirely upon an interior state of soul, and was wholly independent of external circumstances. These might be favorable or not, but they could not enter into the sanctuary of the soul, its inmost and deepest shrine, where the armed man, secure, kept his court in peace. The peace of the world meant that I had all that I desired, the peace of Christ that I desired no more than all I had. The peace of the world was largely in its cause negative; it implied the absence, the careful removal, of every form of trouble, evil, distress; it was a peace through circumstance. But the peace of Christ depended wholly, under the grace of God, on the attitude of the soul. It was built upon a firm foundation of the will never to be troubled or dismayed. It was compatible with every form of suffering, with every privation, with failure in every line of life. It was compatible even with discontent. . . .

This contradiction is achieved by the soul which realizes the meaning of the will of God, and the ensuing peace arises from the absolute acceptance of that will. . . . I accept the will of God, and the rest does not matter. I labor to produce my best; I am discontented, but never discouraged. I may be a failure, but never a disappointment: for the first I do not hold myself responsible, but for the second I do. The first depends more upon external circumstances, the second wholly on my attitude of soul. The peace, then, of Christ is within the will, unaffected by outward conditions, sustained alone by conscious devotion and submission to the Father that sent me.

WHEN Our Lord Jesus is present all things are liking, and nothing seemeth hard to do for His love; but when He is absent, all things that are done for His love are painful and hard. When Jesus speaketh not to the soul, there is no faithful consolation: but if He speak one word only, the soul feeleth great inward comfort. Did not Mary Magdalen rise soon from weeping when Martha shewed her that her Master Christ was nigh and called her? Yes, truly. O that is a happy hour when Jesus calleth us from weeping to joy of spirit!

THOMAS À KEMPIS

THE PRINCE OF PEACE

ANONYMOUS

OUR Lord has no grander or truer title than that of the Prince of Peace. The first word spoken on earth at His birth by the angels was, "Peace." "Let not your heart be troubled, nor let it be afraid," He said at His last supper. "Peace I leave with you, My peace I give unto you"; and on the first Easter Day He saluted His disciples with the words: "Peace be to you"; "and then He showed them His hands and His side." Here is the secret of it. We must keep these two sentences together if we would understand the Peace of Christ, "which the world cannot give." It is not the peace of inactivity or of freedom from pain and care; that is the peace which the world seeks to give. It may be sweet for a time like a drug that lulls sharp pain, but it is a mockery, leaving us empty-handed and unsatisfied. The peace of Christ is the peace of a soldier fighting on the field of life, beneath his captain's eye, sure of victory, and who can show his hands stained and pierced with the sword of the love of God, not closed with the dead key of love of self.

The peace of Christ means self-possession, the act of holding the mighty forces within us well in hand, of framing our lives on the manifest will of God, and keeping our eyes fixed on Him for direction.

Till the day break, and the shadows retire, I will go to the mountain of myrrh and the hill of frankincense. (Cant. iv.6) That is to say, till my soul escape out of the shadows and darkness of this world, till the bright day of eternity dawn upon me, my resting-place, my shelter, the home of my heart, shall be on the mountain of myrrh, on the hill of frankincense; there to embalm with the myrrh of a devout remembrance the wounds of my Lord crucified, and there with the frankincense of prayer to look on Him Whom I have pierced.

THE REV. PETER GALLWEY, S.J.

"A KING HAS GONE FORTH"

SUSAN L. EMERY

THE French scholar and Christian, Frederick Ozanam, once said that if God has, as of course He has, some mysteries yet unrevealed to us, no doubt they are secrets of mercy; and when we look very deeply into the awful tragedy of Good Friday, a solemn joy takes possession of our souls; in no figurative sense we *glory* in the cross of our Lord. For, if we read the office for Holy Week with this thought of triumph and joy uppermost, we shall be struck with the frequent occurrence of a key far other than the minor in the great chant of the Missal. It flashes upon us that, hidden behind the dark curtain of the shame and pain, a King has gone forth to the battle, riding the strange white steed of the Apocalyptic vision; the name of the King, Faithful and True, is the Word of God, and His eyes are as a flame of fire, and on His garment and on His thigh is written: King of kings, and Lord of lords. And, through and above the yells of the murderous multitude, rises the voice of a far greater multitude, as the voice of many waters, and as the voice of great thunders: "Alleluia! for the Lord our God the Omnipotent hath reigned!"

As our Leader He leadeth us down, He leadeth us on Himself as the Way, and He bringeth us to Himself as our home. . . . In Him thou seest both thy labor and thy reward; labor in His passion, reward in His resurrection.

ST. AUGUSTINE

WALKING WITH THE STRIDE
OF GOD

THE REV. WALTER FARRELL, O.P.

ORDINARY, routine, even mediocre Catholic life is a noble thing, far outstripping liberality. Liberality, after all, deals with the small change of life; and we too often part with our trifles reluctantly. But we do part with them at His command. We grumble, groan, fidget, are ashamed and embarrassed; but we are back at His feet again and again with the gifts in our hands. We do give up the Sunday sleep, we do elbow our way into crowded churches on torrid days, we do sit stoically through long, dull sermons, we do kneel down and tell the things that only God can know.

And by those very things we proclaim again and again that He has first place in our hearts. We confirm the momentous fact of our love, confirm it unquestionably day after day. And this means that again and again we have put self to one side to work for our "other self" who has so won our hearts. We do not merely say we love Him; we prove it, prove it to the hilt.

Our reluctance and regret, the fruit of our pettiness, have done just this: they have distracted our minds from the nobility of our acts, from the fact that our lives are a high romance where blows are struck resoundingly, bridges burned in spite of the cost (though not without the cost being counted). The joy of battle, honor, and high surprise is there to be savored; the taste of it all instantly sponges the bitterness of regret and reluctant surrender from our mouths. Thus we can maintain that

45

reluctance only by cheating ourselves of the romance of Catholicity, the pride of family, the joy of high endeavor. But even then the royal blood triumphs and puts its eternal mark of heroism on our every action.

In other words, heroism is not rare in the twentieth century; indeed it is a common thing, as it has been in every century since the Son of Mary walked among men. It is only in a world empty of Christ that heroes must be few and far between; for only in that world is the individual of no value, only there is he condemned to meaningless routine and skies that hold no stars for his reaching hands. In a world that makes room for the Son of God, men and women walk with the stride of God to the goal of God; they may grumble at the pace and sigh at the height of the goal, but nothing that earth or hell has to offer can stop them.

We respond to the love of the Sacred Heart, though we fail to match that divine generosity, still clinging to our trifles. Yet the very realization of the response we are making, of the heroism of this ordinary life, is itself the broom which sweeps our hearts clean of the dust of trifles. We can be small, in other words, only by forgetting that we are being big; we can be discouraged at our failures only by cheating ourselves of the joy well earned by the routine task of tracing the footsteps of Christ. Our lives can seem dull, routine, colorless only if we glue our eyes to the window that looks out on a world empty of Christ, neglecting the divine Guest for whom we have built the house, and whom we entertain faithfully, though sometimes with scant courtesy.

IT IS with Christ that we journey, and we walk with our steps in His footprints. He it is who is our Guide and the burning Flame which illumines our paths; Pioneer of Salvation, He it is who draws us toward heaven, toward the Father, and promises success to those who seek in faith. We shall one day be that which He is in glory, if by faithful imitation of His example, we become true Christians, other Christs.

ST. CYPRIAN

III

So we, being many, are one body in Christ,
and every one members one of another.

Romans 12:5

THE LIFE WE SHARE

THE REV. LEO J. TRESE

St. Paul says, "For as in one body we have many members, but all the members have not the same office; so we being many, are one body in Christ, and everyone members one of another." And Christ, St. Paul later adds, "is the head of one body."

We read that over once or twice, and we say, "Yes, what a beautiful figure of speech. We are all united in Christ, like the different parts of the body are united under the direction of the head. What a very expressive metaphor to describe the unity of all Christians in Christ!"

We can see what the idea will lead to, in action. If each of us is a member of the same body, then each of us will be working always for the good of the whole body, and for the good of every other part of the body. . . .

48

It is different from the *physical* Body of Christ—the Body He took from the Virgin Mary, the Body which we receive sacramentally in Holy Communion. And it is ever so much different from a mere *moral* body—one in which the members are joined together simply for a common purpose or by a legal statute. . . .

Every single one of us has become, by Baptism, an individual cell in that very special Body which Christ has chosen to fashion for Himself. It is the Body in which He perpetuates Himself in the world, the Body in which He lives and works among men.

It means that the angels and saints, looking down from Heaven, see me and my neighbor as more truly a part of each other and a part of Christ than my own hands and feet are a part of me. Looking closely at a newspaper picture, we see that it is made up of thousands of tiny dots, all combining to form the photograph which attracts the eye. So all of us are incorporated in Christ by Baptism; together we form His Image. Only, in this case it is a living Image, a vital, growing, dynamic Body. It is the Mystical Body of Christ. . . .

The Mystical Body of Christ has a soul, too. The Soul of the Mystical Body is the Holy Ghost. It is the Holy Spirit Who unites each of us individual cells with each other, and with Christ our Head. "Christ," says Pope Pius XII, "is in us through His Spirit, Whom He gives to us and through Whom He acts within us, in such a way that all divine activity of the Holy Spirit within our souls also must be attributed to Christ." . . .

That means that the Third Person of the Blessed Trinity, Divine Love personified, is in *me,* whole and entire. He is in me with all of His Gifts and all of His Fruits and all of His Virtues. It is this invisible but real and pulsating life, this sharing in God's own life through the Holy Spirit, which we call "Sanctifying Grace."

To share in that Life, I must of course be united to the Body. A hand that has been chopped off at the wrist is a dead hand, because the soul no longer is present in it. Similarly, if I am cut off from the Mystical Body, the Church, by unbelief or excommunication—then I am not a part of the Body, I do not share in the life of the Body. . . .

This, then, is the Mystical Body: Christ the Head, we the members (or better, perhaps, the cells) and the Holy Ghost the soul. . . .

Our whole idea of the Catholic Church is transformed . . . once we have grasped the doctrine of the Mystical Body of Christ, because of course the Mystical Body *is* the Church. They are just two different names for the same thing. . . .

The state of sanctifying grace is the normal condition of health, to be expected of each member of that Body. It means that I am sharing in the pulsating life of the whole Mystical Body, because the Holy Ghost, the soul of that Body, is within me.

It means that every Mass which the Church offers in my name and for my needs—hundreds of thousands of Masses every day in every part of the world—every one is a heart-beat of the Mystical Body, pumping into my soul the grace by which I live and grow. Every Divine Office that is recited, every liturgical prayer that is said by priests and religious around the world, all of them are for me; in all of them I have a part.

THE Church is Christ Himself. The Church is the plenitude, the accomplishment of Christ, his body and his real and mystical development—is Christ in His totality and plenitude. Thus among the works of God the Church occupies the very place of Christ; the Church and Christ —they are the same work of God.

DOM A. GREA, O.S.B.

"A LIFE REALLY LIVED"

ORESTES BROWNSON

WE WHO live at this day do not communicate directly with Christ Our Lord. We do it, and can do it, only through the medium of others. The Apostles and Disciples lived in personal intercourse with Him, and therefore communed with Him directly and immediately as their object. By this direct and immediate communion, his Divine human life became infused into their life. Others by communion with them partake of the same life. The succeeding generations participate in it by communing with its predecessor. Thus by communion the life may be infused through all men living contemporaneously, and transmitted to the latest posterity. . . .

This Divine-human life is one and identical in all who receive it, for it is a real life really lived, not merely desired by the heart or assented to as a doctrine by the reason. It enters really into the life of their life. All life is organic, and consequently all who live this life are moulded or formed in one body, living one and the same life, the life of Christ, and therefore rightly termed his

51

body, the CHURCH, as the Scriptures expressly teach. Hence I have the Church, not as an association, an organization, or mere aggregation of individuals, but as an organism, one and Catholic,—one because its life is one, Catholic because it includes all who live the life, of whatever age or nation, and because all men in every age and nation may by communion have it. The life of Christ is not only life, but the principle of life, and operating in the body assimilates individuals, as the human body assimilates the particles of food eaten. It is then no sham, no illusion, but the real body of Christ, a real living organism, and in some sense a continuation of the Incarnation.

ABOVE all Christ is the life. His words and example were to endure, not in memory alone, as do the words and deeds of national heroes of the past; "My words shall not pass." Through century after century He lives on in the life and activities of His MYSTICAL BODY, counseling, healing, and forgiving, even as He did in Galilee. He has not left us orphans. He abides with us today and will be with us all days, even to the consummation of the world. Truly does His divine life course through the souls of the faithful and prompt them to share with Him mankind's burdens of sickness, sorrow, and privation.

PATRICK CARDINAL HAYES

"MEMBERS OF ONE ANOTHER"

THE REV. GERALD ELLARD, S.J.

SUPPOSE we focus our attention for a moment on this *consciousness* of worshipping as a member of the Body of Him whom St. Paul calls our Liturgist. I go to Mass on Sunday morning to dedicate myself to God in the form of a material gift, for I recall that the basic idea of sacrifice is the service of God by a gift which stands for self. Just as I am about to enter a pew, I see a person who offended me a few days ago, so I give her a meaning look and go to another pew. But as I kneel down I am ashamed of myself for did not Christ say something about leaving one's gift at the altar and going first to be reconciled to an offended brother and only then coming to offer the sacrifice? In my present endeavor then to present my body "a living sacrifice, holy, pleasing unto God" (Rom. xii.I), I propose that the oblation of my service will be the fulfilment of God's will in the matter of Christian patience and charity. So at the Offertory I present my penny's worth of bread and wine in gifts that stand not only for myself and my present good resolution, but for the priest at the altar, for every soul in the church building, for every soul in the world-wide Church itself. Next to me is the landlord, and he is putting his gift on the altar in token of conformity to God's will in the matter of decent housing. Behind me is a laborer, a labor leader in fact, and he is offering himself for the perfect observance of the law of Christ in the relationships of master and man. I note nearby a banker, whose bread and wine signify his willingness to fulfill the mind of Christ as to the stewardship of our goods. By ourselves we are weak and shrink from sacrifice, but the Stem supports us, and so the altar is heaped with our poor crooked selves in the form of common bread and wine. By these offerings we express our willingness to practice self-control, to shoulder the cost of a Christian education, to assume the full responsibilities of citizenship, to extend the hand of fellowship to those of other races and other nationalities, and, in a word, to dedicate to God a union of minds and hearts, which we call in the Canon "the oblation of our service." As our gifts are put on the altar we pray that in a contrite heart and humble spirit we may be received by God and may be made partakers of His Divinity, Who vouchsafed to share our humanity. Then, in the process of giving, the bread and wine, that stand for all of us, are caught up with Christ's great Gift and become the Body and the Blood. . . .

And so at Mass we press forward to the Banquet Table, sacramentally if possible, or at least spiritually, to eat of the one Bread that makes us all one body. Banker and laborer, educator and politician and industrialist, the proud, and self-centered, the unforgiving, all partake together of the good things that God has prepared for us. And it chances I find next to me at the railing that very person I snubbed on entering the church. Arising from communion, I follow and kneel beside her and praise God present in her, as well as in myself, for I know now what St. Thomas meant when he said that the effect of the Sacrament is union with the Mystic Body. We leave the church together, thankful that the Light which is the life of man, hath made us understand that we are members of Christ and members of one another.

THE sense of isolation, of dwelling as strangers in a foreign land, is lost when we grow conscious at Mass or Benediction or at the reception of any of the sacraments, that we are bridging over all times and places. All the world over, what we see and hear and are saying is being witnessed by others besides ourselves. We are not lonely travellers toiling after some lost trail, but a huge army, whose uniform and whose battle-songs are the traditions of our race. We enter into the inheritance of all the saints. All that is best in literature, art, religion, is swept up and gathered into one—the wonders of the Mass, the depth of the Psalms, the night-prayer of Compline, the radiance of the office of Prime, the consoling tenderness of the Office for the Dead. Here Hebrew, Greek, Latin are like three solemn kings who bring their gifts to Christ. Out of all nations have come the creators and preservers of the liturgy; and these bring with them the spirit and the genius of their own peoples. All find there some lot or part in the magnificent yet simple services.

THE REV. BEDE JARRETT, O.P.

THE UNIFYING SPIRIT
OF CHRIST

THE REV. IGNATIUS W. COX, S.J.

CHRIST is extending Himself; working out the fruits of His incarnation in every land; meeting in His mystical body the same forces of good and evil He met in His earthly days. This divine life is Catholic and therefore universal. It is in Rome, in Paris, in Berlin, and London and New York and San Francisco. It is found in the African forest, in the Indian jungle, in the Chinese hamlet. It is in the palaces of the rich and the slums of the poor. It is the same in moral ideal, in dogmatic belief, in its sacramental system, because it is the life of Jesus, the way, the truth and the life. It is the same in its fountain source. It is the divine life lived by Peter and Paul, by Jerome and Augustine and Benedict; by Francis of Assisi and Dominic and Ignatius of Loyola, by Teresa and the Little Flower of Jesus, by De Sales and Vincent de Paul and John of the Cross. It is the Divine Life, the ideals of which were ever present to Joan of Arc and Thomas More, and Edward the Confessor, and Louis of France; to Dante and Francis Thompson, to Columbus and Marshal Foch. It is the communion of the saints; it is the unity for which Christ prayed, the union of men with God and men with one another through the one divine life of Christ. It is the solidarity lost by Adam and brought back by the redeeming blood of Christ; the at-one-ment of man with God and man with man in the abiding love of Christ. "One body and one Spirit . . . one Lord, one Faith, one baptism. One God and Father of all, who is above all, and through all, and in us all." Eph. 4:4–6.

THE most solitary hermit is not really a Christian if he does not pray for the Kingdom of God to be spread in this world. A Christian is never alone, and he is always responsible for his brethren. Not only is he not alone, but his relationship to others is not merely that of an individual who happens to be in contact with them; we are bound up with one another; we are social to our very core on every level of life, natural and supernatural. Owing to our communion in faith and charity as members of Christ's Mystical Body, there should be a circulation of life among us, in which each gives out as much as, or even more than, he gets. This giving out, for the growth of our neighbors and the increase of the whole Body, can be called, in a wide sense, apostleship. Each of us has a mission of radiating the supernatural life to all those God puts in our way.

THE REV. PIE-RAYMOND RÉGAMEY, O.P.

COMPANIONSHIP IN CHRIST

THE REV. JOHN W. LYNCH

THERE is no such thing as a Catholic who is completely strange to any other Catholic. In being related to Our Lord we are already introduced to each other. That is what Paul meant by the Mystical Body of Christ, but approached from the idea of a human association, of a wide, varied company of people who hold ties among themselves, the dogma becomes vivid and human and immensely enriching.

Within the Church we hold the same bundle of doctrine; we do live by the same code, we do become holy in the same Sacraments, but in addition we all belong to a companionship that is very real and very good. Nationality does not matter, race does not matter, condition of life does not alienate. There are no boundary lines on the earth or in time, for the association breaks through time and death and physical disappearance, and it holds everywhere, and always.

The ideal of durability is mentioned, and hoped for, and intended, in all good bonds among human beings. We say: "I shall always be your friend." We say: "You can always count on me." Or, "I am your friend and I shall never fail you." It's the *always* that is the ideal, the pledge and the test. The notion of *forever* is forever in what we want in our loves.

The splendor of the Faith is precisely here: Our Lord is always there, Our Lady is always our own, the bonds with the Saints, with fellow Catholics are always our own, the same, and will endure forever. God did manifest His love for us in the concept and in the establishment of His Faith on the earth, but His love took into account what we are and what we need. The Faith is not an outside thing imposed on men: it meets the needs of men as they are, and it fits our inside nature.

"It is not good for man to be alone," said the Creator. In the Faith He has given His Son, His Son's Mother, His Own great friends, and all of us together, that we be not alone.

A CHRISTIAN BROTHERHOOD

PIUS XII

NOTHING more glorious, nothing nobler, nothing surely more honorable can be imagined than to belong to the Holy, Catholic, Apostolic and Roman Church, in which we become members of one Body as venerable as it is unique; are guided by one supreme Head; are filled with one divine Spirit; are nourished during our earthly exile by one doctrine and one heavenly Bread, until at last we enter into the one, unending blessedness of heaven. . . .

True love of the Church, therefore, requires not only that we should be mutually solicitous one for another as members of the same Body, rejoicing in the glory of the other members and sharing in their suffering, but likewise that we should recognize in other men, although they are not yet joined to us in the Body of the Church, our brothers in Christ according to the flesh, called, together with us, to the same eternal salvation. . . . While Our heart overflows with the sweetness of the teaching of the Apostle of the Gentiles, We extol with him the length, and the breadth, and the height, and the depth of the charity of Christ, which neither diversity of race or customs can diminish, nor the trackless wastes of the ocean weaken, nor wars, whether just or unjust, destroy.

(JUNE 29, 1943)

THE knowledge of our holy religion will enkindle in you a love of the Church. . . . It is the Church, not of one race or of one nation, but of all those who truly believe in His name. The more you dwell upon its teachings, its practice, and its history, the stronger will be your sense of unity with the multitude of believers throughout the world. You will clearly understand that the true interests of each part, of each diocese and parish, are the interests of the Church Universal. "And if one member suffer anything, all the members suffer with it; or, if one member glory, all the members rejoice with it. Now you are the BODY OF CHRIST, and members of member" (I Cor. xii, 26–27).

JOINT PASTORAL, AMERICAN
BISHOPS, 1919

A TREASURE HOUSE FOR SOULS

THE REV. F. P. LE BUFFE, S.J.

Jude, the servant of Jesus Christ, and the brother of James, to them that are called, being beloved in God the Father and kept for Jesus Christ.

St. Jude I. 1.

"KEPT for Jesus Christ!" What thoughts that phrase evokes! God has placed in this world a great treasure-house, His Church, and into that Church, against which even the gates of hell cannot prevail, He has placed me to be guarded and "kept" for Him until He calls me home to be safe with Him in Heaven for all eternity. My soul is so "precious" to Him that, when Adam had thrown away my chance for Heaven, He became man for me that I might have another chance to be with Him unendingly.

His stay on earth was not an easy one, He led an obscure life and worked as a village carpenter that His example might emphasize for me just how much He valued my soul. Then, lest even that might not be proof enough to me, He suffered the most cruel death that man has ever invented. That is how "precious" I am to Him.

But He did not then leave me alone and unguarded to make my way home to Him. He founded His Church as His other self, His Mystical Body, and made me a member in that Body wherein I am shielded by its doctrines, and safeguarded and nurtured by its Sacraments. From the hour of my birth until I close my eyes in death, there are always plentiful means of grace to keep me near Him and draw me even closer to Him.

"Kept for Jesus Christ!" That is the explanation of each big and little thing in the Church, of each great and small grace He gives me. No loved one has ever been more "precious" to any lover than I am to Christ. No lover has ever guarded his "precious" one the way Christ guards me.

"Kept for Jesus Christ!" What a conviction to help me keep my balance when the pleasures of life would attract me too much! What an inspiration in life's dark hours to steady me against discouragement and to move me to "make good" in the eyes of my "tremendous Lover"!

IV

You are the light of the world. A city seated upon a mountain cannot be hid.
St. Matthew 5:14

THE LIGHT FROM THE MOUNTAIN TOP

THE MOST REV. JOHN CUTHBERT HEDLEY, O.S.B.

THE Lord Jesus went up from Mount Olivet on Ascension Day, and we have Him no more in the flesh. But when He was taken from our sight, another form came down from the heavens; a form of beauty, of brightness, and of power. She lighted upon the mountain top. . . . She was sent by that Jesus Who promised He would not leave us orphans, and she was the creation of that Spirit of Jesus Who shook the house upon the Day of Pentecost, and Who sent out into the streets the twelve men with the fire upon their brows. And her name was the Law of the Lord Jesus Christ. Her light streams from her lofty mountain upon all that there is in the world. Except so far as the malice of gainsayers hinders her, she makes herself felt on things little and things great—on intellect and work, upon men and their dealings with one another; on "all the tall and lofty cedars of Libanus, and upon all the oaks of Basan; and upon all the high mountains and all the elevated hills; and upon every high tower and every fenced wall; and upon the ships of Tharsis, and upon all that is fair to behold." This is the prophetic description of the effect of the Christian revelation in the world. The cedars of Libanus represent the men of genius of the human race. The lofty hills are the heights of human industry and achievement. The high towers are human pride—pride of race and pride of person. The ships of the great seaports are human interests of every kind. And the fair and beautiful things mean all human pleasure and delight. Christianity must touch and transform them all.

Among all the instances of harmony, and of law, which the Creator has given us after His own image, the most remarkable is that which He set up when He came on earth, the most perfect is that which exists in His Church. In the awful music of her doctrines, in the deep wisdom of her precepts, in the majesty of her Hierarch, in the beauty of her Ritual, in the dazzling lustre of her Saints, in the consistent march of her policy, and in the manifold richness of her long history,—in all of these we recognize the Hand of the God of order, luminously, illustriously displayed. In her whole and in her parts, in her diversified aspects, the one same image of law and of rule ever confronts us, as in those crystallized substances of the physical world, which, both in the mass and in the details, consist in a reiteration of one and the same structure.

JOHN HENRY CARDINAL NEWMAN

THE CATHOLIC COMMUNITY
AND THE INDIVIDUAL

RT. REV. ROMANO GUARDINI

ALL that Christ was, all that He taught, did, created, and suffered, is contained in these words—He has established the Kingdom of God. The Kingdom of God means that the Creator takes possession of His creature, penetrates it with His light; He fills its will and heart with His own burning love and the roots of its being with His own divine peace, and He moulds the entire spirit by the creative power which imposes a new form upon it. The Kingdom of God means that God draws His creature to Himself, and makes it capable of receiving His own fulness; and that He bestows upon it the longing and the power to possess Him. . . .

The Church is the Kingdom of God in its suprapersonal aspect; the human community reborn into God's Kingdom. The individual is 'the Church,' in so far as the aim of his life is to assist the building up of the community, and he is a member, a cell of it. . . .

The Kingdom of God, however, has a subjective side as well. That is the individual soul, as God's grace takes possession of it in that private and unique individuality by which it exists for itself. The Church embraces a man as he reaches out beyond himself to his fellows, capable

64

and desirous of forming in conjunction with them a community of which he and they are members. The individual personality, however, is also based upon itself, like a globe which revolves around its own axis. And as such, also, God's grace takes possession of it. By this I do not mean there exists in human beings a sphere which lies outside the Church. That would be too superficial a notion. It is truer to say that the whole man is in the Church, with all that he is. Even in his most individual aspects he is her member, although only in so far as this individuality and its powers are directed to the community. His whole being belongs to it; it is in its social reference—his individuality as related to his fellows and incorporated in the community. But the same individuality has an opposite pole. His powers are also directed inwards to build up a world in which he is alone with himself. In this aspect also he is the subject of God's grace. . . .

The nature of the community as Catholicism understands and realizes it, is not such that individual personality has to struggle for self-preservation against it. It is not a power which violates personal individuality, as Communism does, or any other variety of the totalitarian state. On the contrary, Catholic community presupposes from the outset and requires the free individual personalities as its components. In particular the Church is a community of beings, which are not simply members and instruments of the whole, but at the same time are microcosms revolving on their own axes, that is, individual personalities. . . .

The Church then is a society essentially bound up with individual personality; and the individual life of the Christian is of its very nature related to the community. Both together are required for the perfect realization of the Kingdom of God. . . .

From all this one fact emerges. The personal life of the Christian is engaged to its profoundest depths in the Church and affected by her condition. And conversely the Church is to an incalculable degree affected by the spiritual condition of her members. . . . Between the individual and the Church there is an organic solidarity of the most intimate kind. The same Kingdom of God lives in the Church and in the individual Catholic.

The sacramental and sacrificial system of Christianity puts perfect purpose and poise and order into the restless religious yearning of the *nature of man* as we know it. It alone imparts the *supernatural life* in a complete system of sanctification, wherein all life's needs and aspirations are met and furthered. It alone allows an expression, perfect from every point of view, to man's humble homage; it alone brings to actual accomplishment man's longing to put himself into communication with, to unite himself with, God. Only Catholicity gives full play to the need of bodily as well as spiritual homage, enabling man to enlist in his worship color and sound and fabric, lights and incense, oil and water, bread and wine.

THE REV. GERALD ELLARD, S.J.

THE FAITH'S EARTHLY
REWARDS

THE REV. JOHN W. LYNCH

Now the whole teaching: *"My Kingdom is not of this world,"* and the undeniably obvious doctrine: *"We have not here a lasting dwelling place,"* are basic to religion. Heaven is very much part of the plan. . . . Heaven is the fulfillment of the human person in the measure of his own capacity. . . .

Catholicism begins Heaven here and now. The rewards are immediate, a matter of daily enrichment, and we ought to note the simple fact that non-religious living, so prevalent in our times, is thin, shallow, and petty when compared to religious living, and that lack of depth and size is its chief characteristic. The Faith actually gives a bigger life to live. Remove the Faith, or narrow its practices, and life, this week, this month, diminishes. Anybody can be glad when it is May; the Catholic is glad with the added joy that May means Our Lady, and the inner, half-secret happiness that is the sound of her name. The lilacs take on an air of tribute, the fresh blooms acquire a spiritual significance, and the brighter mornings mean more than springtime.

Night prayers and the bedside examination of conscience are more than duty; they indicate that this casual, anonymous day contained adventure, and that it is filed away as part of a total story. Without religion there would be no story, and if no story, then no hero running risks, conquering hazards, winning triumphs. The Sunday Mass is not just an obligation; it means that you do count in the vision of God, that you are an individual, and that you are important enough to be missed, even in the presence of vast crowds, if you are not there. You have a place in the scheme of things, and the place is your very own.

Certainly the Catholic enjoys the trout stream, the lazy leisure with the Sunday papers strewn about, the late sleep, the sunny fields of golf, the ride in the car, the day with the children, but all these are twice as much fun if they are not alone but rest on the solid foundation of the worship of the Mass. What ought to be seen is that for the Catholic, Sunday is not just the papers and the day off, nor merely a break in the routine. Sunday is that . . . plus.

I have nothing but sympathy for newspaper reporters, and especially for those reporters who write for the society pages, but I have often observed how helpless, how inept, how trivial the society reporters are when they must describe a Catholic marriage. There the story is, with perhaps a photograph of the bride. . . . The papers report the trimmings; they miss the reality.

This is a romance that religion has ennobled and deepened and made rich. Here is the union of two souls helping each other on the way to Heaven. The words, "until death do us part" have glorious honesty in them. This man and this woman belong to each other. There will never be other flowers, other lists of bridesmaids, other pictures in the papers. This is a vow . . . forever. The pledges are enshrined in a Mass that is their Mass, in a Holy Communion that is *their* Communion. Christ is here as He was at Cana. Divorce does not lurk like a blight in the background. The current one-out-of-three percentage has no dismal threat here. This is not tentative, nor half-hearted, nor fragile, and there is quite another blessing than the wistful saying of "Good Luck." Religion is the main theme of a Catholic marriage, and it makes all the ribbons and the laces and the society reports look just like ribbons and laces and society reports. The Catholic wedding does not depend upon them.

And the abstinence on a Friday is not just a small observance of a small ritual. The Faith puts meaning in one day of the week as Christ put meaning in one day in all time. Meat on Friday would be as dust in the mouth. St. Christopher rides in a car; Our Lady's medal is worn like a badge; religion adds retreats to conventions; and religion puts a Missal among the books of the month that the clubs select.

We could continue. The Faith has quite a lot to do with actual living, and I suppose the genuine Catholic rarely thinks of Heaven at all; at least I am sure he never thinks of it as the sole reward and justification for his life. The Faith gives too much now. Heaven is the last great endowment, but it is not waiting all by itself.

A child has an immortal soul behind his laughing eyes; the three meals are salted with Grace; the calendar turns from Feast to Feast, and Season to Season, in the liturgy; and death has the great Requiescat to give it peace.

THE Church has herself become, in a subordinate sense, our way, our truth, and our life, for she conducts us to Christ, for in her teaching she dispenses unto us the word of Christ, for in her sacraments and sacramentals she communicates to us the divine sap of Christ.

DOM COLUMBA MARMION, O.S.B.

69

THE COMFORT OF CERTITUDE

RT. REV. ROBERT HUGH BENSON

GOD has not left us comfortless: He has planted His Vine
and safeguarded her against error. He has established an
authority which speaks with His voice.

And the whole of my observation confirms the theory.
It is written not on paper, but in the lives and hearts of
men. I see a unity here, unlike any other unity in the
world; I hear a voice consistent with itself and louder
than all the cries of conflict, and a message that is the
same for simple and wise alike; I see a Figure moving
through the ages, overshadowing every country, and bearing on herself the marks of the LORD JESUS; and I
hear millions of voices acclaiming her as divine. Her
Children are not required to be infallible; they are not
asked to expect personal illumination from heaven on
all points of doctrine; one thing only is given—certitude
that she is what she claims to be; one thing only is asked
—a simple act of faith in her mission. . . .

Scholarship is not asked of me, nor eloquence, nor in-
genuity; no more is required than was required of Mary
and Martha and James and Andrew, and which all can
give—that, looking upon this Figure, I should recognize
it as from GOD, listening to the message I should acclaim
it as divine; and that my highest joy and widest freedom
should henceforth be found in sitting at those feet, re-
signing my self-will, and learning what the LORD GOD
will say.

THE Catholic rests not on his own frailty, but on the voice of millions uttering united testimony. He stands with them on the rock of ages, whose foundation is Christ's promise. He hears the winds of persecution howl, and is awakened to vigilance, and wraps his garment of Christianity closer about him. He looks out upon the waters of contradiction how their waves rise and fall and bellow, crossing in strife, and mingle, and have each their time. He sees each billow, swollen and crested with pride, as it comes and is dashed and broken against the rock, and retires and disappears.

THE MOST REV. W. BERNARD
ULLATHORNE

THE MIRACLE OF THE CHURCH

RT. REV. ROBERT HUGH BENSON

"IT IS my glory," cries the Church, "that I make dead things to live. I take the dead music of the Jews, and it blossoms in flowers of plainsong; I catch up the dying language of a Latin people, and I make it live, when to all others it has been long dead; it thrives in my liturgy, it generates new words in my theology, it glows on the lips of my preachers, it is the tongue in which my foreign priests communicate with me and with one another. At Pentecost the miracle that showed the wisdom of GOD was that men of one language spoke many; in the twentieth century after Pentecost my miracle is that men of many languages speak one.

I sweep up the debased architecture of the Roman Empire, and out of it I build my basilicas. I seize to myself the dying philosophy of Aristotle, and recreate it alive to make my meaning plain. I am ready, as I have always been, to take the ephemeral things of men, their dress, their methods, their modes of thought, and to use them, if it suits my purpose, for the manifestation of my divine life.

The whole world lies about my roots, and I suck out of every country and age what befits my energy of life.

For I am more than the oak and the mustard-tree; I am the very Vine of GOD, brought out of Egypt long ago; my seed fell in a ball of fire with the sound of wind; and from that moment I have lived indeed. I thrust my white shoots in the darkness of the catacombs, and forced my way through the cracks of Caesar's falling palaces; my early grapes were trodden under foot, rent by the wild boar in the amphitheatre, spoilt by little foxes, crushed in the wine-press of rack and prison; I am blown upon by every wind that blows, by calumny and criticism from the north, by passion and fury in the south and west. I am pruned year by year with sharp knives forged in death and hell, yet grasped by the hand of the Father who is my husbandman. And yet I live, and shall live, till my Beloved come down to taste the fruits of the garden.

For I am planted by the river of salvation, watered by the tears and blood of saints, breathed upon by the spirit of GOD who alone can make the spices to flow forth. More than that, I am mystically one with my Beloved already; it is His Heart's blood that flows in my veins; His strength that sustains me; for He is the Vine, my boughs are His branches; and I am nothing save in Him and them. It is for this cause then that I spring up indomitable; that I stretch my boughs to the river; and my branches to the sea, that my shadow is in all lands; that the wild birds lodge in my branches, the dove and the eagle together; that the fierce beasts couch beside my roots, the wolf beside the lamb, and the leopard by the kid. It is for this that I am older than the centuries, younger than yesterday, eternal, undying and divine."

EACH CHURCH IS THE ALL-EMBRACING CHURCH

THE MOST REV. JOHN CUTHBERT HEDLEY, O.S.B.

THE people of God are now the whole world; and wherever there are souls of men, there also is by right the one and all-embracing Church; and wherever one church is, holy places can be multiplied, sanctuaries set up, and altars raised; and in every place where the Universal Church thus takes unto herself an outward shape and a material habitation, there is the dream of the patriarch realized, and heaven is brought into communication with the earth, and the earth with the heavens.

This church of yours has all the endowments, the prerogatives, and the glory of the Church Universal. It has the Church's stability and security; the Church's spiritual unction and fulness of grace; it has the same Presence and Word which is the Church's life; and, like the Church, it lifts up hearts to God and draws down God to the heart. Any one who passes its threshold, if he is instructed, knows this. Any stranger, even from another

73

hemisphere, even from the remotest and least known shores, if he is a Catholic, knows what to find within these walls. This altar is the altar he has always known, and these rites are familiar to him; and even if the tongue, or the vesture, or the observances be strange, he knows that God is in this place—God's word, God's presence, God's operation, God's mercy. He knows that in this place there is the universal Catholic truth, the universal Catholic teaching, the universal Catholic sacrifice, the universal Catholic Sacraments. And he knows that all that the Church was meant to bring to the universal world, this church can bring to him in particular, and to those who gather beneath its roof.

And yet you are not wrong in calling it your church. It is yours; and by a title far more real, because so far more spiritual, than any claims of material ownership can confer. It is yours because it is bound up with the history of your spirit. For the spirit, as we all know, has a thousand points of contact with this universe of matter. For this very reason it is that there is a visible Church, a Priesthood, Sacraments, and the great dispensation of the Holy Eucharist. And, therefore, it is not surprising—it is most natural—I will go further, and say it is right and just—that the walls and the roof of your own church should be dear to you, and that you should love the choir and the altar which have been, through so many years, the symbol and visible means of the nearness and the merciful work of the Lord your God.

OUR SUBLIMATION IN THE
COMMON LIFE OF GRACE

THE MOST REV. FULTON J. SHEEN

WHEN . . . I am asked what the Church means to me, I answer that it is the Temple of Life in which I am a living stone; it is the Tree of Eternal Fruit of which I am a branch; it is the Mystical Body of Christ on earth of which I am a member. The Church is therefore more to me than I am to myself; her life is more abundant than mine, for I live by union with her. She could live without me for I am only a cell in her body; but I could not normally live without her. I live only as a part of her, as my arm lives only as a part of my body. So absorbing does she become that her thoughts are my thoughts; her loves are my loves; her ideals are my ideals. I consider sharing her life the greatest gift God has ever given to me, as I should consider losing her life the greatest evil that could befall me. Dependence is the very essence of my creaturely existence, for no man is sufficient unto himself. I am not a speck in a moral void, nor a wanderer without a home, nor an isolated unit in creation; rather am I dependent on the God-appointed destiny whereby I share my love of God with others who love God in the unity of the Mystical Body of Christ. . . .

There is no destruction of nature by grace, but only its elevation to another order. Tears are a common fountain for joy and sorrow. Passions too are common outlets for virtue and vice. It is not a different passion that makes a man a saint, from that which makes a man a devil; it is the same passion going in a different direction. The Church then in embracing our lives within her common life does not destroy our personalities—she does not even destroy our most wicked passions. She transmutes them by the magic of her Sacraments, provides new outlets, fixes new goals, and digs new channels. The heroes of the world are not different from martyrs; the same natural courage which would make a man die for Caesar on a battlefield, the Church would transmute into a supernatural courage which would make him die for Christ. The bigots are all potential missionaries, for the same zeal that makes them unwittingly serve falsehood can be elevated by the Church to make them serve Divine Truth. The great scientists are all incipient theologians for that same curiosity, which drives them to a knowledge of secondary causes, the Church transmutes by leading them to a knowledge of the First Cause which is God. We would not say that the hero who became a saint, nor the bigot who became a missionary, nor the scientist who became a theologian lost their personalities once incorporated into Christ's body, any more than we lost our personalities once we became citizens of a nation. But we would say, that in their union with that common life of grace, they had found the sublimation of their distinct personalities, and the crown of their individual selves.

How men seek in vain, in their friends, what the Church alone and her consecrated priests can supply. Many pressed with the want, make even strangers their confidants, and yet find no light, no peace, no answer. Some yield to despair of ever finding it; others, in the hope of discovering an answer, have entered upon a false and diabolical mysticism; others, again, to drown their feelings of their higher nature, who only seem, like fiends, to harry their bosoms, have yielded up their souls to a voluptuous unconcern. Not one has gone on steadily in the path of a divine life. Those who have not gone back, stand, as it were, upon enchanted ground; they seem to themselves to advance, but it is only a charge; they seem to announce new truths, but it is only a tame repetition; they appear to live, but it is a life without freshness or hope. They are encircled and imprisoned by self.

There is no other progress in life than heavenward. But to progress toward God, two things are necessary. First, the knowledge of the way to God. Secondly, a divine guide. The Church affords both. The first is her dogma; the second, is her spiritual directors.

THE REV. I. T. HECKER

THE CHURCH'S APPEAL TO THE BEST IN HUMAN NATURE

THE MOST REV. JOHN LANCASTER SPALDING

THE efficacy of a religious organization to keep pure religious faith alive and active is the highest test of its worth, and the Catholic Church when tried by this test stands pre-eminent. Her power to speak to the mind, the heart, the imagination, the whole man, is proclaimed and dreaded by her enemies, while those who believe in her are stirred to tender and grateful thoughts at the mention of the name of her whom they call Mother. She is dear to them for a thousand reasons. Has she not filled the earth with memorials of the soul's trust in God? Who has entered her solemn cathedrals and not heard whispering from higher worlds? Her liturgy, her sacred rites, her grave and measured chants; the dim lights that ever burn in her sanctuaries; the mystic vestments with which her ministers are clothed; the incense diffusing a hallowed fragrance through the long withdrawing aisles; the bells that morning, noon, and night repeat the Angel's salutation to Mary and seem to shower blessings from Heaven—all this speaks to the soul, subdues and softens the heart, until we long to bow the head in prayer and give free course to the gathering tears.

Can we not read in the countenances of those who love her truly, the story of lives of patience and reverence, purity and mildness? How unwearyingly do they labor! How serenely when death comes do they rest from their labors! What a Heavenly spell has she not thrown, does she still not throw, over innumerable souls, creating in them habits of thought, love, and deed, against which theories, of whatever kind, are advanced in vain! They have made experiments; they have tasted the waters of life; they know and are certain that it is better to be for a single day in the holy place of the Lord than to dwell for a thousand years in the habitation of sinners. Has she not the secret of teaching the poor and unlearned the higher wisdom—the wisdom that lies in the spiritual mind and the lowly heart; making them capable of feeling God's presence and viewing all things in their relations to Him Who is eternal; ennobling them to forget their nothingness in the consciousness of co-operating with Him for ends that are absolute, under the guidance of Heaven—appointed leaders, comrades of the noble living and the noble dead; certain that though they die yet shall they live? Thus she turns her true children to righteousness, lifting the individuality of each from out the crushing mass of matter of men; giving them deep convictions of the sacredness and worth of life, of the possibilities that lie open to the meanest soul if he be but converted to God, who even in the most degraded can still see some likeness to Himself.

The Church has power to attract and hold the most different minds. In all the centuries since Christ was born, among all the races of men, she has found followers and lovers. She impresses by her long descent, her historic continuity, her power to adapt herself to an ever-varying environment, by the force with which she resists foes whether from within or from without; at all times maintaining her vigor, despite the corruptions of her children, and the hatred and persecution of the world; thus manifesting herself as the city of God, the Kingdom of Christ, a spiritual empire in which there is an imperishable principle of super-natural life and of indefectible strength. The unity of her organization and government, the harmony of her doctrines, the consistency of her aims and purposes, the sublimity of her ideals, the persistency of her efforts to mould the minds and hearts of men into conformity with the will of God, make appeal to what is best in human nature.

THE CHURCH IS FOR ALL

THE REV. ALBERT H. DOLAN, O. CARM.

CATHOLIC lay people, yes, Catholic priests and sisters and brothers, often are, in spite of their membership or rank in the Church of God, uncharitable, narrow, rigid, and they often make a disagreeable and painful impression upon others. There is no doubt of it—many Catholics are characterized by prudery, vulgarity and an imperfect sense of honor. . . .

Although these sad truths fill us Catholics with shame, still from another point of view they fortify and strengthen our faith. Yes, actually, when I contemplate the spectacle of the membership in the Church of Christ (some few ideal Catholics but the majority imperfect); when I contemplate that spectacle, it sometimes makes me want to fall down on my knees in reverent devotion. . . .

As I contemplate the spectacle sometimes I am filled with shame and sometimes with reverence. Let me explain both attitudes. First, why should the spectacle fill us with reverence? For this reason: to see how utterly Christ Our Lord in His love delivered Himself up to men, to all men, when He founded His Church, and to see how truly heroic is the obedience of the Catholic Church to her Founder when she desires to take into her membership all men, all types of men. She dares to take upon herself the burden of human nature just as it is, to take into her fold, at God's orders, all manner of men. She dares to deliver herself up to the burden of carrying in her vast arms the masses, the multitude, the proletariat, all classes including the mob, the elite and the riffraff, the so-called upper and lower classes, the literate and illiterate, the cultured and the ignorant, the refined and the crude—and thus expose herself to being misunderstood, expose herself to degradation and shame.

How could the Church do otherwise, and be the Church of Christ? "As the Father hath sent me, I send you," Christ said. And to whom was He sent? To sinners. "I am not come to call the just but sinners" (Matt. 9, 13), He said. So must His true Church embrace not only the just but also the sinners. . . .

If you search for the just in the Church you will find them today; and as for the power of the Church to produce perfectly balanced characters and the sanest holiness, read the lives of the legions of saints, and there you will find a partial answer to the question we are discussing. So much for the just.

Now for the imperfect and sinful. They must be present in the Church of God. Does it require any profound reasoning to perceive that truth? With whom did our Lord surround Himself? Did He surround Himself with the elite of His day, with the philosophers and the wealthy and the cultured? He did not exclude them. Some of them, like Joseph of Arimathea, were His friends; but generally the elite—the Scribes and doctors of the law, the Pharisees and the Sadducees—were His enemies. He invited them, He preached to them, but they rejected Him. With whom did He surround Himself? To whom did He chiefly minister? To sinners. Yes, to sinners. So much so that again and again He suffered the reproach that "He was the friend of publicans and sinners." "Why doth your master eat with publicans and sinners?" (Matt. 9, 11). Such was the reproach suffered by our Lord by reason of His ministrations to sinners. And such is and must be the reproach of the one true Church of Christ—namely, that she too harbors sinners in her fold.

Is it not clear that if there is to be a Church of God, a Church of God, mark you, that Church must be for all? All are children of God; all are God's creatures; all were created by Him, redeemed by Him. . . .

Moreover, our Lord gave His own description of His Church. He compared it to a net gathering bad fish as well as good; to a field in which there were weeds as well as good grain; to a banquet to which were invited not only the wealthy and the cultured but also beggars and the lame and the crippled from the highways and byways. Yes, there can be no doubt of the truth that the Church of God must be for all men, just and sinners. . . .

The true Church of God must contain not only the cultured but also the crude. Who composed the inner circle of our Lord's closest friends? The refined and cultured were not excluded, as witness the wealthy Joseph of Arimathea, who provided the place of our Lord's burial, and Martha and Mary and Lazarus. But whom did He choose for His Apostles? Fishermen. And for the chief of His Apostles?—again a fisherman, Peter. And did their close relationship with Christ—daily, hourly companionship with Him—transform them into perfect men and loyal followers? Why, one of them betrayed Him (Judas) and another denied Him (Peter) and with the exception of John they all deserted Him in the hour of His need. Is it strange then, is it not rather to be expected, that His Church would duplicate His own experience, and that just as daily association with Him did not transform His Apostles into perfect men, so membership in His Church, with all the intimate privileges which that membership involves, will not necessarily transform all Catholics into perfect specimens of nature or of grace? The Church of God must transform some into such perfect specimens; it must possess the power of effecting such a transformation and elevation. But what our Lord Himself did not accomplish in all His followers we cannot expect the Church to achieve in all her members.

But we inquire further: Why should this be so? It is a necessary consequence of the truth that the Church of God must exist for all. When I say it must exist for all, I mean, to give one instance only, it must exist not only for the brilliant but also for the dull. And one of the many reasons why there are Catholic churchgoers who remain narrow and uncharitable and selfish is because many of them are unintelligent. They are intellectually incapable of perceiving fully what their membership in the Church of God ought to do for them and in them and with them. The beautiful doctrine of love of neighbor, based as it is chiefly on the doctrine of the Mystical Body of Christ, the thoughtless do not fully understand. There are other doctrines too which have delighted the minds of the most gigantic intellects of every century which are only half-understood by the stupid. Ignorance explains why the Church of God does not transform many. But would you exclude the ignorant from the Church of God, the Father of all? No, they must be there.

Similarly, there are people who are by nature light, frivolous and shallow. They have never taken life seriously; they are utterly incapable of appreciating the finer things of life; they immerse themselves only in what is frothy and superficial. Would you expect that the religion of Christ would take hold of them as it does the deep thinker? Such shallow people are incapable of a great, enduringly loyal human love; how then can they be capable of loving Christ as He has been loved down through the centuries by men who saw in Him not one far removed from them, but a living Person? One whom it was possible for them really to love? And again would you exclude the shallow and the artificial and the frivolous from the Church of God, the Father of all? No, there must be a place for them there also. What place? Both they and the ignorant find in the Church not as much as the thinker finds, whose brilliant mind is completely fascinated and satisfied by Catholic doctrine, but they find what God chiefly intends they should find; sufficient means to save their souls and, more than that, sufficient means to accomplish also what God intends for them in this life: union with Him. Does God actually seek union with the shallow and the stupid? Would He be God if He did not? He is the Father of all. . . . When we grasp that truth we can bow in reverence, realizing that with God there is no "forgotten man." His Church must contain men forgotten by all except Him, neglected by all except Him.

Now let us go deeper into the subject. That the true Church exists for all means that she allows and encourages everyone to set out on the road of her ideal (Christ's ideal) of perfection. She encourages everyone to set out on that road, even though he takes along with him the queerest baggage. What queer baggage? Stupidity and ignorance, which alone have been responsible for keeping so many of the undiscerning from respecting piety. What other baggage? Bad taste, inner vulgarity, narrowness, fanaticism—and that baggage has kept many out of the

Church, many more from respecting the Church. Why? Because they are not clever enough, nor perhaps humble enough to study and reason, until they see that the Church of God must be for all. . . .

Every single individual without exception carries the whole encumbrance of a nature not as yet purified, not as yet fully controlled, prone at times to error, betrayal and disloyalty. Are we not all aware that we have not permitted God fully to work His way with us as our religion teaches us we should? And for that shall we blame God, or our religion, or ourselves? Do we not all cherish dreams of living up to the high and beautiful ideal of conduct which our Church has held up to us from childhood? And if we have failed to realize those dreams, may we not fairly expect to see all around us Catholics who like ourselves have not realized their dreams? If we have to confess the same sins now that we had to confess ten or twenty years ago, and if we are lenient in our judgment of our failure, should we be surprised if other Catholics about us are not completely transformed by the religion of God?

It is not that our religion has failed us; we have failed our religion. We know full well that great transformation would be accomplished in us if we would only do what we have been taught to do—for instance, get down on our knees for frequent prayer, make a thorough daily examination of conscience, spend some time reading Catholic books which would develop in us a great love for our Lord in the Blessed Sacrament and a tender devotion to our Blessed Mother. But no, we neglect those things which would bring out all that is noble and best in us and affect enormously our daily behavior and conversation. We neglect these things which we know would result in our religion dominating our daily lives. . . .

Very many of these apparently inferior people extract more good from the Church than many superior people. Many of these so-called inferiors who are a scandal to the aesthetic eyes of some Catholics and some outsiders, many who are of limited intelligence, illiterate or semiliterate, are so transfigured and ennobled by the Church that they lead a life which moves in the highest regions of the sublime, far above what we would expect, far above their own natural "comprehension." In those high regions these men and women of inferior parts achieve works which are outside the range of ordinary observation, and are incredible unless you know them as their confessor knows them, or read their lives; as for instance, the life of the celebrated Matthew Talbot.

When you are visiting a New York church some time, observe closely some scrubwoman at silent prayer before the Blessed Sacrament and you will know what I mean. Very often we encounter a life of closest union with God on the part of men and women who are called "the common people"—and sometimes I think that these people are more impressive than the interesting converts with brilliant minds with whom we dress our shop windows. But we do not expect that non-Catholics or even many Catholics will see the living, compelling beauty and dignity which our religion does bring even to the poorest, most stricken, most destitute of illiterate people. Many of us are color-blind to this kind of beauty and see only barrenness and wreckage where we priests and confessors see (are forced to see) radiance and shining splendor. Many look on in pity and horror, whereas we look on in reverent envy of what God has done for those humble folk. We must not forget the many of low degree whose lives are illuminated and ennobled by our religion.

The man of low degree often furnishes a better example of the educative powers of Christianity than his superior does. Some will say: The former has much to gain and nothing to lose whereas the latter has much at stake and much to lose, just as the slaves of ancient Rome became Christians more easily than their masters, even though the latter became Christians too. But let it be said in reply, that for the inferior and the superior, for the slave as well as for his master, the stakes are precisely the same—the same thing—namely, self—and each stands to gain the same thing—namely, God; union with God.

WHERE but in her [the Church's] bosom do you find from elder ages to our own day, men and women, of every nation, of every rank, leaving all, father and mother, houses and lands, and offering up their uttermost action and possession, and feel ennobled while so doing? Is not this fact written on every page of the annals of the Catholic Church, and borne witness to in our own streets by the Sisters of Charity? How explain this incontestable fact, unless it be that the Catholic Church alone has "the power to charm and command the soul, as the laws of nature control the activity of the hands,—so commanding that we find pleasure and honor in obeying?" . . .

Most assuredly a Religion which can count its martyrs by the millions, and whose noble children glory in strewing fresh branches of palm at her feet, must have so pro-

nounced the august laws of moral being as to fill their
ears, and make them feel ennobled by the offer of their
uttermost action and passion.

THE REV. I. T. HECKER

THE CHURCH'S MANY PATHS
TO SANCTITY

THE REV. BEDE JARRETT, O.P.

WHEN I say that the Church is pre-eminently holy, I do
not mean that I am a saint, but I do mean that, if I want
to be a saint, in the Catholic Church there are held out
to me numerous aids to spur me on to the perfect love of
God. There are the daily Masses, the many sacraments,
the daily visit to the Blessed Eucharist which the ever-
open Church invites, the countless confraternities and
guilds which are willing and eager to satisfy every ideal
that can ever have come into my mind; or, indeed, if
that which I wish to see established does not yet exist,
there is no reason why I should not myself begin it. Saints
without number, among whom I can surely find those
whose lives most appeal to me as the way in which I too
could be brought to serve God best, are to be found in
the list of her canonized children, who are canonized
that they may be an example to me in my labors. Then
by this doctrine I profess belief in an ever-increasing
number of blessed souls who here or in the other world
unite with me in the grand work of following in the footsteps of Christ. Like a huge army with even pace, and

with the impetus that comes from a great movement, I feel that with them the way is made more easy; that the long weary journey seems shorter, and the help that each affords the other adds to the general goodness of all. I am surrounded by this influence, which should overcome that feeling of loneliness that causes so much discouragement to human hearts. My own character and temperament require my own special mode for getting to God, but the grace of God is poured out so prodigally in the Church that I have never any need for bewailing my inability to adopt other people's ways. The Church is so great that somewhere I can find that which makes appeal to me, and I shall be led along my own path to Him.

THE SERVANTS OF GOD

JOHN HENRY CARDINAL NEWMAN

NIGHT and day, sick or well himself, in all weathers, off he is, on the news of a sick call. The fact of a parishioner dying without the Sacraments through his fault is terrible to him; why terrible, if he has not a deep absolute faith, which he acts upon with a free service. Protestants admire this, when they see it; but they do not seem to see as clearly, that it excludes the very notion of hypocrisy.

Sometimes, when they reflect upon it, it leads them to remark on the wonderful discipline of the Catholic priesthood; they say that no Church has so well ordered a clergy, and that in that respect it surpasses their own; they wish they could have such exact discipline among themselves. But is it an excellence which can be purchased? Is it a phenomenon which depends on nothing else than itself, or is it an effect which has a cause? You cannot buy devotion at a price. "It hath never been heard of in the land of Chanaan, neither hath it been seen in Theman. The children of Agar, the merchants of Meran, none of these have known its ways." What then is that wonderful charm, which makes a thousand men act all in one way, and infuses a prompt obedience to rule, as if they were under some stern military compulsion? How difficult to find an answer, unless you will allow the obvious one, that they believe intensely what they profess!

St. Paul called the clergy the Ambassadors of Christ. When they declare the authoritative teaching of the Church they announce the truth of God.

This constitutes the great comfort and security of Catholics. They know, they do not conjecture. They have certitude, not probability. They are not searching for the light; they have it.

THE REV. MARTIN J. SCOTT, S.J.

"THE HOME OF YOUR SOUL"

THE MOST REV. W. BERNARD
ULLATHORNE

The Church is the home of your souls. In the Church Christ always is to be found, the loving Father of your soul, your loving Entertainer, who washes from your feet the soil contracted in the world's ways, who provides for you the spiritual table, who provides for you a place of repose. The Church is the home of your soul, and wherever you go the Church spiritually follows you as with the very spirit of Christ. Even the material Church, unlike in this to your domestic home, is to be found in almost every place where you come, and have need of her ministrations. If your domestic home has enriched your heart with all your best human affections, and if there is no sacrifice which you will not make for the maintenance and protection of that home, you know that whatever is purest and most elevated in those affections has flown into them from your spirtual home—the Church. Less importunate in its demands upon your resources, it is more venerable, it is yet more sacred, it is more enduring; for when your earthly home knows you no more, when your body is committed to the dust, the Church, according to all your hopes and aspirations, shall be the everlasting home of your soul. Hence that Catholic love of the Church, as the representative of God, as the home of every pure and faithful soul. Hence there springs up a constant renewal of interest for the well-being of the Church. And here we see why the poor love the Church so much, for whereas they have nothing, yet in the Church they have all things.

THE dawn was breaking, a dawn of youthfulness and purity—and a celestial clarity lit up the horizon before me. This time I knew where I was going. I was going toward the Catholic, Apostolic and Holy Roman Church.

I was going toward the dwelling of peace and of blessing, I was going toward joy, toward health; I was going, alas, toward my cure. And then, thinking of this true mother who for so many years had been awaiting me, back there across two continents . . . I wept with happiness, love and gratitude.

Yes, it was a magnificent truth which was calling me back there in my gentle homeland. The whole Christian order appeared to me in a rejuvenated atmosphere; an immense and majestic temple—founded on solid rock —a temple of Reason and divine Wisdom stood before me, and all the lines of this temple were so straight, so pure, so united that in its presence one could desire nothing more than to live eternally in its shadow, far from the enchantments and the vanities of this world.

ERNEST PSICHARI

THE EXAMPLE OF THE MAGI

DOM COLUMBA MARMION, O.S.B.

IT HAPPENS at times that the stars disappear from our sight. . . . The soul then finds itself in spiritual darkness. What is to be done then?

Let us see what the Magi did under these circumstances. They directed their course towards Jerusalem, the capital of Judea, the metropolis of the Jewish religion. Where, better than in the holy city, could they learn what they sought to know?

In the same way, when our star disappears, when the divine inspiration leaves us in some uncertainty, it is

God's will that we should have recourse to the Church, to those who represent Him amongst us, in order to learn from them the path to be followed. This is the dispensation of Divine Providence. God loves that in our doubts and in the difficulties of our progress towards Christ, we should ask light and direction from those whom He has established as His representatives.

In submitting the aspirations of our souls to the control of those who have the grace and mission to direct us in our seeking after divine union, we run no risk of going astray, whatever be the personal merits of those who guide us. At the time when the Magi arrived at Jerusalem the assembly of those who had authority to interpret the Holy Scriptures was composed in great part of unworthy members; and yet God willed that it should be by their ministry and teaching that the Magi learnt officially where Christ was born. Indeed, God cannot permit a soul to be deceived when, with humility and confidence, she has recourse to the legitimate representatives of His sovereign authority.

On the contrary, the soul will again find light and peace. Like the Magi going out from Jerusalem, she will again see the star, radiant and splendid, and, also like them, full of gladness, she will go forward on her way.

THERE is a King's Highway, and that is the Church of God and the pathway to truth.

ST. EPIPHANIUS

93

SIGNED WITH THE MARKS
OF GOD

RT. REV. ROBERT HUGH BENSON

FOR I see through her [the Church's] eyes, the eyes of
God to shine, and through her lips I hear His words. In
each of her hands as she raises them to bless, I see the
wounds that dripped on Calvary, and her feet upon her
altar stairs are signed with the same marks as those which
Magdalene kissed. As she comforts me in the confessional
I hear the voice that bade the sinner go and sin no more;
and as she rebukes me or pierces me with blame, I shrink
aside trembling with those who went out one by one,
beginning with the eldest, till Jesus and the penitent
were left alone. As she cries her invitation through the
world I hear the same ringing claim as that which called,
"Come unto me and find rest to your souls"; as she
drives those who profess to serve her from her service I
see the flame of wrath that scourged the changers of
money from the temple courts.

As I watch her in the midst of her people, applauded
by the mob shouting always for the rising sun, I see the
palm branches about her head, and the City and Kingdom of God, it would seem, scarcely a stone's throw away,
yet across the valley of Kedron and the garden of Gethsemane; and as I watch her pelted with mud, spurned,
spat at and disgraced, I read in her eyes the message that
we should weep not for her but for ourselves and for our
children, since she is immortal and we are but mortal
after all. As I look on her white body, dead and drained
of blood, I smell once more the odor of the oint-

ments and the trampled grass of that garden near to the place where He was crucified and hear the tramp of the soldiers who came to seal the stone and set the watch. And, at last, as I see her moving once more in dawn light of each new day, or in the revelation of the evening, as the sun of this or that dynasty rises and sets, I understand that He Who was dead has come forth once more with healing in His wings, to comfort those that mourn and to bind up the broken-hearted; and that His coming is not with observation, but in the depth of night as His enemies slept and His lovers woke for sorrow.

THE POETRY OF THE RITUAL

CARYLL HOUSELANDER

MAN cannot live only in spiritual terms, for he is matter too. If the realities of invisible Order, and the movement of the power of divine Love are to be brought into his consciousness and made to take hold of him, as they must be for his integrity, they must be expressed consciously in the whole of his nature. . . .

Therefore God has given him the Church and its ritual, that the invisible world may be visible to him, the intangible tangible, the soundless music audible.

The prayers of the Church are the agelong poetry of mankind, lifted above the perfection of poetry, for they are the prayer of Christ on earth. That is what the ritual means, with its ordered movements, its wide encircling gestures of love, its kiss of peace, its extended arms of sacrifice.

Every step in the sanctuary is counted, every pace measured. The vestments clothe man's emotions in the colors of mourning and of joy, of the blood of the Lamb, and the snow of Tabor.

The liturgical year moves through seasons of Christ-life as the natural year moves through seasons of natural life. It imposes a sweetness of order upon the human heart, measuring its sorrow and its joy, its waking and its sleep. It prevents man from being swamped and carried away by the excess of his emotions, and yet it carries him forward into an immensity of energy infinitely greater than his own.

THE Church herself is the most sacred and august of poets. Poetry . . . is a method of relieving the over-burdened mind; it is a channel through which emotion finds expression, and that a safe, regulated expression. Now what is the Catholic Church, viewed in her human aspect, but a discipline of the affections and passions? What are her ordinances and practices but the regulated expression of keen, or deep, or turbid feeling, and thus a "cleansing," as Aristotle would word it, of the sick soul? She is the poet of her children; full of music to soothe the sad and control the wayward,—wonderful in story for the imagination of the romantic; rich in symbol and imagery, so that gentle and delicate feelings, which will not bear words, may in silence intimate their presence or commune with themselves. Her very being is poetry.

JOHN HENRY CARDINAL NEWMAN

ASH WEDNESDAY TO EASTER

THE REV. JOHN W. LYNCH

IT IS the Springtime part, the Lenten part of being Catholic. Some hopeful, eternally young and undefeated inner response of the soul is here. We are glad that this has come again, and looking ahead, even in the very beginning of the season, we are conscious of what awaits us at the end in the great climax of the Holy Week.

These days are not merely times of penance, of fasting, of additional abstinence. This is not merely a season when we all decide to discipline ourselves. There is an anticipation in these weeks, a sense of waiting, a feeling of promise and a progress toward a magnificent fulfillment. That's what makes Lent for us: it leads somewhere. A triumph, a victory, a tremendous, crashing drama lie at the end of it. Already we feel its power. We do not fast just for the sake of fasting. All this heightened and more intense life of the Church does not proceed in a vacuum. We know what's ahead of us. We are moving toward a crisis and the day will come when the Church will cry: *"Hosannah to the Son of David: blessed is He who cometh in the name of the Lord,"* and we will hold palm branches and stand again at the moment when all time and eternity come to a focus. It is Springtime again in the Faith.

We shall see again the whiteness, the hush, the ineffable calm of a Holy Thursday when the bells ring and then are silent as the movement of Redemption turns to the unveiled cross of the Good Friday. The Church will be empty, the Tabernacle door swung wide, the linens stripped, the lamps put out. Then early in the dawn, the priest, like an everlasting prophet, will move with fire in his hands from the church porch to the interior, to the gates of the sanctuary. The lamps will be relighted from the fire. The long telling of God's plans will be recited in the twelve Old Testament prophecies. Slowly, deliberately after the blessing of water and a Baptismal font, after a twice repeated Litany, in measured certainty, the priest of Christ will approach the altar for the long delayed moment of utter bliss. *"Gloria in excelsis,"* he will sing, and all the earth must hear him.

The bells ring out "Alleluia!" and the Church which seemed dead comes alive. It is the Day of Resurrection, and all the delighted air, the new lift and surge in life, the young infectious gladness of Spring will be justified and made real.

It is all beginning again, and a new light is in our sky.

"A HOUSE OF LIGHT"

FATHER JAMES, O.F.M. CAP.

HE WHO would see the Church must view it from within. From without, the Church is a visible society whose marks, as we designate them, are the windows through which the light streams forth. From within, once the door has been closed upon the darkness of unbelief, the Church is seen as a house of Light whose centre is the Real Presence.

This is the doctrine which unequivocally is the faith of the one, true Church, that Jesus Christ in Person, Man and God, resides under the appearances of bread and wine. If we think of the Sacred Host, our very senses point to the Real Presence. . . .

There is no isolating this aspect of the Holy Eucharist from its context in the Sacrifice and Holy Communion. The whole doctrine is a unity in which we can discern different aspects. But we do regard the sacred species, the veils about the Presence, as a challenge to divine energies in our being. The Master once said: "Wherever the body shall be, thither will the eagles also be gathered." . . .

A cloud is but a challenge to the eagle that would fix his gaze upon the sun. What the sun is to the material world, the Real Presence is to the Church. . . .

While Holy Eucharist ministers to the Spirit in human conditions, being the Food of charity, the Holy Spirit ministers to the Real Presence by gifts which enable men and women to penetrate, and taste, the sweetness of the Real Presence. When that happens, one begins to realize that in the humblest Church we are but one degree removed from heaven; the roof of the House of Light is the empyrean of Eternal Skies. In common with the celestial court, we possess Jesus, God and Man, the Same Who is present to saint and angel in the full splendor of beatific vision, and to us on earth in the unwavering light of the Church's faith.

In the light of day the little lamp that burns before the tabernacles of the world may seem of small account. But when the darkness comes, then flames of light leap up to send their rays into distant corners of the Church, and far out into the night, as witnesses to a Presence.

GOD needs not the temples we build to him; of man and his works, He is for ever independent. But we who crave for God, and who, without Him, perish like the brute and have no hope, must have sanctuaries, religious rites and symbols, to prevent the heavenly spirit of faith and love from escaping and losing itself in boundless and empty space. . . . It is the House of God not because it is consecrated to His worship, but because He dwells there really and truly under the sacramental veil; and it is His divine presence which gives to the whole edifice its form, its appropriateness, and its meaning, as the mind of God creates, moves, and harmonizes the universe. The vital principle in the Christian temple is the Real Presence. Take this away and it is a body without a soul. Therefore the whole edifice grows out of the tabernacle, and draws from it use and beauty, as from the heart the members are developed and by it nourished.

THE MOST REV. JOHN LANCASTER
SPALDING

THE POWER OF THE LITURGY

J. K. HUYSMANS

WINTER had come and at Val-des-Saints the cold was unbearable. . . . Waking at half-past three, he again tucked himself under the eiderdown and dozed in comfort until four-o'clock, when the bell rang faintly out in the night. It was the cloister bell to rouse the sleeper; five minutes later, other bells rang; then after ten minutes silence, the bells began again, slowly, to strike three hundred strokes. . . . "There is no need to hurry," thought Durtal. "In conscience I am only bound to go to the first Mass on Communion days, but I should be sorry to miss Lauds;" and so saying he dragged himself out of bed. . . .

The quarter of an hour walk to the church seemed never to end; but, jogging along, he reached the porch. There the light through the keyhole served as his guide, glowing like an ember in the darkness. Gleefully he put out his lantern and lifted the latch.

As he entered from the gloom, the aspect at the far end of the nave shone with splendor. Shaded lamps above the stalls threw a light on the motionless monks, and as their chants of piety and of praise rose up in the midst of a dreaming village while the tempest raged without, the effect was one of celestial radiance, an enchanting glimpse, as it were, of a world beyond our own. . . . If Durtal had ever entertained any doubts as to the power of the Liturgy, he had to admit its presence in this grand service, which induced in those who heard it a kind of ecstasy or spiritual intoxication and prepared them for entering more fully and actively into the holy and eloquent mystery of the Mass.

And at the end of Lauds, in the silence of the choir, while the monks knelt with bowed heads, the Angelus rang out its triple peal, and as the last strike resounded through the night all rose, and the priests went to vest for Mass.

LITURGY, THE EXPRESSION OF A DIVINE PERSONALITY

DOM VIRGIL MICHEL, O.S.B.

When the Catholic worship is mentioned, especially under the term "liturgy," many persons think immediately of the external grandeur with which it is enacted. In the dramatic unfolding of the liturgical worship all the devices at the service of man are pressed into the service of God and are employed to increase the splendor and beauty of the worship, to enhance its impressiveness. This is but a further development of the fact that the liturgy is the expression of Christ's priesthood, is the expression of His divine personality in His mystical body the Church. "All the evil comes from this, that people do not love Jesus enough. Jesus is not loved because He is not known. But Jesus is beautiful, He is true, He is good; and it is necessary, therefore, that the priesthood properly display to the eyes of the people the beauty of Jesus by the splendor of its worship, His truth by the clearness of its teaching, His goodness by the charity of its works. There is the program of all true priestly action." (Tissier, *Semaine liturgique de Maredsous*, p. 130). . . .

Human nature is so constituted that internal acts alone are difficult for man to sustain; they are not the full expression of the man until they find their completion in external action. Man naturally reveals his inner thoughts and wishes by means of external actions. Without the latter the former are ordinarily incomplete, and neither of long duration nor of great vigor. . . .

From all these standpoints the external aspects of the liturgy, the words and actions, the material things used, become properly important in the services of the Church. To neglect them is to give incomplete homage to God. Hence we can understand why the great liturgical pope, in inaugurating the liturgical renewal, spoke of the leading duty of every local church as "without question that of maintaining and promoting the decorum of the house of God." (Pius X, November, 1903)

LITURGY is certainly a sacred thing; for by it we are elevated to God and joined with Him; by it we give testimony of our faith and bind ourselves to Him in most solemn homage for benefits and assistance received, of which we are constantly in need. Hence there is a kind of intimate relationship between dogma and sacred liturgy, and likewise between Christian worship and the sanctification of souls.

PIUS XI (1928)

THE LITURGICAL YEAR

DOM VIRGIL MICHEL, O.S.B.

THERE is a rhythmic ebb and flow running through the liturgical year as through all else in the world. The universe of the heavens has its changing cycles and periods; the solar system gives us our four seasons and the earth gives us the regular recurrence of night and day, the rhythms of which are copied by the various forms of life here on earth. In life itself there have been the vast cycles of species coming into existence in geological time and again disappearing; the stages of youth, maturity, old age in the individual; the seasonal changes in many forms of life; the daily periods of wakefulness and sleep; and the smaller alternations of the rhythmic pulse-beat of breath and blood. Likewise in the liturgical or church year we have the larger seasonal divisions of Advent, Christmas, Epiphany, Septuagesima, Lent, Passiontide, Eastertide, and Pentecost with its longer aftermath; and again the regularly recurring Day of the Lord, and within each day the recurring rhythm of the different hours of the divine office. In all these cycles there is also a progressive change of sentiments and moods, based on special dogmas and mysteries, a changing series of eternal truths accompanied by a corresponding atmosphere of joy and adoration, admiration and wonder, sympathy and compunction, mortification and repentance. The whole spiritual life in all its wondrous variations thereby comes to view and realizes itself in the members of the mystical body ever in intimate union with their divine head Christ.

THE Mass, the hymns, the rites, the benedictions, the sacraments, the offices, and the celebration of the seasons —all this vast body of liturgical functions in a word— what is it in reality if not the faith prayed, the faith confessed, the faith chanted in the concrete, palpable, living reality that is the Christian community united to its pastor?

ABBÉ AUGUSTE CROEGAERT

A NON-CATHOLIC VISITS A
CATHEDRAL IN ITALY

EPHRAIM PEABODY

As ONE sits in the dim twilight of the arches—the soft strains of the distant organ and the scarcely-heard chants of the priests in a remote chapel floating through the shadows and mingling with one's musings—the vast church seems to dilate above,—solemn, magnificent, an abode of the most High, detached from the fretted and fevered human life without its walls. Beneath such a pile, all men are reduced to an equal level; and while one watches the worshippers of every class scattered over the great space, and kneeling at the different altars, each apart and by himself uttering his devotions, it is impossible not to sympathize with them and with the spirit of the place. *You want no words. A sermon, in which man addresses men, would be an offense. It is a temple, not for man's teaching, but for God's worship.* One cares not even to hear any distinct utterance of prayer, and is glad that the human expression of the sentiment of devotion is in a foreign tongue. The true language is found in the architecture, and in the solemn cadences of the music; and devotion falls so back on upon its simplest, sublimest, and universal emotions, that no other language is needed. As among great mountains, which alternately oppress you with a sense of sadness and humility, and inspire you with their grandeur, but admit no intermediate feelings, so the cathedral seems to be either that of weakness and humble trust, or, while one forgets himself and thinks of God, that of loud thanksgivings, of majestic anthems, and exultant adoration. And the place grows more sacred to you. These walls have stood a thousand years, and in all that time perhaps no day has passed in which desponding hearts have not sought strength, and sinful hearts implored God for pardon. The atmosphere is throbbing with the profoundest emotions of human souls. You would trifle with yourself,—it would be trifling with humanity no less than with God,—not to regard such a place as holy.

ART SPEAKS TO A SOUL

THOMAS MERTON

I NEVER knew what relics and what wonderful holy things were hidden in the churches whose doors and aisles and arches had become the refuge of my mind. Christ's cradle and the pillar of the Flagellation and the True Cross and St. Peter's chains, and the tombs of the great martyrs, the tomb of the child St. Agnes and the martyr St. Cecilia and of Pope St. Clement and of the great deacon St. Lawrence who was burned on a gridiron. . . . These things did not speak to me, or at least I did not know they spoke to me. But the churches that enshrined them did, and so did the art on their walls.

And now for the first time in my life I began to find out something of Who this Person was that men called Christ. It was obscure, but it was true knowledge of Him, in some sense, truer than I knew and truer than I would admit. But it was in Rome that my conception of Christ was formed. It was there I first saw Him, Whom I now serve as my God and my King, and Who owns and rules my life.

It is the Christ of the Apocalypse, the Christ of the Martyrs, the Christ of the Fathers. It is the Christ of St. John, and of St. Paul, and of St. Augustine and St. Jerome and all the Fathers—and of the Desert Fathers. It is Christ God, Christ King. . . .

The saints of those forgotten days had left upon the walls of their churches words which by the peculiar grace of God I was able in some measure to apprehend, although I could not decode them all. But above all, the realest and most immediate source of this grace was Christ Himself, present in those churches, in all His power, and in His Humanity, in His Human Flesh and His material, physical, corporeal Presence. How often I was left entirely alone in these churches with the tremendous God, and knew nothing of it—except I had to know something of it, as I say, obscurely. And it was He Who was teaching me Who He was, more directly than I was capable of realizing.

These mosaics told me more than I had ever known of the doctrines of a God of infinite power, wisdom and love Who had yet become Man, and revealed in His Manhood the infinity of power, wisdom, and love that was His Godhead. Of course I could not grasp and believe these things explicitly. But since they were implicit in every line of the pictures I contemplated with such admiration and love, surely I grasped them implicitly—I had to, in so far as the mind of the artist reached my own mind, and spoke to it his conception and his thought. And so I could not help but catch something of the ancient craftsman's love of Christ, the Redeemer and Judge of the World.

THE LESSON OF CHARTRES

RAÏSSA MARITAIN

ON OUR return from the country, we stopped three days in Chartres to visit the Cathedral. . . .

The three days were spent in very close contemplation of the architecture, the statuary and the glass of the most French of churches, which has always remained for us the most beautiful cathedral in the world. Indeed, we spelled it out letter by letter like a Bible.

Since that first visit we have gone several times to Chartres, and each time the Cathedral has presented a new aspect to us. Sometimes it was all beauty, sometimes all piety. . . .

But in its first aspect, in its plastic language, it was for us a master-teacher of theology, of sacred history and of exegesis. It repeated what *Le Salut par les Juifs* had just told us: that the two Testaments are united in the person of Christ; that the Old prefigures the New and is its basis, just as the New is the fulfilment and the crown of the Old. . . .

The book of the Cathedral revealed to us sublime and familiar and tender things. I am thinking, for instance, of a sculptured group representing the creation of man. Christ is fashioning him with love, this first man, whose head, still vague, rests upon the knees of God. I can still see the beautiful, pensive face of God "creating the world." We see only this august countenance; the creation is as yet wholly in the mind of God, but we can perceive its unmarred beauty; it shines through the expression of the divine features, like the bottom of a lake whose waters are crystal clear.

And the windows of Chartres! Who does not know their beauty? We saw them from below and from above, circling the nave by the triforium. We were surfeited with splendor. Alone, having taken leave of our chance guide, we went to rest ourselves near the naïve images about the altars, close to the Virgin Mother dressed in satin and gold, lighted by the flame of the candles and the oil lamps. There everything was so humble, so calm. The majesty of the place, the sacred presence of the Mysteries, which the heart felt, blended into a pure repose of love and of simplicity. And we were inclined to believe that the unity and harmony of so much lofty beauty could have as its foundation only the unity of truth.

ART AND CATHOLICISM

JACQUES MARITAIN

THOSE who by their art desire to serve the Truth which is Christ are not pursuing a particular human end but a divine end, an end as universal as God Himself. The more they live their faith, the more spiritual their inner life becomes, the more deeply rooted they are in the Church, the higher do they rise above human limitations and the conventions, opinions, and special interests of particular social groups; so that, with a fuller understanding of the pure spirituality and universality of the action of God in their souls, their art and their thoughts are purged of all human narrowness, to be thenceforth concentrated upon the boundless Love which is and acts on earth as in Heaven. This is what men who are utterly ignorant of the Faith or deceived by an excess of appearances are incapable of understanding; in zeal for souls they see merely a human effort at domination, an attempt to serve the interest of some sect or clique. They cannot see that those who take part as Christians, because they are Christians, in the works of the mind, are not engaged in *clerical* philosophy or *clerical* art, or in *confessional* philosophy or *confessional* art. There is in this sense no Catholic philosophy or Catholic art, for Catholicism is not a *particular statement of faith* any more than it is *a* religion: it is *the* religion, confessing the only omnipresent Truth. Yet their art and philosophy are Catholic, that is to say genuinely universal. . . .

I believe it to be impossible outside Catholicism to reconcile in man, without diminishing or forcing them, the rights of morality and the claims of intellectuality, art or science. Morality as such aims only at the good of the human being, the supreme interests of the acting Subject; intellectuality as such aims only at the Object, its nature, if it is to be known, what it ought to be, if it is to be made. What a temptation for poor human nature to be faithful to one only at the expense of the other! True, we know, *haec oportebat facere, et illa non omittere;* but how shall the children of Adam keep the balance? Outside the Church and its divine life it is natural that moral and religious zeal should turn man against the mind, and it is natural that zeal for art and science should turn man away from the eternal laws. Socrates's judges, Luther, Rousseau, Tolstoi, and the Anglo-Saxon pragmatists, are in one camp; in the other Bruno, Bacon, the great pagans of the Renaissance, Goethe himself, and Nietzsche.

Catholicism orders our whole life to Truth itself and

subsisting Beauty. In us it places the theological virtues above the moral and intellectual virtues and, through them, gives us peace. *Et ego si exaltatus fuero, omnia traham ad meipsum.* Christ crucified draws to Himself everything there is in man: all things are reconciled, but at the height of His heart.

Here is a religion whose moral exigencies are more elevated than those of any other, inasmuch as only the heroism of sanctity can fully satisfy them, and which at the same time more than any other admires and protects the mind. I may say it is a sign of the divine origin of that religion. A superhuman virtue is necessary to secure the free play of art and science among men under the supremacy of the divine law and the primacy of Charity and so to realize the higher reconciliation of the *moral* and the *intellectual*.

ART'S HIGHEST MISSION

THE MOST REV. JOHN LANCASTER SPALDING

RELIGION and art are allies. Between them there is no antagonism, as there is none between theology and science. This truth the Catholic Church has ever proclaimed. . . . In her universal life she embraces all the arts, gives to them harmony and special ends. Her sacred edifices are not alone the temples of the living God; they are also the sanctuaries of art which point heavenward. Her sublime conceptions of God and man have revealed a new world of thought and sentiment. She has clothed the highest truth in the most perfect beauty. Spiritual in all her teachings and aspirations, she understands that the visible is but the symbol of the unseen; that we must stand upon the solid earth before we can rise to higher worlds; and that this is not a sensuous but a reasonable creed which holds that God cannot be worshipped in spirit and in truth except by signs and symbols. For what else is thought, what else is language. Our truest conceptions of God and of the soul are but symbols. . . .

No human act can be wholly spiritual. We ascend by a law of our nature, from the visible to the invisible, from the sensible to the supersensible. A purely spiritual religion would be to man an inaccessible and unreal religion. There can be no faith where there is no thought, nor thought without language; and language is addressed primarily to the senses. There can be no authoritative religious teaching without a church, and an invisible church is no church at all. The sectarian protests against the alliance of religion and art can be justified only by ignoring the most essential fact of Christian history, which is the manifestation of God's power and beauty and holiness in human form. To take from the Church her symbolism is to deny the humanity of Christ. In our invisible society what becomes of His incarnation, miracles, and whole systems of things invisible visibly manifested—the symbolism of divine truth, love, wisdom, justice, in their relation to man immortal but sinful.

The union of the soul with God, through faith, hope, and love is the first and highest aim of religion; but faith, hope, and love, like all the deep emotions of the human heart, tend irresistibly to incorporate and express themselves in symbols and acts. . . .

Through the long centuries, year after year, with love's

unerring instinct, the Church leads her children along the sacred way the Blessed Christ did tread, lingers over each hallowed spot in joy, in thankfulness, in sorrow, or in triumph, nor feels the deadening weight of time nor the fatal curse of distance.

Art's highest mission is to reveal to the world Jesus Christ in His birth, in His life, in His death, in His beautiful and perfect conception of the divine mind. He is God, the all-beautiful, made manifest. Purity and gentleness and grace, with power and majesty combine to make Him the fairest and noblest figure in history, to whom the whole world bows in love and adoration. . . .

As the Christian religion is the fullest revelation of the soul, it ought to produce the highest art. Since human nature has been transfigured and recreated by the immediate and personal union with it of God Himself, art ought to be able to disclose the soul and permit us to gaze upon the divine possibilities which in it lie latent. It may no longer linger in form and color and motion, as if these were its abiding home. It is wedded to the soul and must soar or die. . . . True art, like heroic souls, lifts itself above its embodiment and, rising into the world of the eternal and the infinite, unwraps itself of the vesture woven in the roaring loom of Time. It leaves behind all passion and desire, all enjoyment of sense, and reposes supremely blest in that which, unchangeable, is yet never the same. It aims not merely at the beautiful, but seeks the true and the good.

Without this union of virtue with beauty there can be no Christian art. All its purposes are holy. Its mission is not to multiply the pleasures of the fortunate, but to comfort the unhappy, to raise to heaven eyes weighed down by sorrow or blinded by the vulgar, garish world;

to reveal to all who despair of this life the certain and immortal triumph of those who suffer in faith and hope and love.

There is no art for art's sake. It exists for man, and can be worthy only by being useful.

MUSIC THAT MOVES TO DEVOTION

ST. PIUS X

SACRED music, being a complementary part of the solemn liturgy, participates in the general scope of the liturgy, which is the glory of God and the sanctification and edification of the faithful. It contributes to the decorum and splendor of the ecclesiastical ceremonies, and since its principal office is to clothe with suitable melody the liturgical text proposed for the understanding of the faithful, its proper aim is to add greater efficacy to the text, in order that through it the faithful may be the more easily moved to devotion and better disposed for the reception of the fruits of grace belonging to the celebration of the most holy mysteries.

Sacred music should consequently possess, in the highest degree, the qualities proper to the liturgy, and in particular sanctity and goodness of form, which will spontaneously produce the final quality of universality.

It must be holy, and must, therefore, exclude all profanity not only in itself, but also in the manner in which it is presented by those who execute it.

It must be true art, for otherwise it will be impossible for it to exercise on the minds of those who listen to it that efficacy which the Church aims at obtaining in admitting into her liturgy the art of musical sounds. . . .

These qualities are to be found, in the highest degree, in Gregorian Chant, which is, consequently, the Chant proper to the Roman Church, the only chant she has inherited from the ancient Fathers, which she has jealously guarded for centuries in her liturgical codices, which she directly proposes to the faithful as her own, which she prescribes exclusively for some parts of the liturgy, and which the most recent studies have so happily restored to their integrity and purity.

On these grounds Gregorian Chant has always been regarded as the supreme model for sacred music.

(1 9 0 3)

GREGORIAN Chant is a spiritual music which has no role other than its association with the liturgy of the Church. It is free of all else other than this association; the sole influence to which it is subject is the liturgy, with all that the liturgy embodies in its Latin text, which acts not only as melodic generator and model of constructive form, but which, in the intimacy of this union, at times reverses the role and yields to the exigencies of the melody. Whether it be performed in the church, school or concert hall, it still remains liturgically spiritual music in the character of its sentiment; nor has it reason for existence, properly speaking, other than its association with the liturgical text.

MARIE PIERIK

"A PERFUME OF CHRISTIANITY"

KENELM HENRY DIGBY

THE music as well as the poetry of the Catholic Church seems like a faint echo of that primitive language in which man spoke to God in the state of innocence, the sounds of which can revive in some manner those powers of sentiment and virtue, which the Creator placed in his heart. . . . While the Gregorian Chant rises, you seem to hear the whole Catholic Church behind you responding. It exhales, says Généroult, a perfume of Christianity, an odor of penitence, and of compunction, which overcome you. No one cries how admirable! but by degrees the return of those monotonous melodies penetrates one, and as it were impregnates the soul; and if to these be added personal recollections a little sad, one feels oneself weep, without ever dreaming of judging, or of appreciating or of learning the airs which one hears.

I HEARD a *Tantum Ergo* this morning in the convent chapel at Benediction. Thought floated with the sound, and carried me out and out beyond the earth to the choirs of the Seraphic Spirits. Music is the "Lost Chord" that has strayed hither from heaven. If one or two mortals on this grain of sand in the Universe can produce such ravishing melody, what imagination can reach the faintest outer bounds and limits of the harmonies that breathe before the throne of God from the vast choirs of all the Spirits of the Universe.

CANON P. A. SHEEHAN

"LIKE THE DIVINE BREATH"

THE MOST REV. JOHN LANCASTER
SPALDING

THE organ, the master instrument, is the voice of the Christian Church, "the seraph-haunted queen of harmony," sounding like an echo from a mystic and hidden world. How full and deep and strong it rolls out its great volume of sound—an ocean of melody! How it bursts forth with irresistible power like the hosts of stars when first they wheeled into their orbits and shouted to God; and how, with a veiled and mysterious harmony, it wraps itself around the soul, shuts out all noise, and composes it to sweet, heavenly contemplation. It is tender as a mother's yearning, and fierce as the deaf and raging sea; sad as angels' sighs for souls that are lost; plaintive and pitiful as the cry of those who in purgatorial fires cleanse their sins; and there its notes faint and die, until we hear their echoes from the eternal shore where they grow for ever and ever. With the falling day we enter the great cathedral's sacred gloom, and at once we are in a vast solitude. The high pillars rise in giant strength, upholding the high vault already shrouded in the gathering darkness, and silence sits mute in the wide aisle. Suddenly we have been carried into another world, peopled with other beings. We cease to note the passage of time, and earth, with its garish light and distracting noises, has become a dream. As the eye grows accustomed to the gloom we are able to observe the massive building. Its walls rise like the sides of a steep mountain, and in the aisles there is the loveliness and mystery of deep valleys into which the sunlight never falls. From these adamantine flanks countless beings stand forth, until the whole edifice is peopled with fantastic forms, upon which falls the mystic light, reflected from the countenance of angels, patriarchs, apostles, virgins, martyrs, who from celestial windows look down upon the new-born world. In the distance we see the glimmering taper that burns before God's presence, and then suddenly a great volume of sound, like the divine breath infusing life into these inanimate objects, rolls over us, and every stone from pavement to vaulted roof thrills and vibrates; each sculptured image and pictured saint is vocal; and from on high the angels lend their voices, until the soul, trembling on the wings of hope and love, is borne upward with this heavenly harmony, and, entranced in prayer, worships the Invisible alone.

A VISIBLE SOCIETY WITH A
SOUL

DÉSIRÉ JOSEPH CARDINAL MERCIER

YES, the Church of Christ, placed upon a height, is visible to all! "A city seated upon a mountain cannot be hid." The Messiah appeared upon the scene of history during the brilliant reign of Augustus. He sent His Apostles to the four points of the compass, and three centuries after He had said to them, "Going, therefore, teach ye all nations," the Gospel had indeed spread East and West. Everywhere it had its martyrs; everywhere it had its apologists, its doctors; its chief Pastor held his See in the very centre of civilization, and the Master of the Roman Empire, having become a disciple of the successor of St. Peter, declared himself at Nicaea the official protector of the first Ecumenical Council.

While contemplating in spirit this truly wonderful development of the Church, my eyes rested on the silent tabernacle, where Jesus remains hidden under the Eucharistic veils, and the contrast between the splendor of the victory and the effacement of the Victor made me better understand that the visible society of which we are members has a *soul;* that the spirit which animates this society would have it turn its gaze inwards; that the life of the true Christian is indeed an *interior life.*

V

*Now therefore you are no more strangers
or foreigners; but you are fellow citizens
with the saints and the domestics of God.*
                              Ephesians 2:19

THE SAINTLY FELLOWSHIP

THE REV. KARL ADAM

THE way of the saints leads from earth through the place
of purification to heaven. It is a lonely way. We travel
it in the fellowship of the body of Christ, growing and
blossoming in the fullness of Christ, giving and taking
one from another "according to the grace that is given
to each member." . . . When the Church speaks of the
Communion of Saints she is thinking primarily of this
interaction, of this confluence of the powers of Jesus
that work in His saints, of this supernatural inter-
change of graces, of this solidarity of life and movement.
. . . All the saints are bound together, over and above
their personal functions, by a close community of life
and sentiment, by a fellowship and sympathy in sorrow
and joy. Being members of Christ, their souls do not

stand before God as isolated units. However individual may be the character of their sanctity, yet it is still the life of a member of Christ and as such belongs to all. . . .

So pervasive and so creative is God's glory that it does not shine only in the face of His Only-begotten Son, but is reflected also in all those who in Him have become children of God, and therefore illuminates with unfading radiance the countenances of the blessed. So we love them as countless dewdrops in which the sun's radiance is mirrored. We venerate them because we find God in them. "Their name liveth unto generation and generation. Let the people shew forth their wisdom and the church declare their praise." (Ecclus. xliv, 14–15). And because God is in them, therefore are we confident that they can and will help us; for where God is, there is our help. They do not help us through any strength of their own, but through the strength of God, and they help us only so far as creatures may. . . .

The Catholic fellowship in faith does not mean merely that all the members of the Church loyally profess one and the same faith, presented to them by apostolic authority, that they share the same luminous ideal, the same effective rule and the same fruitful sources of spiritual life. It means more than that. It means that there is a solidarity and partnership of the faith, a reciprocal interaction and fruitful influence, which by intimate and pervasive action makes their external union an inward communion in faith, a communion which out of the depths of the common experience of the faith is ever expressing itself anew in a single "credo" of the mystical Christ. This solidarity of Catholic belief manifests itself in two ways. On the one hand it communicates the inwardness and strength of your personal faith, the "power of God" that you experience in your own conscience, to other members of the Body of Christ, in ever new impulses and stirrings, and makes them the vital experience of ever wider circles. On the other hand, this solidarity of the faith, returning so to say upon itself, becomes a fertile soil and fruitful womb, which impregnated by the infallible teaching of the Church produces a constantly richer appreciation of supernatural truth. . . .

The life of faith, that life which is the supreme goal of the Church's preaching, the one thing necessary, the supernatural fruitfulness of the faith, all intimate experience, all consolation, all confidence, all nobility and lofty courage: these things do not belong to any privileged individual, but to the community, to the fellowship of all those who by baptism have been born again in Christ. Faith becomes living, and the seed of preaching strikes root and grows and bears fruit in the fellowship of the members of Christ. The spirit of the faith is never an isolated or an isolating thing, but always a spirit that presses towards fellowship, because it is derived from the Spirit of God, the Spirit of union and love. If the authorities of the Church are the instruments and bearers of the truth, it is by means of the community that the truth becomes life. . . .

Communion of Saints—what a glad and blessed light illumines it! It is the hidden treasure, the secret joy of the Catholic. When he thinks on the Communion of Saints his heart is enlarged. He passes out of the solitariness of here and of there, of yesterday and of tomorrow, of "I" and "thou," and he is enfolded in an unspeakably intimate communion of spirit and of life, far surpassing his needs and dearest wishes, with all those great ones whom the grace of God has forged from the refractory stuff of our humanity and raised to His height, to participation in His Being. Here are no limitations of space and time. From out of the remote ages of the past, from civilizations and countries of which the memory is now only faintly echoed in legend, the saints pass into his presence, and call him brother, and enfold him with their love. The Catholic is never alone. Christ, the Head, is ever with him, and along with Christ all the holy members of His Body in heaven and on earth. Streams of invisible, mysterious life flow thence through the Catholic fellowship, forces of fertilizing, beneficent love, forces of renewal, of a youthfulness that is ever flowing anew. They pass into the natural, visible forces of the Catholic fellowship.

WE BELIEVE in the Communion of Saints and that by this communion our insufficiency is made good. If indeed we love God in His saints, the saints themselves, urged by the claims of their own charity, will communicate to us their happiness with God.

ST. BERNARD OF CLAIRVAUX

WHEN we no longer have any personal reasons nor any relish for living, but live only for God and in Christ so as to supply our share in the common work humbly and generously, that is the moment when life becomes useful and fruitful. For "in the Church the union of souls is so profound that nothing which cooperates in

123

the common welfare is accomplished without a common effort."

This doctrine consoles and gives value to those barren and, as it were, paralyzed existences of life-long invalids, whose sole role in this world is to suffer from their own incapabilities. It reinstates in their efficacy seemingly unsuccessful efforts, and readjusts the balance of those false and intolerable situations which are prolonged without any hope of an issue. It justifies those unwilling accomplices of sin, which they are forced to suffer to avoid a worse catastrophe or harm falling upon children.

THE REV. VALENTIN-M. BRETON,

O.F.M.

''A SPIRITUAL TREASURY''

JOHN L. STODDARD

THE Father smiled. "I am going," he said, "to reveal to you a very beautiful and consoling feature of the Catholic Church. All Catholics, and many Protestants also, repeat every Sunday in their Creed the words: 'I believe in the Communion of Saints.' . . . Catholics make a great deal of this doctrine; and among the privileges connected with it in their minds is that of a spiritual treasury of saintly merits."

"A spiritual treasury!" I responded in astonishment; "what is its nature, and what are the merits which it contains?"

"Picture to yourself," he answered, "a fund, founded originally by Christ, but still increased by separate contributions, large and small, paid by charitable souls.

Imagine that this fund is used to ransom captives from detention, and to relieve the needy and suffering." He paused. "Do you see where we are coming to?" he asked.

"Not yet," I answered; "please continue."

"You said just now," resumed the priest, "that there are pious souls, who do far more by deeds of mercy and self-sacrifice than is required to discharge the temporal punishment due for *their own* sins. But shall the super-abundant merits gained by them remain unused? Not so; the Church believes that all such merits, credits, satisfactions—call them what you will—are gathered up by God into a fund of mercy, love and grace, which Christ can then apply, together with His own essential merits, to struggling, suffering souls either in this world, or in Purgatory."

"Was this a custom of the early Church?" I asked.

"It was her custom from the very earliest time. A striking illustration of it was given by the Christian martyrs, who often wrote from their prisons to the Church, entreating that, by reason of their own courage in confronting death, the time of penance inflicted on their lesser brethren might be shortened. Gradually then, as these and other martyrs passed to their rewards, the practice was extended, so that such superabundant merits might be gathered into the 'Treasury of the Church,' to be applied either to those who are attempting to discharge their debt of temporal punishment here, or else to those still suffering in Purgatory.

"God wishes us to pray for others, as well as for ourselves . . . 'Bear ye one another's burdens, and thus fulfill the law of Christ.' There is thus formed a tender bond of sympathy between ourselves and the Church suffering, as well as with the Church triumphant."

THE Church is *one* in heaven and on earth. The stern of the vessel no doubt is still in the darkness. But the prow advances, shining into the living light of eternal glory. Our stammerings are amplified by the praise of the Saints, and the succour of their loving kindness as it shines upon us calms our trembling hearts. How could they fail to love who are at the heart of love, or to act who possess the fulness of life? But if they are such loving brothers, it is because God is infinitely more loving: Our Father.

THE REV. MAURICE ZUNDEL

A SPIRITUAL COOPERATIVE

THE REV. JOSEPH RICKABY, S.J.

BY "SAINTS" in this connection is meant us members of the Church, whether on earth, in heaven, or in purgatory. The saints in heaven help us, we help the souls in purgatory, and on earth we help one another. The help here spoken of is spiritual help, in order to eternal salvation,—a definition not to be taken to exclude the corporal works of mercy rendered by Christian to Christian in a Christian spirit. Every virtue is facilitated and called into exercise by the Communion of Saints: it is easier for the individual Christian to believe, to hope, to love, to be patient or pure, because of the multitude of his fellow-Christians believing, hoping, loving, practicing patience and purity with him. Nor is this a matter of mere external edification. Of course we are helped to virtue by seeing the virtuous behavior of our fellow-

Christians, but so are pagans also helped; nay in point of natural virtue the pagan may edify the Christian. But the Communion of Saints means not mere external edification, but an inward grace apart from anything to strike our senses. The Christian in England is in communion with the Christian in China, and is helped by the patience, fortitude, and purity of that Chinaman whom he has never seen or heard of. It is as when a number of men are pulling at a rope; each is helped by the pulling of all the rest; and of course the harder each man individually pulls, the more the task is facilitated for his fellows. The Christian [i.e., Catholic]—I speak particularly of the living member of the Church, the Christian in the state of grace,—the Christian then is never alone in his well-doing, but in every act of virtue that he does he has the whole Church at his back. The Church is helping him, and he is helping the Church. St. Thomas says (2a 2ae, 64, 6): "The life of the just man makes for the preservation and promotion of the good of the community." And St. John Chrysostom insists on the utility to the Church of the solitaries of the desert, or of what we now call the Contemplative Orders. The mere leading of a good Christian life, though you may be palsied and blind, is a service rendered to all other good Christians on earth, and to the souls in purgatory, and a glory to all the saints in heaven. . . . To die in the Communion of Saints and, opening your eyes in the next world, to find yourself still in that Communion of Saints, is to be saved. Your death in that case has been a passage from the Church Militant to the Church Triumphant, or Suffering. We are not in communion with the lost.

THE whole Church assumes the sinner's burden, so that by applying to one who is doing penance the [merits] which superabound in her through the contributions of all, she expiates his faults as though she were absorbing them in a mixture of collective mercy and virile compassion.

ST. AMBROSE

"THIS WONDERFUL COMMERCE"

THE REV. BEDE JARRETT, O.P.

IT SEEMS like a strange vision of the Apocalypse to conceive that vast intercommunication of living and dead, such as this Catholic doctrine proclaims. To unite in one single body the living that follow the teaching of Christ, and that vast crowd of dead that in Heaven or in Purgatory follow for ever the Lamb, is an idea that is overwhelming in its very extent. . . . The dwellers over all the earth, different and even antagonistic, in language and climate and culture; and those suffering souls, bodyless, expectant of release, glad in the midst of all their woe, longing for the end of their exile; and that throng who praise God unceasingly and look down with brotherly compassion on the repentance of sinners on earth—how or in what are these to be established in unity? . . .

Where shall we find this common bond? It is not in faith, for in heaven faith has passed into knowledge, and the Church has no jurisdiction beyond the grave. It is not in hope, for there can be no hope where the higher gift of possession has been obtained. It can be only in love expressed by prayer. It is, indeed, by prayer that all these are made one. This conception under which we view the world is really marvellous; it gives an entirely new outlook upon life, for we see how between heaven and earth are passing ceaselessly great streams of prayer, petitions from wearied and anxious souls rising upwards, borne along by the hands of angels, strong cries and tears from hearts in anguish that beg for courage to bear their cross or for the chalice to pass, the grateful thanks of those whose voices have been heard and their favors granted them, and those whose words are no more than a great paean of praise at the marvels wrought by the mercy and majesty of God, and a conscious acknowledgement that God is wonderful in His saints. So, too, from earth and heaven steal up to the throne of Omnipotence, the prayers of sinners and saints for their dear dead: there are hands uplifted in worship, hearts afire with friendship, sufferings of mortal life gladly borne for the hastening of their loved ones' release. . . . To feel in the company of the saints, to feel our oneness in Christ with all Christians [i.e., Catholics], to be sure that death does not sever or part, is indeed consoling to man, whose greatest fear is the dread of loneliness. . . .

Over all the world that is split into different languages, there is still one common tongue to every Christian. Here, then, surely I shall get to feel that there can be no real loneliness; that I am not left alone to fight out my battle, for there are countless hosts who watch me, interested in my welfare and applauding my efforts. There are the well-wishes of my fellows in the Christian [i.e., Catholic] Church who pray daily, as I pray for the whole Church. . . . While earth sleeps or wakes, through the busy day and the long watches of the night, this wonderful commerce goes on through the medium of endless prayer.

WE LEARNED that sanctity invisibly unites all the living members of the Church,[1] and that this *Communion of Saints* is the bond and the life of the Church's mystical body, and gives it its note of sanctity, independent of the imperfections and faults of some, or of most, of the members of the visible Church—the Church whose head is Christ, whose soul is the Holy Spirit, but whose members are born sinners like all men since the Fall; the Church which exists wherever there is a holy soul, militant on earth, suffering in Purgatory, or glorious and blessed in eternal life.

RAÏSSA MARITAIN

"ONE UNITED HOUSEHOLD"

SUSAN L. EMERY

THE Catholic Church is one great family, one united household, although part are in heaven, and part on earth, and part in the realm of the waiting souls in their place of purgation and patient peace. Everywhere is one love of the Heart of Jesus; everywhere one Divine Spirit, animating all; everywhere one heavenly Father, Whose tender care is all-embracing and unforgetting. The

[1] Sinners are members of the Church as well as saints. Ed.

Church triumphant, the Church militant, the Church in purgatory,—what are all these but one Church, bound by a common tie to a common head? . . .

Therefore she binds all nations into one. Happy, indeed, are the eyes that see the things which we see! Look at the family life in the Catholic Church everywhere, not the family as divided into separate households, but the one, united, world-wide family of the household of the faith, bound by its marvellous strong tie everywhere to the centre of its unity, God's chosen representative of His own divine paternity, Christ's own vicar and vicegerent, the Holy Spirit's mouthpiece, the Pope at Rome. Amor Roma: beautiful and holy anagram! Rome rhymes with home, and all roads lead there, Jew and Gentile, bond and free, black and white, rich and poor, flock to the bosom of the Catholic Church and call her mother; new converts meet her sons and daughters, and declare that they find themselves each among his own people, and in his Father's house. Over and again, as on the first Pentecost, men enter into the true fold, and stand there in rapturous amazement, saying: "How hear we every man our own tongue wherein we were born!" For every tongue beneath the sky belongs to her; and each of us hears, in her musical accents, his mother's voice. . . .

No man is ever alone in that vast communion which is named the Catholic Church and the Communion of Saints.

Alone? Every saint in heaven is our brother, our sister. We speak to them with words of human affection; we ask them to help us, and we believe that they are strong to help, and that their prayers avail with God. It is their names that are given in Baptism to our children; we

keep their feasts with rejoicing; we make personal
friends among them, know this saint better than that
one, and expect to see them and know them face to face
at last.

Alone? Our dead go from us, we lay them with tears
and kisses beneath the sod. But *alone*—when we meet
in the Heart of Jesus; when our prayers and communions and Masses can reach them? Speak, St. Augustine!
"One *never* loses those whom one loves in Him Whom
we can never lose." Truly may we say, in the words
of today's [Twelfth Sunday After Pentecost] gospel:
"Happy are the eyes that see the things which we see!"

VI

For by grace you are saved through faith.
Ephesians 2:8

"A RAY OF DIVINE BEAUTY"

THE REV. M. JOSEPH SCHEEBEN

THE grace of God is a ray of Divine beauty, infused from Heaven into the soul of man, and penetrating its innermost nature with such a bright and beautiful light, that the soul delights the eye of God, is most tenderly loved by Him, is adopted as His child and spouse, is elevated above all limits of nature from earth to Heaven. By grace the soul is received into the bosom of the Eternal Father, and at the side of His Divine Son participates in His nature, His life and glory, and inherits the realm of His eternal happiness. . . .

It would follow, then, that man ought to be more thankful to God for the smallest share of grace, than if he had received the perfections of the highest spirits and were made king of Heaven and of the whole world, with full possession of all power and dominion. How infinitely superior in value, then, is grace to all the riches of this earth! . . .

Indeed, we may well say that grace surpasses all natural things in a manner similar to God Himself. Grace is nothing but the heavenly light, which from the depths of the Divinity diffuses itself over the rational creature. . . .

Thus the work of grace is the greatest wonder of God's omnipotence. It is greater than even the creation of the natural world out of nothing, and can only be compared with that unspeakable act of God the Father, by which He produces from all eternity His own and equal Son, and in time unites with Him a human nature. As supernatural, sublime, and full of mystery as is the generation of Christ, so supernatural and mysterious is the infusion of grace into our soul, because, in the words of St. Leo, we thereby "participate in the generation of Christ." . . .

In grace God wills that we ourselves, with His assistance, prepare our soul for it, receive it from His hand, preserve, cultivate, and increase it.

O wonderful greatness which God has given us, taking our soul unto Himself as His spouse, that by the power received from Him she may produce in herself the image of God and become the child of God! O wonderful power which God has granted His Church, to communicate His grace to her children by her teaching and her sacraments! . . .

Every degree of grace that we acquire raises us up higher above our nature, unites us more closely to God, and causes us to ascend ever more above all the heavens. . . .

The glory of Heaven, in which the blessed see and enjoy God, is nothing else but the full development of the grace that we possess. Grace is the fountain, springing up unto everlasting life; it is the root, of which the blossom and fruit is beatitude; it has, then, the special privilege, that this beatitude depends upon it and is founded upon it. . . .

As long as you do not see God face to face, you cannot see the image of His Divine nature in you. Grace is, so to speak, the dawn of the light of the Divine Sun; wait only until the Sun itself rises, until it develops in you its whole splendor, until it penetrates and glorifies you with the glow of its heat, and your glory will delight you the more, the longer it has remained hidden from you. Until then, you must, after the words of the Apostle, walk by faith and not by sight, believing the unfailing promise of God. . . .

In grace you have the pledge, aye, the root of your future glorification in soul and body. If you still sigh in the servitude of the flesh, if you feel depressed by suffering and frailties, sigh with the Apostle after the freedom and glory of the children of God, where even your flesh will be spiritualized, and in the fulness of perfection, free from all suffering and fear of death, beautiful as the sun and swift as the eagle, you will feel the power of grace and possess in the fullest abundance all those perfections which you perceive in visible things.

"LIFE WITH GOD"

THE REV. WILLIAM LAWSON, S.J.

WHEN you bend your mind to a serious consideration of supernatural life, you are startled by the boldness of some of the expressions used about it. That phrase of St. Peter's, "sharers in the divine nature," is bold and startling. But it is meant by him to be a plain statement of a truth of doctrine: and that is what it is. Nor is it alone. The Apostles St. John and St. Paul express the same truth in similar words which they learnt from Our Lord: and the Church speaks the same truth with equal boldness. How else can they state a staggering truth but in words which shake the mind?

Our Lord begins by telling us that we must receive from Him a new life—a life so real that it can be acquired only by a new birth. The life is given by the Holy Ghost, with the water of baptism to be a sign of the new birth. God is our Father because He created us. He is our Father in an even more intimate way because He brings us to a higher life: "for of His own will He hath begotten us by the word of truth." (James i.18)

To share in the divine nature cannot mean that the divine nature is parcelled out, each of us receiving a portion of it. The divine nature is one and indivisible: it *is* God. We remain what we are, human, created limited. But the statement that we share the divine nature is not an empty exaggeration. It is an inspired expression of the truth that grace raises us to a supernatural level on which we can enter into the Family Life of the Blessed Trinity. Grace is the life we have from Our Lord through the Holy Ghost. It gives us the reality of family likeness, so that God the Father recognizes us as brethren of Our Lord and as His own children. . . .

With that transformed human nature, lifted now to the divine level, we are specially united to the Blessed Trinity. We see God with a new power of vision. We have the beginning of that power which will be completed in eternity by the light of glory in our direct beholding of God, the Beatific Vision. . . .

Grace really is supernatural life, life with God, in the Family of the Blessed Trinity. Is that life worth living?

ETERNAL LIGHT FOR THE SOUL

DOM ANSCAR VONIER, O.S.B.

SANCTIFYING grace is the fitness, divinely received, in the human soul, to see God one day, as He is in Himself, and to be happy in this vision of Him. Sanctifying grace may be said to be the education or elevation of the created spirit, making him capable of seeing the beauty of God, when God will come to him and tell him: "Behold here I am, the God of thy heart." . . .

Sanctifying grace in the human soul . . . gives the created spirit eyes for God's hidden glory; it gives him a heart vast enough to enter into the joy of a God Who dwells on high. It is then this conformity of the created spirit with the Uncreated Spirit, enabling the created spirit to understand the Uncreated Spirit, which we call sanctifying grace.

Sanctifying grace is therefore a permanent state of the spirit, a state destined to last for ever. Just like the spirit himself, it is unending from its very nature. God never takes it away from the soul, through a direct act of His omnipotence.

It may be lost through the act of mortal sin on the part of the spirit.

Sanctifying grace is the divine light in the soul whose radiance can never fail; but the lamp in which it is burning may be broken to pieces, the light itself would have been burning for ever, as it is eternal light. . . .

Sanctifying grace is entirely divine in its origin. Through a direct act of His omnipotence, God causes it to come into the human soul. It is so high in its nature, and lies so deep in the human soul, that nothing short of mortal sin can touch it.

Sanctifying grace may exist, and does exist in the soul, before the soul awakens to reason, as in the baptised infant. When reason has been dimmed and obscured by some cerebral infirmity, it remains. Outwardly, those unhappy people appear to be unreasoning children; inwardly they are the temples of the Living God. . . .

Santifying grace admits of progress. It grows more and more abundant in the faithful soul, through the divinely assisted acts of spiritual life. The building up of character has been made the religious watchword of many in our own days. No expression could be more Catholic, provided we give it a meaning vast enough to be useful for eternity. Our divinely assisted acts, as we have described them above, when speaking of actual graces, are a constant building up of moral character. Through them man becomes the *homo quadratus*, the square man, whom the ancient philosophers envied for the perfections of his moral character.

But there is a building up of character unknown to pagan philosophy and modernized Christianity. It is this: every virtuous act, prompted by the Holy Ghost, brings about in the depths of the human soul an increase of sanctifying grace; and thus makes the transitory virtuous act result into something higher than itself: a more complete possession of the unchanging participation of the Divine Nature. This is the only true building up of moral character according to Catholic theology.

THERE is within us a truly supernatural principle, a pure gift of God, a divine form, which inclines us as it were naturally and so easily and pleasantly to live the life of God. In other words, we become *naturally divine.*

THE REV. Y. E. MASSON, O.P.

OUR HIGHEST HAPPINESS, OUR GREATEST GOOD

THE REV. M. JOSEPH SCHEEBEN

GRACE, which makes us saints, gives us the highest and only happiness that we can possess on earth. . . .

There is, first, the hope of heavenly happiness, which alone, if we had nothing else, would render our heart more happy than the full enjoyment of all earthly goods. The mere consciousness that the heavenly joys infinitely transcend all idea and conception of the human soul, and that, on the part of God, they are infallibly certain —this consciousness alone is powerful enough to perfectly comfort and quiet our heart.

But in grace we possess the highest and infinite good, not only by hope, but in truth and reality in our very heart, and we may already embrace it and taste its sweet ness. By grace we bear God truly and substantially in us, call Him our own with perfect right, and hold Him so firmly, that no power in Heaven or on earth can rob Him from us. By it we embrace Him with the arms of holy charity, press Him to our bosom, enclose Him in our heart, and are so penetrated by Him, that we are one heart and one soul with Him. By the union with God in grace, we already enjoy the highest delight and the sweetest pleasures, which so far surpass all sensual pleasures, as Heaven surpasses the earth; we possess the greatest wealth in possessing Him Who has created all and whose greatness knows no limit. . . .

Above all, however, grace gives us that sweet, heavenly peace which the Son of God has brought upon earth, the peace of Christ, of which the Apostle says: "Let the peace of God, which surpasseth all understanding, keep your hearts and minds in Christ Jesus."

GRACE is nothing else but a certain beginning of glory in us.

ST. THOMAS AQUINAS

THE FIRST GRACE

THE REV. BENEDICT WILLIAMSON

THE supernatural life is a gift, not a reward, hence this supernatural life can be received by the child. A gift is something given quite freely, depending not on the dispositions of the receiver but those of the giver. With Grace the Giver is God. And He gives His Grace to the grown man or the new-born babe. . . .

This Sacrament of Baptism is the door through which souls are admitted into the Kingdom. . . . The Act of Baptism is the Actual Grace, and it puts the child into the state of Grace by the infusion of Sanctifying Grace. From that instant the child is taken up into the supernatural state, and has been made partaker of the Kingdom of Heaven.

If the child dies the soul goes straight to Heaven, because there is nothing to hinder her flight thither. This inner invisible operation is the essential side of the Sacrament. It is no mere meaningless form, as some may think, but a most tremendous act pregnant with eternal consequences. . . .

This first Grace given through Baptism is a passage from death to life, a translation of the soul out of the kingdom of darkness into the light and liberty of the children of God.

GRACE COMES TO THE
MARITAINS

RAÏSSA MARITAIN

On April 5th we told Léon Bloy of our desire to become Catholics, surrounding this desire, it is true, with all sorts of naïve restrictions. . . .

We still thought in very truth that all this could be a matter between ourselves and God and our godfather. We dreaded all externalization.

Although the speculative debate was ended for us, we still had many feelings of repugnance to overcome. The Church in her mystical and saintly life we found infinitely lovable. We were ready to accept her. She promised us Faith by Baptism: we were going to put her word to the test. . . .

While the spectacle alone of the sanctity, and that of the beauty of Catholic doctrine had occupied our thoughts, we had been happy in heart and mind, and our admiration had grown by leaps and bounds. Now that we were preparing ourselves to enter among those whom the world hates as it hates Christ, we suffered, Jacques and I, a sort of agony. This lasted for about two months. Once, during those months, I heard in my sleep these words, said to me with a certain impatience: "You have only to love God and serve Him with all your heart." Later I found these words in the *Imitation*, which I had not then read.

Léon Bloy had sent us to a priest of the Sacré-Coeur Basilica, "the very image of a child and martyr, whom you will love," he had written to Pierre Termier. Father Durantel awaited our decision.

Our suffering and dryness grew greater every day. Finally we understood that God also was waiting, and that there would be no further light so long as we should not have obeyed the imperious voice of our consciences saying to us: you have no valid objection to the Church; she alone promises you the light of truth—prove her promises, put Baptism to the test. . . .

Suddenly our decision was made. Purely for reasons of convenience—I had a journey to take—we chose the 11th of June for the Baptism. . . .

On June 11th, . . . all three of us betook ourselves to the Church of Saint John the Evangelist in Montmartre. I was in a state of absolute dryness, and could no longer remember any of the reasons for my being there. One single thing remained clear in my mind: either Baptism would give me Faith, and I would believe and I would belong to the Church altogether; or I would go away unchanged, an unbeliever forever. Jacques had almost the same thoughts.

"What do you ask of the Church of God?"
"Faith."

We were baptized at eleven o'clock in the morning. . . . An immense peace descended upon us, bringing with it the treasures of Faith. There were no more questions, no more anguish, no more trials—there was only the infinite answer of God. The Church kept her promises. And it is she whom we first loved. It is through her that we have known Christ.

I think now that faith—a weak faith, impossible to formulate consciously—already existed in the most hidden depths of our souls. But we did not know this. It was the Sacrament which revealed it to us, and it was sanctifying grace which strengthened it in us.

WE ARE set free, through grace, from time and place, from the imprisonment of matter, not by flight, not by rejection of them, but through new understanding of their meaning. In their own right, in relation to themselves, created things are deprived of the value that in a purely human view they were accorded, but in exchange they too, in their degree, acquire new value as means through which God manifests His glory.

ROSALIND MURRAY

THE INFUSION OF TRUTH

THE REV. GERALD VANN, O.P.

IT IS not just an abstract knowledge of truth that is given in the sacrament of Baptism; it is the abiding presence of the Truth. God is with us, and in us. And to be faithful to the faith is, therefore, to live always in that presence, and to find in it both the motive force and the standard of judgment for all life and all action.

What is essentially given is thus the power of entering into the kingdom, the power of heaven. When the human being is thus filled with the life of God he has within him precisely the life which is heaven, though he has it only in germ; and all that he does, his thought and willing and prayer and action, can increase that life within him and make him more and more heavenly himself. . . .

But it remains true that to live the life of God is, in fact, to find a new earth, to see the earth as the habitation of His glory, to see all things in Him and Him in all things. . . .

All that sense, which you find so strongly marked in the early Church, of the power of the God-life in man to heal sickness and suffering and to tame the wild brutality of created things, the power to restore and heal the world by goodness and love, is simply an affirmation of the importance of baptism for the world as a whole. True, the power it gives is primarily a passive power, the power to be a child of God: but that power itself creates a responsibility. You were a slave; now you are free; and therefore you have the responsibility of the free man.

"OUR DIVINE ADOPTION"

DOM COLUMBA MARMION, O.S.B.

BAPTISM is as it were the spiritual birth by which the life of grace is conferred upon us.

This life is a participation in the life of God; it is, of its nature, immortal. If we possess it here below, we have the pledge of eternal beatitude; if we have it not, we are forever excluded from the Divine fellowship.

Now, the regular means, instituted by Christ, whereby we are to be born to this life, is Baptism which thus constitutes the Sacrament of adoption. Plunged in the sacred waters, we are there born to the Divine life. God, in making us partakers of His nature in so liberal a manner, by a gift infinitely exceeding all we could hope or expect, creates us, so to speak, anew. We are—it is the great Apostle's expression—"a new creature." . . .

Baptism is the efficacious sign of our Divine adoption; by Baptism we truly become the children of God and are incorporated with Christ. It opens the door to every heavenly gift. Remember this truth: all God's mercies towards us, all His condescensions proceed from our adoption. When we turn the gaze of our soul towards the Godhead, the first thing that is unveiled to us of the eternal counsels regarding us, is the decree of our adoption in Jesus Christ; and all the favours God may shower down upon our souls here below, until the day when He communicates Himself to us for ever in the beatitude of His Trinity, have for their first link this initial grace of Baptism, to which they are attached. At this predesti nated moment, we entered into the family of God. At the hour of our baptism, Christ engraves an indelible character upon our soul, we receive the pledge of the Divine Spirit. . . .

This Divine, God-given life is only in a state of germ. It must grow and develop in the same way as our renunciation of sin, our "death to sin" must unceasingly be renewed and sustained.

Our whole existence ought to be the realization of what Baptism inaugurates. By Baptism, we communicate in the mystery and divine virtue of Christ's death and risen life. "Death to sin" is wrought; but on account of the concupiscence remaining in us, we must maintain this death by continual renunciation of Satan, of his suggestions and works, and the solicitations of the world and the flesh. Grace is the principle of life in us, but it is a germ we must cultivate; it is that kingdom of God within us that Our Lord Himself compares to a grain of mustard seed which becomes a great tree.

St. Augustine says, God has a greater desire to give us His graces, than we have to receive them. The reason is, because God is of His own nature infinite goodness. Hence He feels an infinite desire to impart His goods to us. Hence St. Mary Magdalene de Pazzi used to say, that God feels as it were under an obligation to the soul that prays to Him; because by prayer it opens to Him the way by which He can satisfy His desire of dispensing His graces to us. . . .

We have a God who loves us to excess, and who is solicitous for our salvation, and therefore He is always ready to hear all who ask His graces. The princes of the earth, says St. Chrysostom, give audience only to a few; but God gives audience to all who wish for it.

ST. ALPHONSUS DE' LIGUORI

THE HOLY SPIRIT WITHIN US

THE VERY REV. JOHN G.
ARINTERO, O.P.

We live a life in which the Spirit . . . since He is the Spirit of Truth, enables us to know this life truly and makes us call God by the name of Father. He imprints on us the divine seal and fashions us in the like-

147

ness of the only-begotten Son of God. He anoints us and makes us truly anointed Christs in the image of Jesus. He dwells within us, although in a hidden manner, as the vivifying principle, and constitutes the pledge of eternal life. Without destroying our nature or our personality, but rather enriching them, He renews, transforms, and deifies us, making us one with Jesus Christ, our Saviour, as members of the Mystical Body, all of whom live one and the same life. This life resides fully in Christ as Head and thence, according to the measures of His giving and the dispositions which are found in His distinct members, it is poured forth and redounds to all. When these members, having rid themselves of all obstacles, receive this life in great abundance, the Spirit who animates them will give them clear testimony that they are sons of God and, as such, co-heirs with Jesus Christ.

THE POWER OF CONFIRMATION

THE REV. BEDE JARRETT, O.P.

ONCE I have been marked with the grace of Confirmation, I have had set up in my soul a power, a force, that never runs dry or can be drained or even wholly affected by sin. When I do wrong the grace ceases to work, but it does not cease to exist; so that as soon as I have reconciled myself to God, back again comes the flood that Confirmation for good and all established within me. Hence the value of it does not consist simply in the day of my reception of it, but is to be made use of all the days of my life. The indwelling of the Spirit of God, begun in Baptism, is now made perfect, and the wonderful Sevenfold Gifts of God are put into my charge, so that with me it lies whether I have the benefit they can confer or not. . . .

The object and effect of this sacrament was to make me strong, that this strengthening of me was to be achieved by the abiding Presence of the Holy Spirit, and that this abiding Presence was to continue for the whole of my lifetime. As the need endures, so must the remedy endure. This sacrament, therefore, is tremendously alive.

THE union of the Spirit [i.e. the Holy Ghost] is not effected by His drawing near according to place. Shining on those who are purged of all dross, He makes them spiritual through union with Himself; and, as bodies become bright and shining when a ray of light falls upon them, and from their brilliance they diffuse a new lustre, so souls that possess the Spirit within themselves are illumined by the Spirit, themselves become spiritual and send forth grace to others. . . . Hence the likeness to God and that than which nothing more sublime could be desired, that you should become God.

ST. BASIL

THE GIFTS OF THE
HOLY SPIRIT

THE REV. RICHARD L. ROONEY, S.J.

WHAT the Holy Ghost effected in the Apostles, that Christ would have Him do in you. Briefly it comes to this: Christ speaks; the Holy Ghost explains. Christ acts and lives; the Holy Ghost expounds, illuminates, interprets the significance of Christ's deeds. For real insight into Christ's words and works you must have the Holy Spirit. Without Him you would be in darkness, you would understand *nothing*. Without Him you would be too cowardly to do anything, even if you did understand what Christ did and was and what He wanted you to do and be. The Holy Ghost teaches, strengthens, and energizes you actually to relive Christ. . . .

Catholicism is a creed and a code and a cult that give men a way of life. Because Catholicism is so at variance with your natural instincts, it requires that you have special helps for your living it. Those helps Christ left in the sacraments of His Church. It is by means of the sacraments that the Holy Spirit causes the life of Christ to flow from Him into those souls who are to be made at one with Him, who make up His Mystical Body. . . .

The Holy Spirit is a unique teacher. All others who teach have to remain outside their pupils. They can transfer their ideas to their students only over the bridge of language and illustration. Not so the Holy Spirit. He actually comes right into your souls. As long as you allow Him, He will remain within you, dwelling in your souls,

150

laboring in His infinite and mysterious way to form you to the likeness of Christ.

From His dwelling place within you the Holy Spirit looks about Him. He sees:

(1) that you are human beings, having everything that belongs to a human.

(2) that the grace which He poured into your hearts at baptism, or that is restored when you lose it by sin, or that He made to grow by the other sacraments, has made you something more than human persons. By reason of His grace you are now divinized, made godlike in your beings, *in what you are*.

(3) that along with this grace, He has given you virtues, new powers, faith, hope and charity, and as a result you can be divine not only in what you are but also *in what you do*. Your actions can now harmonize with your beings.

Your divine teacher might very easily have stopped after He had made you divine in what you are and in what you do. He is however divinely generous. He would lavish on you everything that He can and still have you remain creatures. There is one thing that remains for Him to add, one further finishing touch: He can make you perfectly acceptable to God the Father and completely like to God the Son. He has made you divine in your *being*. He has made you divine in your *actions,* in *what* you do. It remains for Him only to make you divine in the *way* that you do it. He would grant you even this ability, too.

In addition to all that He has bestowed upon you then, the Holy Spirit from the place of vantage that He holds in your souls bestows upon you seven wondrous gifts. He impresses on your faith-hope-and-charity-virtued souls, on your elevated intellects and wills, these gifts of His. By means of them you are rendered more docile, more pliable to His guidance and aid. By means of them you are made divine in the *way* that you act as well as in what you do.

Even though you are divinized, left to yourselves without these gifts you would find life on the divine plane to which you have been raised possible but quite difficult and quite uncomfortable. By means of these gifts you are put completely at ease with your adoptive Father and in your divine surroundings. By reason of these gifts you can move about this new world into which you have been lifted with the same ease, smoothness, and comfort that Christ, Our Lord God's natural Son, possessed. . . .

The gifts of the Holy Ghost are habits in the way of divine action. They are facilities that the Holy Spirit gives to your virtue-endowed minds and wills, facilities that enable you to do with ease something that would otherwise be hard even though possible. For example, with the virtue of charity you can make an act of love to God. It is not easy for you to do this. But if the gift of piety be added to that virtue, ah then you can make such an act with an ease that you would otherwise never have known.

Finally, the gifts of the Holy Ghost are *dynamic habits*. They look toward action. They do not perfect the soul in being, in what the soul is, as does grace. Rather do they add the finishing touches to the virtues. They give a divine alacrity to your faith-filled minds, not in *what* they think, but in the *way* that they think it. The gifts give you a divine strength in the way that you hope. They add the master touch to charity-enlivened wills, giving those wills a divine warmth in the way that they

love and choose. All the gifts remain vitally and vitaliz-
ingly in your minds and wills, making your minds and
wills more fully responsive to the delicate guidance and
force of the Holy Spirit, who has given you these gifts
for this very purpose. . . .

THE Fathers of the Church speak in exactly the same
terms. The Holy Spirit is the great gift of God and Guest
of our Soul. In giving Himself to us, He makes us share
in the Divine nature and constitutes us the children of
God, saints, Divine beings. He is spoken of as the sanctifying spirit, the principle of celestial and Divine life;
some even go so far as to call Him the form of our holiness, the soul of our soul, the bond uniting us to the
Father and the Son, as that one of the Divine persons by
whom the other two dwell in us.

THE REV. BARTHÉLEMY FROGET, O.P.

ELIZABETH SETON DESCRIBES
THE ACTION OF GRACE

AFTER all had departed, I was called to the little room
next to the sacristy, and made my profession of faith as
the Catholic Church prescribes, and then came away light
of heart, and with a clearer head than I have had these
many long months. . . .

So happy I am now to prepare for this good confession
which, bad as I am, I would be ready to make on the
house-top to insure the good *absolution* I hope for after

it, and then to begin a new life, a new existence itself. It is no great difficulty for me to prepare for this confession, for truly my life has been well culled over in bitterness of soul these past months of sorrow. It is done —easy enough, too; the kindest and most respectable confessor is this Mr. [i.e. Father] O'Brien—with the compassion and yet firmness in this work of mercy which I would have expected from Our Lord Himself. Our Lord Himself I saw alive in him in this venerable sacrament. How awful those words of unloosing after a thirty years' bondage. I felt as if my chains fell, as those of St. Peter's, at the touch of the Divine Messenger. My God! what a new scene for my soul!

On the Annunciation I shall be made one with Him Who said: "Unless ye eat the flesh of the Son of Man, and drink His Blood, ye shall not have life in ye." I count the days and hours; yet a few more of hope and expectation and then! How bright is the sun these morning walks to the church for preparation—deep snow or smooth ice, all to me is the same; I see nothing but the bright little cross on St. Peter's steeple. [St. Peter's Church, Barclay St., New York, N.Y.] . . .

At last, at last, God is mine and I am His. Now let all earthly things go as they will. *I have received Him.* The awful impressions of the evening before! Fears of not having done all to prepare, and yet the transports of confidence, and hope in His goodness. My God! to the last breath of life I will remember the night of watching for the break of day, the fearful, beating heart so pressing to be off; the long walk to town, but every step brought me nearer that street, then nearer that tabernacle, near to the moment He would enter the poor little dwelling so all His own. And when He did come, the first thought

I remember was: *"Let God arise, let His enemies be scattered,"* for it seems to me my King had come to take His throne, and instead of the humble, tender welcome I had expected to give Him, it was but a triumph of joy and gladness that the Deliverer was come, and my defense, and strength, and salvation, made mine for this world and the next. Now all the joy of my heart found vent, and so far, truly, I feel the powers of my soul held fast by Him who had taken possession of His little kingdom.

THE heart that is free and joyful with good-will is better disposed for the reception of grace than the heart that is fettered with sadness and bitterness; for the Holy Ghost is the love and good-will and joy of the Father and the Son, and like naturally loves like.

ST. BONAVENTURE

THE LIGHT OF GLORY

DOM ANSCAR VONIER, O.S.B.

IT IS *my* mind that will see God as He is in Himself, the very mind that is thinking now, whilst writing this; and it will see God, because it will be capable through God's grace of seeing Him, as my bodily eyes are capable now of beholding the picture opposite me. This wonderful act of Beatific Vision is the act of man, it is not the act of God. Moreover the degree of Beatific Vision will depend entirely on the intensity of that great endowment. We shall see what our eyes will allow us to see.

The doctrine of the light of glory is the noblest and highest instance of that essentially Catholic conviction, that man does, in eternity, not what God through an arbitrary disposition makes him do, but what man has made himself capable of doing through the grace of God in mortal life. For the light of glory is merely the sequel of sanctifying grace; it is the same entity, the same supernatural reality; the difference between sanctifying grace and the light of glory, if there be any, would be merely the difference between youth and mature age in the same individual.

This is what may be called the practical human side of *lumen gloriae*. Sanctifying grace is given to us and given to us more abundantly, through the acts of Christian life, done in the body of our mortality.

We have thus a doctrine which is as consoling as it is significant of the value and importance of our Christian lives here below. Through the acquisition of more abundant sanctifying grace we acquire *lumen gloriae;* we acquire the capability of seeing God; we acquire that divine nobility of intellect, that heavenly stability of mind, that makes us fit radically for the vision of God.

EACH grace is not to be rested in, but made a stepping-stone to the next grace. The grace of faith, for example, is but the beginning of life, not its end. It is but an illumination whereby I am made conscious that He calls me higher; and the daily blessings of health, friends, work, and the beauty of nature, and arts and crafts, have to be viewed as daily-given helps to reach His side.

THE REV. BEDE JARRETT, O.P.

VII

"SEEING THROUGH THE EYES OF GOD"

THE REV. WALTER FARRELL, O.P.

FAITH is a view, a superior view opening up truths that only God could know. In itself faith perfects the mind of man far beyond anything else than can come to it in the universe. Yet for all that, faith is an imperfect thing. Although the vision of God should be spread before us, we have not the eyes of God. We are soaring in the heights, but we have not the eagle's power to take in the details of the panorama that unfolds beneath us. We are looking at truths too bright for our eyes, so we move in obscurity. Faith is obscure. By faith a man moves through darkness; but he moves securely, his hand in the hand of God. He is literally seeing through the eyes of God, as a blind man sees through the eyes of his friend, because all that he believes, he believes precisely by reason of the word of the First Truth. The darkness of faith is not a discouragement, a ground for mistrust; it is a promise of that time when we shall no longer see "as in a glass, darkly, but face to face." It is a challenge that can be met only by bending the stiff neck of pride while we listen again to the wise words of a Father as He tells us things our puny experience can never reach. . . .

Moreover, faith brings the comfort of security in the midst of an uncertain world. A woman who has been given the gift of faith stands in the middle of her life somewhat as the pioneers stood in the center of their newly completed stockade; for this gift of faith bars the entrance of the enemy falsehood much more surely than ever did the stockade keep out the Indians. In the emptiness of darkness the stained-glass windows of Notre Dame are no more than a part of that universal blackness; with the morning sun streaming through them they are a blaze of gorgeous color that stops the heart in its beating. Light is the medium by which color is seen. Thus the First Truth is the medium by which men believe; there is no more possibility of falsehood calling that supernatural belief into life than there is of darkness bringing out the glory of color in a stained-glass window. All the smallest details that fall under faith do so only so far as they have an order to God, to the First Truth. To include truth under falsehood is no more possible than to include being under nothing, or goodness under evil. It is not only the *thing* that faith believes but the *very reason* for belief which excludes the possibility of falsehood undermining the foundations which faith gives to man's life. Such is the security of faith. . . .

Faith can be hated for the hard things it demands, and

the acid of distortion may be thrown in its face in a vain attempt to destroy the power of its beauty; it can be the victim of mockery by men in love with their blindness. It can be denied, rejected, lightly tossed aside. But then again, it can be lived up to, cherished, jealously guarded, proudly defended at whatever cost. In the latter case, the world looks on, blind to the beauty of actions that are robed in the splendor that comes from an object so high that properly it belongs to God: the vision of the face of God.

A FEW years ago, I received a letter from a radio listener who said: "I imagine that you from your earliest youth were surrounded by priests and nuns who never permitted you to think for yourself. Why not throw off the yoke of Rome and begin to be free?"

I answered him thus: "In the center of a sea was an island on which children played and danced and sang. Around that island were very high walls which had stood for centuries. One day, some strange men came to the island in individual row boats, and said to the children: Who put up these walls? Can you not see that they are destroying your freedom? Tear them down!

"The children tore them down! Now if you go there, you will find all the children huddled together in the center of the island, afraid to play, afraid to sing, afraid to dance—afraid of falling into the sea."

Faith is not a dam which prevents the flow of the river of reason and thought; it is a levee which prevents unreason from flooding the countryside.

THE MOST REV. FULTON J. SHEEN

FAITH, THE ROOT OF
OUR LIFE

DOM COLUMBA MARMION, O.S.B.

FAITH is a source of joy because it makes us share in the knowledge of Christ. He is the Eternal Word and has taught us the Divine secrets. In believing what He tells us, we have the same knowledge as He; faith is a source of joy because it is the source of light.

It is a source of joy too because it places us in radical possession of future bliss, it is "the substance of things to be hoped for, the evidence of things that appear not." . . . Faith is a seed, and every seed contains in germ the future harvest. . . .

Faith places us in contact with Christ: if we contemplate this mystery with faith, Christ produces in us the grace which He gave to His disciples when, as their Risen Lord, He appeared to them. Jesus lives in our souls; and, ever living, He unceasingly acts in us, according to the degree of our faith and in accordance with the grace proper to each of His mysteries.

Justus ex fide vivit. The just man, (that is to say one who in Baptism has put on the new man created in justice) lives, in so far as he is just, by faith, by the light that the Sacrament of illumination brings to him. The more he lives by faith, the more he realizes in himself the perfection of his divine adoption. Notice this expression carefully: *ex fide.* The exact meaning of this is that faith ought to be the root of all our life. There are souls who live "with faith," *cum fide;* but it is *ex fide,* "by faith," that we must live.

And when we act in all things according to the principles of faith, we become strong and stable because we participate in the Divine infallibility.

IT IS the heart which experiences God, and not the reason. This, then, is faith: God felt by the heart, not by the reason.

Faith is a gift of God; do not believe that we said it was a gift of reasoning. Other religions do not say this of their faith. They only give reasoning in order to arrive at it, and yet it does not bring them to it.

BLAISE PASCAL

"I ASK NOT TO KNOW"

JOHN HENRY CARDINAL NEWMAN

GOD was all-complete, all-blessed in Himself; but it was His will to create a world for His glory. He is Almighty, and might have done all things Himself, but it has been His will to bring about His purposes by the beings He has created. We are all created to His glory—we are created to do His will. I am created to do something or to be something for which no one else is created; I have a place in God's counsels, in God's world, which no one else has; whether I be rich or poor, despised or esteemed by man, God knows me and calls me by my name.

God has created me to do Him some definite service; He has committed some work to me which He has not committed to another. I have my mission—I may never know it in this life, but I shall be told it in the next. Somehow I am necessary for His purposes, as necessary in my place as an Archangel in his—if, indeed, I fail, He can raise another, as He could make the stones children of Abraham. Yet I have a part in this great work; I am a link in a chain, a bond of connexion between persons. He has not created me for naught. I shall do good, I shall do His work; I shall be an angel of peace, a preacher of truth in my own place, while not intending it, if I do but keep His commandments and serve Him in my calling.

Therefore I will trust Him. Whatever, wherever I am, I can never be thrown away. If I am in sickness, my sickness may serve Him; in perplexity, my perplexity may serve Him; if I am in sorrow, my sorrow may serve Him. My sickness, or perplexity, or sorrow may be necessary causes of some great end, which is quite beyond us. He does nothing in vain; He may prolong my life, He may shorten it; He knows what He is about. He may take away my friends, He may throw me among strangers, He may make me feel desolate, make my spirits sink, hide the future from me—still He knows what He is about. . . .

I trust Thee wholly. Thou are wiser than I—more loving to me than I myself. Deign to fulfil thy high purposes in me whatever they be—work in and through me. I am born to serve Thee, to be Thine, to be Thy instrument. Let me be Thy blind instrument, I ask not to see—I ask not to know—I ask simply to be used.

"GOD'S INTERPRETER"

THE REV. J. P. DE CAUSSADE, S.J.

IF WE lived an uninterrupted life of faith we should be in continual communion with God, we should speak with Him face to face. Just as the air transmits our words and thoughts, so would all that we are called to do and suffer transmit to us the words and thoughts of God; all that came to us would be but the embodiment of His word; it would be exteriorly manifested in all things; we should find everything holy and profitable. The glory of God makes this the state of the blessed in heaven, and faith would make it ours on earth; there would be only the difference of means.

Faith is God's interpreter; without its enlightenment we understand nothing of the language of created things. It is a writing in cipher, in which we see naught but confusion; it is a burning bush, from the midst of which we little expect to hear God's voice. But faith reveals to us as to Moses the fire of divine charity burning in the midst of the bush; it gives the key to the ciphers, and discovers to us in the midst of the confusion the wonders of the divine wisdom. Faith gives to the whole earth a heavenly aspect; faith transports, enraptures the heart, and raises it above the things of this earth to converse with the blessed.

Faith is the light of time; it alone grasps the truth without seeing it; it touches what it does not feel; it sees this world as though it existed not, beholding quite other things than those which are visible. It is the key of the treasure-house, the key of the abyss, the key of the science of God. It is faith which shows the falseness of all creatures; through it God reveals and manifests Himself in all things; by it all things are made divine; it lifts the veil from created things and reveals the eternal truth. . . .

Oh, the ineffable peace that is ours when faith has taught us thus to see God through all creatures as through a transparent veil! Then darkness becomes light, and bitter turns to sweet. Faith, manifesting all things in their true light, changes their deformity into beauty, and their malice into virtue. Faith is the mother of meekness, confidence, and joy; she can feel naught but tenderness and compassion for her enemies who so abundantly enrich her at their own expense. The more malignant the action of the creature, the more profitable does God render it to the soul. While the human instrument seeks to injure us, the divine Artisan in whose hand it lies makes use of its very malice to remove what is prejudicial to the soul.

The will of God has only consolations, graces, treasures, for submissive souls; our confidence in it cannot be too great, nor our abandonment thereto be too absolute. It always wills and effects that which contributes most to our sanctification, provided meanwhile we yield ourselves to its divine action. Faith never doubts it; the more unbelieving, rebellious, despondent, and wavering the senses, the louder Faith cries, "This is God! All is well!"

There is nothing Faith does not penetrate and overcome; it passes beyond all shadows and through the darkest clouds to reach Truth; clasps it in a firm embrace, and is never parted from it.

SOMETHING greater than divine philosophy must link the heights and depths for man. It is faith. Faith lowers the heavens to earth. "By becoming Man," said St. Bernard, "God stooped down to man's imagination." But it also elevates earth to heaven. The little child who has faith has a vision illimitable. Material barriers fall away. Earth is lost in a divine perspective. The spirit world, God, the vast empire of humanity's long past, the ascending and descending ladder of Angelic choirs—those are things that stand out in bold relief in faith's vision.

FATHER JAMES, O.F.M. CAP.

THE VITALITY OF FAITH

THE REV. JEAN BAPTISTE LACORDAIRE

I AM tempted to ask you if you are quite sure that divine faith is indeed more difficult than natural faith. You live in an age in which religious faith has undergone, amongst the peoples, an incontestable decadence; you are persuaded that this state of moral misery is the normal state of the human race. It is an error which history does not justify. . . . Humanity has never ceased to present its vows and its fears at the foot of the altars; it has not ceased to uplift to God hands which appealed to Him, hands which have obtained His favors, and which are the cause that, in the book most illustrious and the holiest in the world, God has taken the title of the "Desired of the Nations." The wits have immolated this world-wide faith of their ancestors and of their children to a parricidal raillery; they have lifted against it every arm, that of science and that of contempt, that of lying and that of eloquence; they have had six thousand years against it; the faith of the people has been the stronger; it lives, it is born anew, it speaks to you, it commands you, and your presence here [in Notre Dame Cathedral, Paris] is a submission to the orders which you have received from it. Which of you will die tranquilly if faith has not pardoned him? Which of you will advance without fear towards eternity if faith has not anointed his feet for the passage? Which of you has aught against it save his vices?

Ask not then why religious faith is difficult, but why, at certain epochs, amongst certain peoples, it has undergone diminution? For humanity believes in God as easily as it believes in the existence of matter; it prays to God quite as naturally as it lives. And as to you who are not humanity, and who really find it difficult to believe, consider that we believe willingly what we love, and rarely what we love not. To the question of divine faith is united the question of divine virtue.

THE enlightened soul is a man who, seeing the sunlight hidden by thick mists, does not disquiet himself, because he knows that the mists will pass away, and that the sun, which is always there, will show itself again. Such a soul stands in naked faith: she knows that God will not withdraw Himself so long as she raises no obstacle to His entrance, and she sees that she is ready for that entrance of God so long as she rests in her own nothingness. When she does not perceive His presence she knows that it is only a temporary incapability on her part, and that it will pass away, and that God will manifest Himself again.

FATHER JOHN-EVANGELIST OF
BALDUKE

THE FAITH OF THE HUMBLE

BLAISE PASCAL

THOSE who believe without having read the Testaments, do so because they have an inward disposition entirely holy, and all that they hear of our religion conforms to it. They feel that a God has made them; they desire only to love God; they desire to hate themselves only. They feel that they have no strength in themselves; that they are incapable of coming to God; and that if God does not come to them, they can have no communion with Him. And they hear our religion say that men must love God only, and hate self only; but that all being corrupt and unworthy of God, God made Himself man to unite Himself to us. No more is required to persuade men who have this disposition in their heart, and who have this knowledge of their duty and of their inefficiency.

Those whom we see to be Christians without the knowledge of the prophets and evidences, nevertheless judge of their religion as well as those who have that knowledge. They judge of it by the heart, as others judge of it by the intellect. God Himself inclines them to believe, and thus they are most effectively convinced.

I confess indeed that one of those Christians who believe without proofs will not perhaps be capable of convincing an infidel who will say the same of himself. But those who know the proofs of religion will prove without difficulty that such a believer is truly inspired by God, though he cannot prove it himself.

For God having said in His prophesies (which are undoubtedly prophesies), that in the reign of Jesus Christ He would spread His spirit abroad among nations, and that the youths and maidens and children of the Church would prophesy; it is certain that the Spirit of God is in these, and not in the others.

Instead of complaining that God had hidden Himself, you will give Him thanks for having revealed so much of Himself; and you will also give Him thanks for not having revealed Himself to haughty sages, unworthy to know so holy a God.

Two kinds of persons know Him; those who have a humble heart, and who love lowliness, whatever kind of intellect they may have, high or low, and those who have sufficient understanding to see the truth, whatever opposition they may have to it.

THE light of faith confers upon us undreamed-of enhancement of our vision, an extension of our understanding, an enrichment of our natural powers beyond the power of words to convey; but it is only to be bought at a price, the price of our submission and surrender, the giving up of what we ourselves are or claim to be. Not: "I thank God I am not as other men," but instead: "Behold the handmaid of the Lord."

ROSALIND MURRAY

FAITH AND FRIENDSHIP

THE REV. B. W. MATURIN

A FRIENDSHIP that depends upon constant explanation of everything that is not clearly understood, is not a friendship that can stand the test of trial. Friendship must be based upon such personal knowledge, growing out of mutual affection, that doubt becomes impossible. . . . The Catholic Church has as its end the bringing of the soul into such estimable friendship with God. It may desire as much as anyone else to see deeper into the mysteries of life, it may be as keen as possible in its research, using every power at its command to probe further, but the devout Christian is able to possess his soul in unruffled calm, assured that all he may ever know or not know can never disturb his confidence in God.

WHO would hesitate to ask of God what He most delights in giving? It is not enough to abstain from all distrust in our Heavenly Father; we must have positive, absolute, most childlike confidence in Him. The act of hope, a thing strictly obligatory on all Christians, is not, as many erroneously think, a mere conjecture based upon motives more or less probable; it is a most sure expectation, a *certainty*.

God has promised heaven to men of goodwill: we should wrong Him were we to doubt either the sincerity of His promise, the faithfulness of His will to keep it, or His power to carry it out.

DÉSIRÉ JOSEPH CARDINAL MERCIER

FAITH IN THE PROVIDENCE
OF GOD

THE REV. WILLIAM LAWSON, S.J.

IT IS a crime to obscure, by worrying, the truth of the Providence of God. Faith tells us all that we need to know for our comfort. We know the power and wisdom and love of God: we know that they are used by God in His personal care of us. There is only one response which is right—to let the certainty of God's loving care outweigh the uncertainties that afflict the human spirit. That is the teaching of Our Lord in the Sermon on the Mount (which so many mention and so few read). He says that His followers must remember always that the power and love of God are with them, looking after them, providing for them, and making their life a peaceful progress (however hard it may be) to eternal goodness and happiness. . . .

It is the teaching of all Christianity, this doctrine of the spiritual serenity of mind and heart which come from faith and hope that are alive. Live your life with courage and power, take care of yourself and your loved ones with all the strength that God has given to you: and when you reach your inevitable limit and can do no more, leave the rest cheerfully and confidently to the Providence of God. That is what the Providence of God is for.

FAITH is like the little night-light that burns in a sick-room; as long as it is there, the obscurity is not complete; we turn towards it and await the daylight.

ABBÉ HUVELIN

FAITH DESTROYS FEAR

THE REV. VINCENT MC NABB, O.P.

Master, doth it not concern Thee that we perish?

Mark, iv;38

THIS is a wonderful scene. I suppose it is night. Night in those regions follows evening as an echo follows sound. When evening comes, already it is night. What is more terrifying than a storm at night? Here is a storm that terrified even these masters of the sea. It is an incident, of course, and a symbol in the little passage of our own craft to the other side of life and death. Storms come suddenly upon us; we never know when our little craft is in danger of sinking. . . . We are never safe, none of us. . . . There is no profession in life that makes life safe. Some sudden storm comes down upon us when perhaps we have been lulled into security by the quiet of the sea.

You and I, of course, are in the boat there, terrified—and the Master is just there—when we say to Him: "Master, doth it not concern Thee that we perish?" Imagine saying that to the Crucified! Yet I don't know

171

anything that is more commonly said against God than that He is cruel. . . .

This is the occasion of His question, "Why are you fearful?" And then, by His further question, He suggests the answer: "Have you not faith yet? Your fear has outrun your faith." Fear is no substitute for Faith. Had they been faithful, there would not have been this fear. Here, in the darkness of the night and in the pitch of this great gale, He speaks of faith and fears. What a very searching question that is for us. If we begin to search the Jerusalem of our fears with lamps, to find out what is the cause of our fears, we may find they are rooted in our lack of faith. Is it true Faith?—firm Faith? something, of course, we would die for (though we don't at all want to die!), something we might well live for. Faith is the one thing worth living for. If a thing is not worth dying for, it is not worth living for.

Our glorious Faith gives us the things that are worth living for. "I believe in God the Father Almighty; and in Jesus Christ, His Son. I believe in the Holy Ghost." Those provide us with the great motives and ends of all human life. When we have Faith, a number of fears begin to be removed. We still fear Death, and physical pain. But when the soul is grounded in Faith, the manner of our fear changes. We are now afraid of the fear; afraid of being afraid. Perfect souls—who realize that Jesus is greatly concerned about their perishing; so greatly concerned that He died for them—are very much afraid of suffering, of the Cross. But they are afraid of being afraid; afraid of getting down from the Cross. They are afraid of yielding; of being conquered under temptation; afraid they may be afraid of the dark, and, under the stress of the storm, they may yield or cry out. That is the greatness of their fear. . . .

Many souls are now fearing because they have never really dealt with the matter of their fears by Faith. They have never brought Faith to bear on their fear and weighed it calmly in the balance of Faith and their relation to Jesus Christ and His shed Blood. If we did that, could we ever turn around to Jesus Christ and say: "Is it no concern to You if we perish?" The Crucifix, if accepted, is the answer; if not accepted, there is no answer. To any evil of suffering there is only one final answer: the Crucifix. Deny that and you have denied all answers. There may be evasions and distractions, but no answer. Is not the modern world seeking, in its despair, distractions from inevitable evil? Most of its pleasures are distractions from inevitable death. Yet when death is accepted, life seems quite happy, full of joy and peace. Instead of overclouding life, the acceptance of death takes all the clouds out; it renders the clouds serene. There are still some fears, but not the great master-fear of death, that seeks to be distracted. If Faith and the Cross do not give the answer, then answer there is none.

NOTHING in this world is so marvelous as the transformation that a soul undergoes when the light of faith descends upon the light of reason. It is like the sunlight coming upon the moonlight and dissipating a thousand shadows and delusions.

THE MOST REV. W. BERNA D
ULLATHORNE

WHEN FAITH IS ASLEEP

ST. AUGUSTINE

THE ship was in danger on the lake, and Jesus slept. We are, as it were, sailing on a lake; neither winds nor tempests are wanting; our ship is nearly filled by the daily temptations of this world. How does this come about, unless it is because Jesus sleeps? If Jesus were not sleeping in you, you would not have these storms to suffer, but you would have inward peace in the companionship of Jesus. What does this mean—*Jesus is asleep?* Your faith, which comes from Jesus, has fallen asleep. Storms arise on the lake; you see the wicked flourishing, the good being tried; this is a temptation; it is an angry wave. You say to yourself, "O God, is this Thy justice, that the unjust are prosperous and the righteous in sorrow?" You say to God, "Is this Thy justice?" And God answers, "Is this your faith? Did I promise you these things? Were you made a Christian that you might be prosperous in this world?" . . . Why are you disquieted by the storms and tempests of the lake? Because Jesus is asleep, that is, your faith, which comes from Him, is slumbering in your breast. . . . Turn, then, your back to that which perishes and your face to that which perishes not. The tempest will not frighten you if Christ is watching, nor will the wave fill your ship, because your faith has power over the winds and the waves, and the danger will pass away.

FAITH IN GOD'S LOVE

THE REV. VINCENT MC NABB, O.P.

ONE of the paradoxes is that we seem to preen ourselves on being so much superior to other centuries in intellectual culture. Yet never was there such a century when men were thinking so much of what they should eat and put on. No wonder things are getting worse. All they can do is to take up or fashion some terrible weapon and go out for blood.

So often human life seems in rags because something is denied it. I will give up all that has ever been written for this passage: "Fear not, little flock." God says to me: "Don't be afraid, Father Vincent." I'd tear up all the works of St. Thomas for that! I'd put them all on the fire!

"You're frightened. Don't be frightened. Poor little soul, you're frightened." I wonder how many of you remember, as I remember, waking up from the sleep of sickness in childish terror, to find a mother's arms round me. "Don't be frightened, my child. What are you frightened of? Dear child, don't be frightened. It's your Mother."

Poor souls now are frightened they will not have enough wheat, or aeroplanes, or young blood to shed on the battlefields. Well, we mustn't be frightened. . . .

Whatever, then, is the cause of our solicitude tonight, we must not yield to it. We must yield to Our Lord. No one loves us as He does, nor so unselfishly. No one has bought us at such great price. We are of great value to Him even if of little value to ourselves. Who of us could value ourselves highly? To Him, even Heaven seemed well lost for love of us; and with desire He desired to prove His Love by death.

So let us be lulled and at peace with the sweetness of these exquisite words of Divine Love.

FAITH is not a thing which one "loses," we merely cease to shape our lives by it.

GEORGES BERNANOS

TO DOUBT IS DIFFICULT

JOHN HENRY CARDINAL NEWMAN

TRUST me, rather than the world, when I tell you, that it is no difficult thing for a Catholic to believe; and that unless he grievously mismanages himself, the difficult thing is for him to doubt. He has received a gift which makes faith easy: it is not without an effort, a miserable effort, that any one who has received that gift, unlearns to believe. He does violence to his mind, not in exercising, but in withholding his faith. When objections occur to him, which they may easily do if he lives in the world, they are as odious and unwelcome to him as impure thoughts are to the virtuous. He does certainly shrink from them, he flings them away from him but why? not in the first instance, because they are dangerous, but because they are cruel and base. His loving Lord has done everything for him, and has He deserved such a return? . . . He has poured on us His grace, He has been with us in our perplexities, He has led us on from one truth to another, He has forgiven us our sins, He has satisfied our reason, He has made faith easy, He has given us His Saints, He shows before us day by day His own Passion; why should I leave Him? What has He ever done to me but good? Why must I re-examine what I have examined once for all? Why must I listen to every idle word which flits past me against Him, on pain of being called a bigot and a slave, when, if I did, I should be behaving to the Most High, as you yourselves, who so call me, would not behave towards a human friend or benefactor? If I am convinced in my reason, and persuaded in my heart, why may I not be allowed to remain unmolested in my worship?

WE SHALL see Him face to face, if we now see Him by faith. Let our faith have eyes, and its truth shall be displayed. Let us believe in Him whom we see not, and rejoicing we shall see, and we shall enjoy Him seen. . . . Prepare your hearts for this vison, prepare your souls for this joy; just as if God willed to shew the sun, He would warn us to make ready the eyes of the flesh. But because He deigneth to show you the aspect of His Wisdom, prepare the eyes of the heart. "Blessed are the clean of heart; for they shall see God."

ST. AUGUSTINE

"HOPE IS THE GREATEST NEED"

THE REV. BEDE JARRETT, O.P.

FAITH is the basis of life, and charity is the crown; but hope is the greatest need. Most of the difficulties of life come because man is so prone to lose heart. . . . The whole of life tends to depress a man who is at all conscious of his capacities, responsibilities, and his failures. He is, then, a great sinner? Not at all. He has lost his faith and love? Most certainly not. What, then, is wanting to him? Hope. He has given up hope; he is disheartened; he is too discouraged to go on. He is very human; oh yes, but he is very foolish also; for when hope is gone, all is over. Failure counts for nothing, defeat, disappointment,—these matter nothing at all, so long as only hope sits patiently, stirring the embers, watching and tending the fire, coaxing the flame, never despairing and never leaving the wind to work its will. That the clouds should come up over the sky, or that darkness should encircle the earth, bring no real terrors, for we are sure that the dawn will come out again and that the sun will break through with its golden glory. . . .

God does not ask from me perfect prayers or perfect sacraments. He does not ask me even to overcome my temper or my want of charity or my untruthfulness. He does not ask these things for He knows He could not get them from me. What, then, does He ask? That I should try to overcome them: only that and nothing more—that I should try day after day, despite failure, repeated and certain, to overcome these obstacles to my union with Him. For goodness consists not in the love of God, but in the attempts to love Him. If, then, I fail, let me not be discouraged, but, realizing my own weakness and confident only in God's strength, let me go on striving my best, for my business in life is really little else than to continue to fail without losing courage or lessening effort. The phrase of St. Catherine should ring always in my ear: "God doth not ask a perfect work, but infinite desire."

HOPE IS DEMANDED OF US

RT. REV. MSGR. RONALD KNOX

THE Christian virtue of hope has nothing whatever to do with the world's future. As it was preached by the first apostles, it meant nothing more or less than a confidence on the part of the Christian that he or she would attain happiness in a future life. The world about them was perishable, and doomed to perish—perhaps in a very short time. The agonies of its dissolution might have terrors for the wicked and the worldlings, none for the believer. The prospect was a warning to us, of course, to live in a way worthy of our vocation, but apart from that, whether the world lasted ten days more or a thousand years was no concern of ours. . . .

Hope is something that is demanded of us; it is not, then, a mere reasoned calculation of our chances. Nor is it merely the bubbling up of a sanguine temperament; if it is demanded of us, it lies not in the temperament but in the will. Indeed, we can hardly doubt that the

Christian is at his best when he is, as we say, "hoping against hope." Hoping for what? For deliverance from persecution, for immunity from plague, pestilence, and famine, from worldly discomforts in general? No, for the grace of persevering in his Christian profession, and for the consequent achievement of a happy immortality. Strictly speaking, then, the highest exercise of hope, supernaturally speaking, is to hope for perseverance and for Heaven when it looks, when it feels, as if you were going to lose both one and the other.

FAITH is not vision, if by vision we mean comprehension and intuition; it is rather the beginning of a new life, the discovery within and without of a new order, of a new and final definition.

THE REV. M. C. D'ARCY, S.J.

VIII

And taking bread, he gave thanks and brake and gave to them, saying: This is my body, which is given for you. Do this for a commemoration of me.

St. Luke 22:19

THE DIVINE DRAMA

THE REV. PAUL BUSSARD

IT WAS the Mass which brought those early Christians together, which quickened the divine life within them and filled them with such courageous enthusiasm that the entire world marvelled at the ease with which they went to martyrdom. It was the Mass which brought them together in the Lord and made them recognize in their neighbor a brother in Christ, so that the whole world marvelled at them, saying, "See how these Christians love one another." The Mass should do the same for us today. Christ is the selfsame today, yesterday and forever. He acts in the Mass today just as He did long ago. Perhaps the reason we do not benefit as much as the early Christians is because we do not approach this great mystery with the same kind of dispositions and understanding. It must become for us the primary source of the true Christian spirit as it was for them. . . .

We know that the Mass is a sacrifice. We know that it is the same sacrifice as that of the cross. We know a great deal about the sacrificial death of our Lord upon the cross. But the entire life of our Lord upon earth was sacrificial. We can say that His life was lived in the shadow of the cross and that the cross was of course the supreme moment of that perfectly lived life of sacrifice. But what was it that our Lord was giving in His life and in His death? The words of St. Paul, repeated in the liturgy of Holy Week, tell us: "Christ became obedient for us unto death, even the death of the cross." And what did He receive? St. Paul continues: "Wherefore God also hath exalted Him, and hath given Him a name which is above every name: that in the name of Jesus every knee should bend."

This rendering of obedience was what Adam, the head of the human race, refused to give and thereby deprived the race of supernatural life. The giving of obedience accomplished by Christ, the second Head of the human race, is what gave back supernatural life to the human race.

But we must not think of our Lord's life and death only in terms of obedience. His oblation of self to God the Father was complete and perfect. He gave all that He was and all that He had, without reservation. . . . Now these actions of our Lord which constituted His Sacrifice are continued in the Mass. The Mass is a true and real Sacrifice. It is identical with the Sacrifice of the Cross. Of course our Lord does not suffer any more. But the *giving,* the rendering of homage to God the Father, the Sacrifice, is exactly the same nevertheless. The Mass is above space and time. It spans the centuries. In it Christ lives and acts just as really and truly as He did in Bethlehem, in Nazareth, in Jerusalem. His Sacrifice is continued.

And the point for us never to forget is that we have a share in it. We "do this" which our Lord does. Christ and His brethren (us) act together. We do not just go to Mass. We take part in the Mass. We are not merely present but we have something to do. . . .

We must, like Him, give all that we are and all that we have to God the Father—our life, our faith, our love, our obedience, our respect, honor, gratitude, and sorrow for sin. These actions of ours then become part of the Mass. They are merged with the Sacrifice of Christ and together made acceptable to God the Father. This is a tremendous truth.

That is our *giving*. And what do we *receive?* God gives us His own divine Son under the form of bread and wine to be nourishment to our souls, to become within us that supernatural life which Christ gained for us on the cross. The giving goes from earth to Heaven, the reception is from Heaven to earth. The Action of Thanksgiving, the Sacrifice of the Mass, is not done by Christ alone, nor by us alone, but by us and Christ together. And to play our part in this divine drama well involves all our energy, all our life. . . .

The Mass . . . is the fulfillment of the desires within us which we cannot explain or express ourselves. It is the bridge between Heaven and earth. In it Christ, the Son of God, the Redeemer, gathers us, the members of His Mystical Body, together, unites us with our feeble good deeds, our imperfect homage, our defective faith, our slipshod obedience and makes of us a not unacceptable gift to God the Father, and then rewards our gift (so imperfect in itself) with a profuse giving of divine life throughout all those persons who constitute the Church, His Mystical Body.

WHAT one of the faithful can have any doubt that at the very hour of the Offering [Mass], at the word of the priest, the Heavens are opened, the choirs of angels are present at the Mystery of Jesus Christ, the lowest things are united to the highest, earthly things with the heavenly, and of the invisible and the visible there is made one?

POPE ST. GREGORY THE GREAT

FROM CALVARY TO THE
END OF TIME

JOHN HENRY CARDINAL NEWMAN

OUR Lord not only offered Himself as a Sacrifice on the Cross, but He makes Himself a perpetual, a daily sacrifice, to the end of Time. In the Holy Mass that one Sacrifice on the Cross once offered is renewed, continued, applied to our benefit. He seems to say, My Cross was raised up 1800 years ago, and only for a few hours—and very few of My servants were present there—but I intend to bring millions into My Church. For their sakes then I will perpetuate My Sacrifice, that each of them may be as though they had severally been present on Calvary. I will offer Myself up day by day to the Father, that every one of My followers may have the opportunity to offer his petitions to Him, sanctified and recommended by the all-meritorious virtue of My Passion. Thus I will be a Priest for ever, after the order of Melchisedech—my priests shall stand at the Altar—but not they, but I rather, will offer. I will not let them offer mere bread and wine, but I Myself will be present upon the Altar instead, and I will offer up Myself invisibly, while they perform the outward rite. And thus the Lamb that was slain once for all, though He is ascended on high, ever remains a victim from His miraculous presence in Holy Mass under the figure and appearance of mere earthly and visible symbols.

A SPIRITUAL OASIS

ANONYMOUS

BEHOLD! in the midst of this desert of sinfulness and helplessness there rises before our eyes *an altar*. A priest ascends the steps; a supernatural, indelible mark is impressed upon his soul. He places upon the altar a chalice and a host. From his lips proceed a few omnipotent words which he pronounces over this chalice and this host—and O wonder! the Body and Blood of the Son of God are present upon the altar. Earth awakens, its exiled children arise; they draw nearer and nearer; they gather about the altar, and from millions and millions of hearts ascend humble and grateful prayers. Songs of praise resound; fervent petitions are heard; and from on high, from heaven's heights, resound melodies that betoken love and forgiveness, blessings and joy. Heavenly spirits proclaim glory to God and peace to men.

What has happened? Why this jubilation, this hope? *Mankind has offered upon the altar the pure, unspotted Lamb to the Eternal Father.* By this Sacrifice mankind worthily acknowledges God's sovereign rights, thanks Him for His gifts, renders atonement for its misdeeds and petitions His help. The Eternal Father accepts the sacrifice of His Son, the homage of mankind: *It is Holy Mass*—the rescuing oasis where, as on another Calvary, God and man meet and offer friendship's hand. . . .

Holy Mass possesses an *infinite value.* The Heavenly Father looked with infinite complacency upon His Divine Son when He accomplished the Sacrifice of the Cross. With the same complacency His eye rests upon every altar whereon the holy Sacrifice of the Mass is offered. From each altar a stream of graces flows out over the whole Church of Christ. Ceaselessly we can draw from this stream of grace in Holy Mass for our life on earth and for our glory in eternity. *How great is the loss that one suffers who passes through life without drawing from this ocean of graces, to which he may so easily have access, the blessings which needs to make him truly happy!* Jesus on our altars offers us His help and His consolations, His blessing and His peace, His goodness and His joy, His suffering and His death, with all their merit. He yearns to come to our assistance in our needs, and *whose need is not great?*

IN HOLY Mass we receive treasures so wonderful and so real, gifts so divine and so costly, benefits so many appertaining to this temporal life, hope so certain for the life which is to come, that without faith it would be impossible for us to believe these assertions to be the truth.

THOMAS B. SANCHEZ, S.J.

LIVING THE MASS

DOM HUBERT VAN ZELLER, O.S.B.

SURELY the reason why the Mass doesn't always have the effect which it should and could have is because it is looked at only and not lived. "Learn of me," says our Lord from the altar, and all we do is to sit there and watch. For as long as the Mass remains for us a duty to be got through, a half-hour in church, an appointment which on pain of mortal sin we cannot afford to miss, we shall never fully benefit from it, or indeed quite realise what it is about. The Mass is not the priest's private prayer which the faithful have to attend once a week so as to maintain their Catholic status. Of course we know well enough that it is not this, we know that it is the Crucifixion over again, that it is the prayer of Christ in which we are privileged to take part, that its merit is infinite, and that it is the most perfect prayer-expression that can be offered. We know all this, but unless the knowledge is effective there is not much point in our possessing it. If the Mass is not a principle of action, a force in the regulation of life, a clue to the meaning of what Christ came on earth to teach, its significance is very

187

largely missed. . . . If the Catholic, then, is to question himself upon his hearing of Mass, the enquiry should be conducted on the lines of "Am I in tune with the Victim of this sacrifice?" rather than "Ought I to use a missal or can I go on saying the rosary?" If Catholics were to live the Mass for that short half-hour, entering into the mind of the Church and the priest and the Subject of the sacrifice, the effects of it would continue throughout the day, and not limit themselves to the time of Mass itself. (I am speaking here of the effects as influencing human thought and conduct, and not from the point of view of what effects a well heard Mass may have in heaven.) Inevitably, surely, that having entered into the mind of Christ at such a time as this, the Catholic comes away more ready himself to offer, to give, to suffer. Having seen whom Christ is praying for, he sees his own place in the fellowship of Christ's Mystical Body.

To ME nothing is so consoling, so piercing, so thrilling, so overcoming, as the Mass said as it is amongst us. I could attend Masses for ever and not be tired. It is not a mere form of words,—it is a great action, the greatest action that can be on earth. It is, not the invocation merely, but, if I may dare use the word, the evocation of the Eternal.

JOHN HENRY CARDINAL NEWMAN

THE INDIVIDUAL'S RELATION-
SHIP TO THE MASS

ANONYMOUS

"MY SACRIFICE and yours," says the priest. Yes, each one of us can truly say, "Holy Mass is *my* Sacrifice." "When you hear Mass," the learned Sanchez says, "remember that this Sacrifice is *your possession,* which is donated to you by God the Father and the Son." If we could realize this, Holy Mass would soon be considered by us the most holy, the most sublime and God-pleasing act of Divine worship.

To the devout Catholic, Holy Mass is not merely a form of prayer,—*it is an act of worship and a sacrifice;* for all who devoutly assist at Holy Mass offer the Divine oblation together with the priest. First of all, there is the great High Priest, the chief sacrificer, Jesus Christ, who Himself offers every Holy Mass to His Heavenly Father. Then there is the officiating priest, who immolates the Divine Victim. Thirdly, there are the faithful present at the Holy Sacrifice, who also have the power of offering it.

One of the greatest graces granted to the children of the Church is that the privilege of offering to the Divine Majesty the sacred and sublime Sacrifice of the Mass is not the prerogative of priests alone, but belongs to the laity as well, to men, women and children. Saint Peter lays stress on this prerogative when he says: "You, however, are a chosen race, a royal priesthood, a holy nation, a purchased people" (I Peter, ii, 9). . . .

Let each of us ever bear in mind: *Holy Mass is my*

Sacrifice; it is *my* work; it is *my* possession. I unite myself with the priest, yes, with Jesus Christ Himself.

PRAYING THE MASS

ST. FRANCIS DE SALES

HITHERTO I have said nothing of the most holy, sacred,
and august sacrament and sacrifice of the Mass; the
centre of the Christian religion, the heart of devotion,
and the soul of piety; a mystery so ineffable as to com-
prise within itself the abyss of divine charity; a mystery
in which God communicates himself really to us, and in
a special manner replenishes our souls with spiritual
graces and favors.

When prayer is united to this divine sacrifice, it becomes so unspeakably efficacious as to cause the soul to
overflow, as it were, with heavenly consolations. Here
she reclines upon her well-beloved, who fills her with
so much spiritual sweetness, that she resembles, as it
is said in the canticles, a pillar of smoke, proceeding from
a fire of aromatic wood, from myrrh and frankincense,
and from all the powders of the perfumer.

Endeavor, therefore, to assist at Mass every day, that
you may jointly, with the priest, offer up the holy sacrifice of your Redeemer to God his Father, for yourself
and the whole Church. "The angels," says St. John
Chrysostom, "always attend in great numbers to honor
this adorable mystery," and we, by associating ourselves
to them, with one and the same intention, cannot but
receive many favorable influences from so holy a society.
The choirs of the Church triumphant and those of the

Church militant unite themselves to our Lord in this divine action, that with him, in him, and through him, they may ravish the heart of God the Father, and make his mercy all our own. Oh, what a happiness it is to a soul devoutly to contribute her affections for obtaining so precious and desirable a treasure!

Should some indispensable business prevent you from assisting in person at the celebration of this sovereign sacrifice, endeavor at least to assist at it by a spiritual presence, uniting your intention with that of all the faithful; and using the same interior acts of devotion in your closet that you would use in some church represented to your imagination.

Now, to hear Mass in a proper manner, either really or mentally, 1. From the beginning till the priest goes up to the altar, make with him your preparation, which consists in placing yourself in the presence of God, acknowledging your unworthiness and begging pardon for your sins. 2. From the time he goes up to the altar till the Gospel, consider the birth and life of our Lord, by a simple and general consideration. 3. From the Gospel till after the Creed, consider the preaching of our Saviour, and protest that you resolve to live and die in the faith and obedience of his holy word, and in the communion of the holy Catholic Church. 4. From the Creed to the *Pater Noster* apply your heart to the mysteries of the passion and death of our Redeemer, essentially represented in this holy sacrifice, and which, with the priest and the rest of the people, you must offer to the honor of God the Father, and for your salvation. 5. From the *Pater Noster* to the Communion, strive to excite a thousand desires in your heart, ardently wishing to be forever united to our Saviour by everlasting love.

6. From the Communion till the end, return thanks to Jesus Christ for his incarnation, life, passion, and death: as well as for the love he testifies to us in his holy sacrifice; conjuring him to be forever merciful to you; to your parents and friends, and to the whole Church; and finally, humbling yourself with your whole heart, receive devoutly the benediction which our Lord gives you through the ministry of his officer, the officiating priest.

THERE is nothing so profitable to mankind, so efficacious for the relief of the suffering souls, nothing so helpful for the attainment of spiritual riches, as the most holy sacrifice of the Mass. In fact in comparison with it all the good works which we perform by day or night, from the most virtuous motives, are of little or no account.

ANTONIO DE MOLINA, O. CART.

ATTENDING MASS IN SPIRIT

ANONYMOUS

THOSE who are prevented from being actually present at the celebration of the Mass may yet draw glorious fruits from this great ocean of grace. For we may assist in spirit at the adorable Sacrifice, just as we may receive Holy Communion spiritually with great profit to our souls. In fact, we may be physically a long distance from the churches where Mass is being offered, and yet be spiritually nearer than one who assists in a careless, distracted manner. And just as we may now offer to God, with greater benefit to our souls, so we may likewise offer up the many Holy Masses which are being continually celebrated day and night, and thereby become partakers in the innumerable graces of the Holy Sacrifice.

It is a glorious, but alas! a sadly unheeded truth, that no moment of the day or night passes but that the Lamb without stain is offered on many altars. In all these oblations of infinite value, we may participate—by having the heartfelt desire to do so. Our good desires are before God as if we really carried them out, and the more fervently we unite in spirit with all the Holy Masses being offered throughout the world, the greater will be the benefits we reap.

MASS IN A GERMAN PRISON

THE REV. HENRI PERRIN, S.J.

PALM SUNDAY (1944). Round 5 a.m. I said Mass. I did not want to do it in the evening, lest the warder should make a late round and find me. At about four-thirty, I woke Raymond who was sleeping on the table, and then Marcel and Remy, who had asked to take part. No one else had shown any wish to do so in the evening—they had come in late and tired, and were going off again at half-past seven in the morning. It was much better not to force them to attend a Mass unwillingly; anyhow, alas, they would not understand. From their beds, which were set up in a circle round the table, they could see the light, and follow me if they wanted to.

Everything was ready. Three handkerchiefs for a cloth; another one, which was quite new, served for a corporal, lying on top of the enamelled tin cup which was to contain the Precious Blood. A candle lit the German text from which I read a passage from Saint Paul, and one from St. Luke. And there were the bread, the water and the wine.

'In the name of the Father . . .' Marcel and Remy could only follow me with memories of long ago, and I recited the psalm alone, and was the only one to make the *public* confession at the beginning of Mass. At the final Kyrie Marcel remembered what he ought to answer. But when I held the sacrifice close between my fingers, I was holding up to God in complete faith the lives of all the men sleeping round me. In an absence of emotion I still find, without the least sentimentality, but simply looking to God in faith, I offered to our Father from the bottom of my heart all the suffering of the prison, and the gloom of all the poor wretches sleeping under its roof; I offered it through Christ, for the forgiveness of all the omissions and sins of men, for the salvation of the world. The others were all asleep, but the whole Church was beside me. At Gethsemane the Apostles slept, and these were my 'apostles'!

A Pole got up, like an animal forced by instinct, to go to the W.C. six feet away from me. He didn't realize that it was not a suitable thing to do. . . . Luckily our ideas of decency and indecency had little in common with God's. We might be scandalized by the incongruity of this man's behaviour, but we ourselves had often come to the sacrifice with our hearts full of bitterness, and that is incomparably worse. The flesh of our hearts is putrid and filthy, says St. Ignatius, and that is why we need the purifying and strengthening of the flesh of Christ. 'Body of Christ, save me . . .' I was alone in this 'communion,' but through the Body of Christ I was in communion with the whole Church and with all my brethren—in this room, in this prison, in all our growing Christian communities. . . . Mass was over. Raymond had not gone, but sat in his corner watching what I did. As he came past me, he just said: 'Your Mass is pretty terrific.' And that was all. In deep silence I watched the windows whitening with the dawn, the dawn of Palm Sunday.

THE Mass is not a mere prayer, although the sublimest of all prayers; not a mere instruction, although the divinest of instructions; the Mass is a divine action, in which the priest represents Christ, and in which Christ presents His immolation to God for man.

THE MOST REV. W. BERNARD
ULLATHORNE

THE FRUITS OF DAILY MASS

THE REV. ANTONIN SERTILLANGES, O.P.

WE HAVE recommended the *spirit of prayer:* where can it get more food than in these morning acts of contemplation in which the mind, rested, not yet caught up afresh in the cares of the day, borne and lifted up on the wings of prayer, rises with ease towards those founts of truth which study draws on laboriously?

If you can hear holy Mass, or say it, will its vastness and fulness not take possession of you? Will you not see, —from this other Calvary, from this Upper Room where the farewell Banquet is renewed,—the whole of humanity standing round you: that humanity with which you must not lose contact, that life lit up by the words of the Saviour, that poverty succoured by His riches which it is your task to succour along with Him, which you must enlighten and do your part to save while saving yourself?

The Mass really puts you into a state of eternity, into the spirit of the universal Church, and in the *Ite missa est* you are ready to see a *mission,* a sending out of your zeal to the destitution of the mad and ignorant earth.

The morning hours thus bedewed with prayer, freshened and vivified by the breezes of the spirit, cannot fail to be fruitful; you will begin them with faith; you will go through them with courage; the whole day will be spent in the radiance of the early light; evening will fall before the brightness is exhausted, as the year ends leaving some seed in the barns for the year to come.

IX

This is the bread which cometh down from heaven; that if any man eat of it, he may not die.

St. John 6:50

THE SACRAMENT OF LOVE

THE REV. I. T. HECKER

THE Catholic Church presents to men the Blessed Sacrament as the answer of the deep cry of the soul after love. She tells us, that in Holy Communion is received God entire—the body and blood, the soul and divinity of our Lord Jesus Christ. . . . There is another reason why God should give Himself to man. It is this: whatever is received as food, must in some way partake of the life it goes to support or sustain; otherwise, starvation and death follow. This is a loss of all attraction and life. Now, in the Christian soul, there is a divine life; a divine food, therefore, is necessary for its support, growth and perfection.

The Catholic Church tells us that we receive the divine food in Holy Communion. Jesus Christ confirms what she teaches. . . .

Thus the Catholic Saviour is not an abstract Saviour, nor a dead Saviour, separated from us by nineteen centuries, but a real, living, personal Saviour, dwelling in the midst of us, even in our very hearts—our heart's life! . . .

The real presence of Jesus Christ in the Holy Communion, connected as it is with the great sacrifice of the Mass, is the central mystery of the Catholic faith. It is the complete, full, and adequate expression of God's love to man. God cannot do more. God cannot love more. If it were not for this, to look for a fuller manifestation of God and His love to man might be admitted; but now to think or dream of such a thing is a mark of folly.

When we consider that God is really and truly present on the altars of the Catholic Church,—that He is the guest of the Catholic heart, its life and its nourishment,—is it to be wondered at that this Church has given birth to so many hero saints, and martyrs, and still continues to do so? Oh, life becomes great, noble, divine, under the influence, and in the participation of so great mysteries! Is it not, we ask, a sufficient evidence of the divinity of the Catholic faith, that it elevates the human heart to the belief, that it receives, in the Sacrament of Holy Communion, Almighty God? Is not this an audacity of faith and love, which none but God Himself can inspire, sustain and perpetuate in poor, weak and human hearts? . . . Is not this the completion of all man's wants, the end of man's supreme desire?

IN NO other action can the Saviour be considered more tender or more loving than in the institution of the Holy

Eucharist; in which He, as it were, annihilates Himself, and becomes food, in order to penetrate our souls, and to unite Himself to the heart of His faithful servants.

ST. FRANCIS DE SALES

THE NEW MANNA

THE REV. WALTER DWIGHT, S.J.

PICTURE the scene of the miracle God worked for Israel. In the midst of the Arabian desert is encamped a host of more than six hundred thousand souls. As the sun is setting groups of men and women, garbed in the flowing, picturesque dress of the Orient, are scattered here and there engaged in excited discussion. Fear is written on their faces and murmurs of discontent fall from their lips. A venerable old man, of majestic bearing, but with an air, too, of singular meekness, moves from group to group, trying to quiet the people. They will scarcely listen to him.

"Would to God," they bitterly exclaim, "we had died by the hand of the Lord in the land of Egypt! Why have you brought us into this desert to destroy us with famine?"

"It is God that has led you hither," we may fancy Moses as gently answering. "Trust Him still. He who has delivered you from bondage, led you dry-shod through the Red Sea, and who lately sweetened for your sakes the bitter springs of Mara, surely will not let you die of hunger now. Have confidence. 'In the morning you shall see the glory of God.' "

199

And see it they do. On awakening the following day the children of Israel are amazed to find the ground about the camp white with a strange substance that had fallen from heaven while they slept. It is like hoar-frost, small as if beaten with a pestle, and in taste resembles flour and honey. "What is this?" they ask one another in astonishment, as men, women and children eagerly gather up and store away as much as they can of the mysterious food. Labor as they will, only a small portion of it can be kept, for the rest corrupts. But there is no need of storing up the manna. Morning after morning throughout their forty years of travel in the desert, until they reached a habitable land, Almighty God fed and strengthened His people with this wonderful celestial bread.

"Your fathers did eat manna in the desert and are dead. I am the living Bread which came down from Heaven. If any man eat of this Bread, he shall live forever." These are the words our Blessed Lord said to the throngs who followed Him just after the first multiplication of loaves and begged Him to give them "always this bread." He contrasts, it will be noted, with the perishable manna on which their long-departed fathers had been fed, a new and living Manna which He would soon give the world, a Bread from Heaven indeed, conferring everlasting life on all who ate of it. Christ kept His promise. Before He died He gave us the Holy Eucharist, a wonderful Bread falling daily from Heaven to give life to the world. . . .

It is, perhaps, scarcely necessary to note how like in color, taste, and form, in the mystery of its origin, in the silent, secret mode of its descent as well as in the constancy of its bestowal, the Blessed Sacrament is to the ancient manna. The Holy Eucharist, too, comes from

Heaven early in the morning, it must be the first food of the day, it cannot be gathered without some labor and exertion, yet no one receives more than his neighbor. To continue the parallel, those who would worthily partake of this nobler Manna must first be delivered by Confession from the Egyptian bondage of mortal sin and by firmly purposing amendment put out of their hearts all longing for the onions and melons of the Nile. That this new Manna, like the old, is food, daily, nourishing, universal food, only infinitely nobler than the old, and that it is meant to feed the soul rather than the body, is almost too plain to need proof. It nourishes, refreshes, strengthens, satisfies and delights the soul. Like wholesome food, the Holy Eucharist repairs the losses that the soul suffers from concupiscence and from the assaults of Lucifer, it heals the wounds that sin has left, and by increasing sanctifying grace, confers new strength and vigor, making God's service joyful, sweet and easy. For in Holy Communion, let it not be forgotten, He becomes our Food who is the very source and centre of all grace and holiness. . . .

Unlike its ancient figure, however, the Holy Eucharist is "hidden manna." Jesus is ever hiding. He was hidden in the old law, He was hidden in the days of His flesh, and now, especially, is He hidden in the Sacrament of the Altar. . . .

Just as those who ate the ancient manna found in it the flavor of the food each relished most, the blessed Manna of the Eucharist will supply the soul with a relish for that particular virtue it needs most. . . .

If we are prudent men we will store up in our hearts against the hour of need all the grace we can; and since the richest source today of Divine grace is Holy Communion, and since we are all in daily need of the grace, we should feel in daily need of Holy Communion, especially since we know how easily it can be had. If we make of this Hidden Manna daily food, as it was certainly meant to be, we shall doubtless find that it will work in our souls results similar to those its ancient type once wrought in the chosen people.

HE IS NEARER TO US BECAUSE
HE IS HIDDEN

THE REV. R. H. J. STEUART, S.J.

IN THE matter of faith in the Blessed Sacrament the most learned theologian has no advantage over the humblest believer. Both know that He is there: the former has, no doubt, a more correct theological apprehension of His Presence, but it does not at all follow that therefore the response of his heart and will and affections to the fact is more complete; indeed, it may well be that it is less so, since the clearness and definition of a mental concept is by no means always the measure of its practical acceptance of a reality. For both it is enough to know that on the altar is Christ, not a picture, nor a statute, nor a relic, nor any other memorial of Him, but His own self, really there.

Well, we believe this, but we remain quite calm about it. We enter our churches, where He is, without a thrill; and we do not hold our breaths when the Tabernacle is opened. In that Presence we can think of other things, and it is often very difficult not to think of other things.

This violent contrast between our belief and our realization is most distressing to us. It awakens again that uneasy fear of unreality in our spiritual life which haunts us all from time to time. It makes us—no, not doubt, but —puzzle over the belief itself. For surely the Real Presence ought to engender in us a real sense of itself; we ought in Communion, for instance, to be aware of something like a shock, a vibration, a repercussion in our very bodies of that almost unthinkable contact—it is more, it is a mixing—of our created being with the uncreated Substance of God Himself? We react to the presence of our own fellow-creatures, and in progressive degree according to their importance to us; they stir us easily to reverence, or love, or fear, or the opposites. But though divine faith should be as compelling as sight, and it makes us here aware of a Presence immeasurably greater than the greatest that we can imagine among ourselves, we yet remain unimpressed.

Of course the fault is in ourselves: it is our weakness, the weakness of children to whom big words are simply troublesome sounds signifying nothing, and who can with difficulty understand what they cannot touch and handle: but then, could not He Who made the blind see and the deaf hear condescend to our childishness and contrive His sacramental presence in some way that would seize our senses and imagination more irresistibly?

Doubtless: but is it not probable that if He did so the Blessed Sacrament would be less instead of more to us: that we might worship, indeed, more reverentially, but on that very account with more formality? A Presence of greater splendor and power would attract, maybe, a readier homage, but at the cost, perhaps, of what is most precious in its intention, freedom and ease of access to it. We should prostrate ourselves in adoration before a Christ visibly enthroned upon the altar, but could we pay Him a three-minutes' visit, on one knee, and speak to Him, anyhow and as they tumble in and out of our minds, of our trifling business of hopes and fears?

One feels, indeed, that He has chosen to be among us in this humble and hidden way precisely because He does not *want* to be specially noticed or ceremoniously approached. For it is only when one is thoroughly at home with others that one can move about amongst them without comment; we stand upon ceremony with those who are strangers or otherwise unfamiliar to us. It is true that the Church surrounds the mysteries of the Eucharist with solemn and dignified rites, and wisely, for thus are they guarded from possible irreverence and desecration, and a uniform scheme of worship is besides established by which is emphasized the universality of His Presence wherever she reaches. These observances are necessary, but none the less they are a concession to our weakness, as is proved by the inevitable decline and collapse of the sacramental sense wherever the solemnities of ritual are despised or rejected.

But even so, what can be more simple and unobtrusive than a Low Mass, and yet, at the same time, like the silent Presence on the altars of our churches, what more dynamic, more pregnant with immensities? Once in a way —it is well, perhaps, that it is not often—the veil drops, and for a fleeting second one believes no more, one sees. It is not meant to last any more than Thabor was meant to last; not for us is it "good to be here" any more than it was for the three Apostles; we, as they were, would be numbed and dazzled if the vision endured: and as they, "lifting up their eyes" when the glory had departed "saw no one but only Jesus" in that shape in which alone He could be to them what He wanted to be, so we, whether on the corporal, in the monstrance, or behind the shut doors of the Tabernacle, can see Him truly, though but with the eyes of faith, in the only way in which, now, He can be to us what He intended when He devised His sacramental Presence. For He preserves His impenetrable disguise of bread, not only because thus we may ineffably feed upon Him while still remaining in the natural order of our being and habits, but also because He can, thus disguised, mix with us unregarded, and therefore the more intimately, as He could never in any living form.

To thrill or catch our breath in the presence of the Blessed Sacrament—though well might we do so—is, therefore, something like violating the careful incognito of a royal prince.

I might be stirred by the company of a saint or of a great hero: but Christ is out of all categories: His pre-eminence over all saints and heroes is not one of degrees, however superlative: even in His humanity He reflects the infinite simplicity of His Godhead: and the truest worship of Him, which is the truest acknowledgment of His Presence amongst us, is not by emotion but by faith. . . .

So, then, we are not distressed that this stupendous reality of Emmanuel, God with us, can be so little real to our earthly faculties and can find so trivial a response in our emotions. He would have it so, because so, in fact, He is nearer to us and we are nearer to His heart's desire. We take His Presence with a simplicity which is a radiation from that Presence itself.

ONE of the chief ends for which God instituted the Holy Eucharist, or perhaps even the very chief, was, to unite Himself to us, or to make us the same with Himself.

ST. ALPHONSUS RODRIGUEZ, S.J.

"GOD WITH US"

THE MOST REV. JOSEPH F. RUMMEL

THE Holy Eucharist is the focal mystery of our Catholic faith, the beacon light whose brilliant rays illumine with rare brightness every phase of Catholic worship, the fountain whence souls draw spiritual life, vigour, and energy, the realization of God's marvelous desire to be with the children of men, the consummation of man's highest ambition to commune with His Maker and to anticipate, in a measure, the enrapturing joy of the beatifying vision of the countenance of God in heaven. . . .

When the Prophet Isaias foretold the advent of the Messias, he said: "Behold a virgin shall conceive, and bear a son, and his name shall be called Emmanuel" (Is. VII, 14). St. Matthew the Evangelist gives us the meaning of this designation, saying: "Which being interpreted, is *God with us*" (Mt. I, 23).

"Emmanuel—God with us," is that mysterious something, which creates in our churches the atmosphere of awe, peace, and confidence that even those perceive at times who have little or no religious faith. To the believing soul it is often sufficient to bask in the sense of the nearness of Christ, knowing that of old, power emanated even from the hem of His garment, mindful that there was a blessing in store for Zacchaeus in the sycamore tree, and consoled in the thought that the publican at the threshold of the temple was not missed by the merciful eye of the Saviour.

"Emmanuel—God with us," draws to the sanctuary and tabernacle the little child that seeks health and healing for an ailing mother or some great grace for a troubled father. In that sacred presence kneel the stalwart youth and the graceful maiden, each to implore light, guidance, and strength in the momentous decision of life's calling, confident that He who dwells within the tabernacle walls hears and sees, understands, and never fails to help. The light that ever burns before the Eucharistic Presence beckons gently, yet constantly and firmly, to all to approach with courage and confidence, repeating figuratively the invitation once uttered so lovingly by humanity's truest Friend: "Come to me, all you that labour, and are burdened, and I will refresh you" (Mt. XI, 28). Watch the frequency with which the doors of churches swing open and shut in truly Catholic centers, and you will realize that myriads of souls must find Christ as ready to hear, heal, and comfort as He was in those days when He walked over the hills of Judea and Galilee.

WHEN you receive Holy Communion, you are taking part in a community banquet; you come to the holy table, not as individuals only, but as members of the MYSTICAL BODY OF CHRIST; not as men merely, but as redeemed humanity; not as yourself alone, but as the Christian living and praying in Christ.

THE MOST REV. R. E. LUCEY

RESTORATION THROUGH THE
BREAD OF LIFE

JEAN LE CHEVALIER DE GERSON

JESUS CHRIST commands you by the mouth of the prophet to return to Him. He promises always to receive you lovingly. He will not despise a contrite and humble heart, had you contemned and abandoned Him a thousand times. If one of your fellow-men gave you this assurance, you would believe him, you would fly to his arms. It is God who now speaks to you. He tells you all this. He promises you forgiveness—nay, He evens commands you to return to Him; and yet in your mistrust you dare not approach Him! You say you are not pure enough.—For that very reason you should flee to the inexhaustible Source of all Purity, that you may be purified. You suffer hunger.—Take the Bread of the strong. It will nourish and quicken your soul. You are ill and languid.—Approach the most loving Physician, who alone is able to heal every malady. You are assaulted with constant temptations against holy purity, and no spiritual exercise is able to free you from them.—Go to Jesus Christ, touch with faith and confidence the hem of His garment, receive the Holy Host, His Sacred Body and Precious Blood, and you will find strength and freedom. Are you entangled in thousands of other temptations which, like the coils of serpents, surround you?—Raise your eyes to the God-Man who bled for you on the cross. His glance alone will heal all your wounds. You complain of your poverty and abandonment.—Fly to the holy Tabernacle. You will there find Jesus Christ your almighty, infinitely rich, and good King, ready to share all His treasures with you. You feel weak, faint, and blind.—But do you not know that this Heavenly King not only invited the lame and the blind to His Banquet, but even compelled their attendance? You bewail your inconstancy and many faults.—Eat this Heavenly Food of the soul. It will restore you. It will make your heart strong and generous. You are sad.—Drink, then, of the Wine that rejoices the hearts of men. Are you confused and distracted?—Seek refuge in Him who calmed the raging billows of the sea, and said to the stormy winds: "Be still!" Fly to Him who alone is the Source of true peace; to Him who gives us the assurance that sufferings and tribulations are our portion here below, and that our hearts will never find rest save in Him. We languish in banishment far from our eternal home.—Receive often the Bread of Angels. It will encourage you and strengthen your faltering steps up the holy mountain of the Lord. What do you fear? Why are you sad? Why disturbed? Hope in God! Put your whole confidence in Him, and He will save you from every trouble and tribulation. He Himself will nourish you and you shall not be confounded. Sighing and lamenting, you ask yourself: "Where is my God?"— Your God is in the Holy Feast in which Christ gives Himself to you as food, in which the remembrance of His Passion is renewed, in which the soul is filled with grace and receives the assured pledge of eternal blessedness!

HIS design in the Blessed Sacrament is not so much that He may give Himself to me as that He may take me to Himself: not so much that I may see Him on the Altar as that He may see me before the Altar: not so much that I may go up to the rails to receive Him as that He may come down to the rails to receive me.

THE REV. R. H. J. STEUART, S.J.

"THE ALMS OF IMMORTALITY"

THE REV. VINCENT MCNABB, O.P.

IF IT requires creative power to be a poet, it certainly requires the creative power of God to conceive of the infinite abyss of love which the Blessed Sacrament is. It is the center of all spirituality, the *Mysterium fidei,* the one mystery which brings out our faith and summarizes for us all the other mysteries of religion, the Unity and Trinity of God, and the Incarnation, Death and Resurrection of Our Lord. It is the Incarnation raised to a higher power. It is God hiding Himself and then going into deeper depths and hiding His hiding-place. It is God's mystery of justice to Himself and mercy to us. It embraces Bethlehem, Nazareth, Thabor and Golgotha. It is almost the omnipresence of the Humanity. In it every mystery which stuns and opens our mind is found. That is why it is called a *wonderful* Sacrament. . . .

To us it is the Sacrament of hope. God has here taken away the immortality of matter and given it a new immortality. In that dead bread and wine we have the "alms of immortality." . . .

When the body of this death of ours is passing into the silent tomb, morning by morning we take hold of the alms of immortality. It seems more dead than the lips that receive It, but It is the well-spring of eternal life and will raise us up in the last day.

GRACE is the light of the soul. To see clearly our way in this dark world, to avoid the many snares set for our feet, we need a great deal of this light. The chief source of this light today is Holy Communion. The warmth that spreads from the Tabernacle we likewise need in abundance, to cause our frozen hearts first to melt with sorrow for our sins and then to glow with love for God. That spiritual strength and energy of which the Holy Eucharist is the readiest source we all sadly need to keep us tireless in doing deeds of kindness for one another, to make us stout of heart in conquering ourselves, to keep our faith alive; for action, movement and resistance are the signs of life.

THE REV. WALTER DWIGHT, S.J.

A KING WHO GIVES AUDIENCE
TO ALL

ST. ALPHONSUS DE' LIGUORI

JESUS CHRIST, in the Blessed Sacrament, gives audience to all. St. Teresa used to say that all cannot speak with the sovereign. The poor can scarcely hope to address him, and make known to him their necessities, even through a third person. But to speak to the King of Heaven, the intervention of a third person is not necessary; all, the

211

poor as well as the nobles of the earth, may speak to Him face to face in the Holy Sacrament. Hence Jesus is called the flower of the fields. *I am the flower of the field and the lily of the valleys.* (Cant. ii.I) The flowers of garden are enclosed and reserved; but the flowers of the fields are exposed to all. "I am the flower of the field," says Cardinal Hugo, in his comment on this passage, "because I exhibit myself to be found by all." With Jesus, then, in the Holy Sacrament, all may speak to Him every hour in the day. . . . The churches are always open: all can go to converse with the King of Heaven whenever they wish. Jesus desires that we speak to Him with unbounded confidence; it is for this purpose that He remains under the species of bread. If Jesus appeared on our altars, as He will on the day of judgment, on a throne of glory, who among us would dare to approach Him? But, says St. Teresa, because the Lord desires that we speak to Him, and ask His graces with confidence and without fear, He has therefore clothed His majesty with the appearance of bread.

THE MUTUAL GIVING IN HOLY COMMUNION

THE REV. JAMES M. GILLIS, C.S.P.

MAN is the highest of creations on this earth. He reaches down into the creation beneath him, takes it up and into himself, imparts to it something of his own superior nature. He assumes minerals, fruits, the flesh of animals, absorbs them, elevates them to a condition of being nobler than their own. That which was inert is made to live; that which was mineral or animal becomes human.

So, in Holy Communion God reaches down to man, lifts him up, unites man with Himself, sharing with him the Divine Nature. "Have I not said ye are Gods?" says Jesus with a holy extravagance greater than that of Tertullian or Augustine or any one else who loves hyperbole. The first consequence of Holy Communion, therefore, is the elevation of man above his own grade of being. St. Augustine pictures God saying to man, "You shall not change Me into yourself, but you shall be changed into Me." In any association of man with man either the better uplifts the worse, or what is base drags down what is noble. In the union of God with man God cannot be debased. He condescends to the dust but the dust cannot soil Him. The imperfections of human nature were not present in the Son of God made man, but they do remain in us after our union with Him.

So, the first moral and spiritual effect of that union should be the lessening of those imperfections and the ultimate result of frequent Communion should be what the spiritual writers call "perfection." Perfection may seem to be impossible, and in fact we confess that it is, and that it remains to the end of our days a goal rather than an achievement. . . . The only way of repaying God who gives His all is to give our all. Nothing less than all we have can satisfy the Infinite. Nothing should satisfy us unless it satisfies Him. . . . Love is all or nothing. In love one gives not something but everything. In Holy Communion, "everything" on the part of God means Himself. He requires in return nothing less than our whole self. . . .

The reception of the Blessed Sacrament imposes yet

another obligation upon the recipient. Quite as important as the love of God is the love of the brethren. We are all blood relatives in the Blood of Christ. . . .

The Holy Communion therefore is not merely a bond of love between God and man, but between man and man. "We being many are one bread," says St. Paul. One Bread and one Blood. The doctrine of the Mystical Body of Christ is based upon the reception of the Body and Blood, the Soul, the Humanity and Divinity in Holy Communion.

THE sacrament of community, Communion, is incomprehensible. In it man is one with God; God is personally united with him, and is given to him as his very own. But with this one God not only one man is united, but all his fellows. And each receives God into his personal being; yet each receives Him on behalf of the other also, on behalf of husband or wife, of children, parents, relatives, and friends—for all those to whom he is bound by ties of love.

RT. REV. ROMANO GUARDINI

REUNION OF MANKIND THROUGH THE EUCHARIST

FRANÇOIS DE CHATEAUBRIAND

IN THE *material* bread and wine we behold the consecration of the food of man, which comes from God, and which we receive from His bounty. Were there nothing more in the Communion than this offering of the productions of the earth to Him who dispenses them, that alone would qualify it to be compared with the most excellent religious customs of Greece.

The Eucharist reminds us of the Passover of the Israelites, which carries us back to the time of the Pharaohs; it announces the abolition of bloody sacrifices; it represents also the calling of Abraham, and the first covenant between God and man. Every thing grand in antiquity, in history, in legislation, in the sacred types, is therefore comprised in the communion of the Christian.

The Eucharist announces the reunion of mankind into one great family. It inculcates the cessation of enmities, natural equality, and the commencement of a new law, which will make no distinction of Jew or Gentile, but invites all children of Adam to sit down at the same table.

The great wonder of the Eucharist is the real presence of Christ under the consecrated species. Here the soul must transport itself for a moment to that intellectual world which was open to man before the fall.

HOLY THURSDAY

FRANÇOIS MAURIAC

HOLY THURSDAY is the day when only one hour is given the Christian to rejoice in an inestimable favor: "The Lord Jesus, on the night in which he was betrayed, took bread, and giving thanks broke, and said, 'This is my body which shall be given up for you; do this in remembrance of me.' " . . .

The anniversary of that evening when the small Host arose on a world sleeping in darkness should fill us with joy. But that very night was the one when the Lord Jesus was delivered up. . . .

We should like to tarry to see on his shoulder the place where St. John's forehead rested, to relive in spirit the moment in the history of the world when a piece of bread was broken in deep silence, when a few words sufficed to seal the new alliance of the Creator with His creature. Already, in the thought of the One Who pronounced the words, millions of priests are bending over the chalice, millions of virgins are watching before the tabernacle. A multitude of the servants of the poor are eating the daily Bread which compensates for their daily sacrifice; and endless ranks of children, making their First Communion, open lips which have not yet lost their purity, and, in the vision of the Saviour, an immense multitude of unchaste persons, of murderers, of prostitutes, regain the purity of their early years through contact with that Host; it makes them again like little children. . . .

The Council of Trent taught that "the same Christ Who offered Himself on the cross, offers Himself up now through the ministry of the priests." This flesh and this blood, delivered for us, in the elements of bread and wine, are being offered up to the Father as a bloodless holocaust. Nothing has changed since the dawn of Christianity except the order of the prayers which precede and follow the consecration and communion. . . .

No man knows himself if he has not looked at his soul in the light of the Host lifted above the ciborium. In that moment the Church, sublimely inspired, puts on the lips of the priest and the faithful the words of the centurion: "Lord, I am not worthy that thou shouldst come under my roof, but only say the word and my soul shall be healed," a prayer that has always been answered since the first day when Christ heard it in Capharnaum. All these misdeeds that the communicant sees at a glance are no longer his; someone else has taken them over since the pardon of Christ has come down on his soul with the absolution of the priest. His misery, far from driving him into despair, helps him to understand how much he has been loved. Such is the sad but precious privilege of the sinner; love has had to seek for his father, to lift him from a lower level. To take heart again, the communicant finds comfort in the fervor he himself experiences and which, perhaps, comes from God. If we love Him, it is a sign that He loves us, for it is a gift of God to love God and He never rewards us for anything that He has not Himself given us. Thus, an almost foolish confidence overcomes all our doubts, our anxieties, and overflows the memories of the defilement of our soul. . . .

The grace of Holy Thursday will be transmitted unto the end of time, unto the last of the priests who will celebrate the last Mass in a shattered universe. . . .

The promise made to us by Christ is renewed each communion. We who are eating this Bread shall not die. As the sheep of His fold, we are being marked out each time more deeply by the Good Shepherd for salvation. We are holding in our hands the token of our victory over evil in our militant life, the token of our everlasting triumph. He who is our Food on earth will be our reward in Heaven; and that Food is already a foretaste of Heavenly bliss.

217

ALTHOUGH a real communion is at the oftenest restrained to once a day, yet you are at liberty to communicate in spirit every hour; and nothing but your own negligence can prevent your receiving this great benefit. And it is worth observing, that a spiritual communion is sometimes of greater advantage to the soul, and more acceptable to God than many sacramental communions performed with little preparation and affection. When, therefore, you are disposed to receive the Son of God spiritually, be assured He is ready to give Himself thus to you for your food and nourishment.

D. LAURENCE SCUPOLI

X

He breathed on them; and he said to them:
Receive ye the Holy Ghost.
Whose sins you shall forgive, they are for-
given them; and whose sins you shall
retain, they are retained.

St. John 20:22, 23

"GOD'S INVITATION"

THE REV. VINCENT MCNABB, O.P.

CONFESSION is something which helps us to *arise*. We hear of Progress. Progress is going on and on and on, but not necessarily going *up*. It might be going down. The Church says: "Come up"—and a much better word. "Come up higher." That is God's invitation. Whenever a soul wishes to get out of the mire of sin, it goes to Confession. The priest has only one medicine. It is the right medicine. Is it the Priest's medicine? He didn't make it. God made it. We have only one medicine, God's; out of God's pharmacopeia. Confession. Begin there—to be forgiven if we are in deep sin—or if we want to go higher; if we have been kept out of sin by the Grace of

God and we feel we would like to be more closely related to God. Our soul may not be in grievous sin. God alone has the secret. But that is the right way to begin. There is God's medicine. . . .

The next thing is to *walk*. We must be self-possessed. Our feet have to be our own. After illness our feet are not our own. We can't walk. But in the spiritual life there is no convalescence. God has found our feet for us. Our feet are now our own. We own ourselves. We have been bought at a great price and then given back to ourselves. . . .

Now our feet are our own. We own ourselves. How wonderful that is! The soul that has used God's institution of Mercy, in Confession, now gets the ownership and possession of his own soul. . . .

By sin we give up possession of our own soul. We have hardly even the leasehold. We are lodgers. It is not our own. It is more or less a furnished flat where sin has gained possession. When that sin has been taken away by God's forgiveness we are once more owners of our own soul. It becomes our own; the house will be *ours*— God's dwelling, and that means HOME. "Home means someone somewhere." Home means love somewhere; and, where God is dwelling, Love is in the heart. Our heart becomes our home, and we are at home with ourselves. . . .

The human heart that has received God's Mercies in Confession becomes full of Grace. Perhaps souls do not realize that the scientific use of Confession will furnish the soul and give it the possibility of challenging everything.

THE SACRAMENT OF JOY

CARYLL HOUSELANDER

THE Sacrament of Penance has a purpose wholly different from that of psychiatry and one which far transcends it. It is one too which can never fail unless the penitent himself deliberately frustrates it by an act of sacrilege.

It is not limited to a certain kind of person, but is for every one; it does not depend on the personality or the skill of the priest; it fulfills its purpose whether he is a man of the deepest understanding of human nature or of none at all.

It is not something experimental which may or may not be effective in a given case, but something absolutely certain which will be effective in every case. It is never an experiment; it is always a miracle.

The purpose of sacramental Confession is atonement—at-one-ment—with God. What happens in Confession is that man, who has separated himself from God, becomes one with Him again. It is an unimaginable impact of love between God and man in which Christ gives Himself to the sinner. To the soul that is dead in sin, Christ's life flows back, and in that sinner's life Christ rises again from death. To the soul that is devitalized and nerveless from habitual sins of weakness, Christ gives an increase of His life, flooding the soul with His vitality and love and changing it as He changed the water into wine at Cana.

The Sacrament of Penance is the sacrament of joy. It is not only the sacrament of joy for the sinner who returns to God and is restored to life and made one with

Christ, but (and this is a mystery far beyond any joy or glory of man's) it is also a sacrament of joy for the eternal Father. He rejoices as the father of the Prodigal Son rejoiced. He sees in the Christ-redeemed sinner, risen from the death of sin and living again with Christ's life, his only beloved Son coming back to Him, clothed in the red robes of his Passion. . . .

The purpose of sacramental Confession is to remove sin, not to remove suffering, though sometimes it does that too. But *always* it does something far more, and for all suffering, not only psychological suffering; it gives a meaning, a purpose, and a power. It changes it from being destructive to being creative. By giving Christ's life, the sacrament gives the redeeming, healing power of Christ's love to the suffering that the forgiven sinner must experience.

THE MERCY OF THE DIVINE PHYSICIAN

THE REV. ALFRED WILSON, C.P.

SOME years ago a non-Catholic woman went to a priest to discuss the Faith. She had, like most non-Catholics, a strong prejudice against Confession. To her it seemed a bugbear, an imposition of priests and a torture-process reminiscent of the Inquisition. She could not conceive the gentle Christ imposing so cruel a yoke on unfortunate humanity.

"You are presuming," said the priest, "that it is a

yoke. Are you so certain that it is a bugbear and not a blessing? To me it seems a most convincing proof of the Divinity of Christ and a magnificent manifestation of His goodness and kindness."

She was taken aback. "How on earth do you make that out?"

"Because," said the priest, "it reveals the Supreme Physician of souls, the Divine Psychologist, Who understands human nature through and through."

"How?"

"When you have done wrong," said the priest, "is not one of your first impulses to tell someone about it? You want to get it off your mind, off your chest. Until you do, you know that you will be carrying a heavy burden; you will have something on your mind. You will have no peace of soul."

"That is true," she said.

"Well, then," he continued, "if that is true, would it not be like Jesus, 'Who knew what was in man,' to institute a Sacrament to enable us to get our sins, our worries, our doubts and fears, off our mind?"

"I never thought of it like that," she said. . . .

It is a pity we need hospitals—but we do. It is a pity we need dentists—but we do. It is a pity that we need the confessional: if we were sinless we would not need it: but we are not sinless and therefore we do need it. Because our bodies get sick, we need hospitals. Because our souls get sick, we need the confessional.

No one goes to the doctor or the dentist for fun, unless he is mad. No one goes to confession for fun. From the nature of the case, confession cannot be easy. The result, not the process, of confession is consoling.

After serious sin, however, we have no alternative but

to confess if we desire to regain undisturbed peace of mind. . . .

But Confession is more than a clinic of psycho-therapy; it is also a Sacrament of Divine Mercy, guaranteeing the pardon of God as well as the pardon of society. It is in no sense an arbitrary imposition, for even the hardest part of it, the obligation of telling our sins, is medicinal not punitive, and is inspired by mercy, understanding, and a desire to help. The medicine is certainly hard to take and not at all palatable, but it is medicine all the same! A kind Lord could not let us off scot-free—it would not be good for us. In this world, however, all penance is designed to be remedial and is never merely vindictive.

Jesus obliged us to confess our sins for our own sake rather than for His. He took the institution of Confession, which is a natural necessity, and safeguarded, facilitated and elevated it, raising it to the dignity of a Sacrament. He made the inevitably difficult task of confessing *as easy as it possibly could be made.* We confess in secret, to any priest we choose; if we like, to one who does not know us and will probably never see us again. We confess in secret to a man who is bound to secrecy. We confess, moreover, to a man who is trained, not merely to listen with tenderness and sympathy, but to instruct, advise and heal.

In the Sacrament of Penance, Christ Himself is the real priest. There, in His capacity of Divine Physician, He forgives sin, pours grace into our souls, removes the traces of past sins, and gives us a title to actual graces in future difficulties.

Confession is simply a Hospital of Souls, where the Good Samaritan, through the instrumentality of the priests, goes about binding up wounds and pouring in oil and wine; a hospital where the Divine Physician displays His healing art.

God's forgiveness is not a pious fiction. The clemency of our Divine Judge is not merely a mantle thrown over our sins to hide their hideousness. Absolution removes from the soul the sins that sullied it, and restores it to that state in which it was before it sinned. The converted sinner is not like that convict whose fetters were worn by St. Vincent of Paul, but whose soul, in the eyes of God and of his own conscience, still bore its guilt. Under the action of redeeming grace sin melts away from the soul like mud-stained snow in a thaw. After the sun has shone on it the soil resumes its firmness, and no trace is to be found of the mire that so lately sullied it. The forgiven soul has the brightness of the soul that has retained its innocence, and the Divine Goodness, with equal complacency, sees itself reflected in both.

DÉSIRÉ JOSEPH CARDINAL MERCIER

"THEY GO AWAY GLAD"

THE REV. BENEDICT WILLIAMSON

There is no need of the human heart, as I can witness from long experience, greater than this, the desire to know with absolute certitude that God has pardoned and forgiven sin. The soul may leave the father's home for long years, strive to forget all about it, try to stifle the voice of conscience in a flood of worldly delights, but a moment comes when she comes to herself and cries out pitifully: "I will arise and go to my father and say: 'Father, I have sinned.'"

The more I have seen of the work of the confessional, the more I realize how Divine it is, and that God alone could have established such a means of meeting between the sinner and the Saviour.

No one kneels in the confessional without sorrow for sin; sometimes the sorrow is but slight, sometimes heart-breaking, but sorrow of some sort there always is.

"Are you sorry?"

"I should not be here if I was not," was the answer of a poor soul once. No, before they kneel there, Grace has already done its work and touched the heart. Then comes the confession, sometimes of a long life of sin; but the relief of it, to open the heart and let it speak at last, to feel absolutely free to sound the very depths of the soul, assured that whatever is told is a secret that will never be revealed. That is one side of the confessional, only one, but a very great one. The priest is never surprised, the quiet voice passionless and unemotional, never gives a hint of horror, no matter how loathsome or terrible the sin; there is something of the tranquillity of the Eternal in the confessional. Then, when it is all over, the quiet voice speaks words of counsel and exhortation, and traces the way to act for the future. Then comes the absolution. What confessor is there who, as he sees the tears of joy and the unutterable happiness that comes over the penitent as the words of forgiveness sound in his ears, has not experienced something of the joy of the angels over one sinner doing penance?

Hour after hour the priest sits while the young and old, men and women, pour forth the story of their frailty, little children very grave and serious over their small failings, the youthful ardent and eager, the middle-aged more matter-of-fact, the old just tottering to the grave; they all come, heavy laden, they all go away glad.

And the priest is never tired, never weary, never impatient; whatever he may have of human weakness it never shows *there;* there he seems the reflection of the inexhaustible patience and pity of God. And indeed such he is, for when he speaks, God speaks, when he forgives, God forgives. He is everything and nothing, nothing of himself, everything as God's instrument to bring the secure assurance of forgiveness to His children.

THERE is in truth a sort of reverence due to sinners, when we look at them not as in their sins, but simply as having sinned, and being the objects of a Divine yearning. It is the manifestation of this feeling in apostolic men which lures sinners to them, and so leads to their conversion. The devotedness of Our Blessed Lord to sinners transfers a peculiar feeling to the hearts of His servants. And when the offenders come to repent, the mark of Divine predilection in the great Grace they are receiving is a thing more to admire and revere and love, than the sin is a thing to hate in connection with the sinner.

THE REV. FREDERICK WILLIAM FABER

CONFESSION IN PRISON

WILLIAM THOMAS WALSH

ONE Sunday morning he got up feeling strangely disturbed and anxious. The bars were drawn, the cell doors open, and he saw some of the men [i.e. convicts] go out, as they were permitted to do, to confess to Father Burke before Mass. He had not intended to follow them, yet he did, feeling bewildered and frightened, but incapable of resisting the impulse that had taken possession of him after all his reasoning. He used to say afterwards that he felt as if some irresistible power had taken command of his limbs and was forcing him whither he would not, to some bitter and humiliating trial.

He waited while several men made their confessions. When it became his turn he went to the little confessional that Father Burke had rigged up in the back of the auditorium, with a prie-dieu and a screen, and kneeling beside the priest he began, with a violently beating heart, to ask himself why he was there. Father Burke looked up, and saw who it was. His freckled face, very pale that morning, betrayed no surprise. He raised his hand perfunctorily and said,

"The Lord be in thy heart and on thy lips, that thou mayest truly and humbly confess thy sins, in the name of the Father, and of the Son and of the Holy Ghost."

Seeing that Stephen still hesitated, he said,

"How long since your last confession, my boy?"

"Nine years."

"Well, it won't be such a job as you think. Let's start with the worst thing you ever did in that time. What was it?"

Stephen began his confession.

Something tremendous had happened to Stephen; something that no one could have imagined without the experience. In that hour when he knelt on the rickety prie-dieu, clutching the edge of his coat while he unpacked his heart of its miseries, his soul was the theatre of a revolution for which he could never find words until, three weeks later, he read the gigantic imagery of the Apocalypse. Sitting hunched on his bed one rainy summer night, while the wind pelted the outer wall, and holding on his knees the Bible Father Burke had given him, he seemed to feel about him the fall and crash of a world, and the rising of a new world out of the ruin; and the mighty figures seemed like the enlarged shadows of his own soul's struggles, past and future. . . .

Thus in the soul of poor Stephen West, life-convict, there seemed to be enacted in miniature the titanic drama of the ages; and when he went back to his cell that fateful morning, healed, cleansed and strengthened, he felt like shouting to the whole world that he had found what all were seeking. Two intolerable burdens, the need of explaining the universe and the shameful tyranny of self, had fallen from his neck like millstones into a sea of compassion, leaving him as lighthearted as a child, as buoyant as a spirit. Nothing seemed difficult now, nothing impossible.

Long afterwards, when his mind turned back to those days and tried to follow the steps which led him from Marxian materialism to the opposite pole of Catholic Christianity, he could never wholly account for what happened to him except on the theory that he had been influenced by a higher power. He was like hard-pressed St. Peter, crying by the Sea of Genesareth, "Lord, to whom shall we go? Thou hast the words of eternal life. And we have believed, and have known that Thou art the Christ, the Son of God!" Standing alone in an immense darkness of doubt and futility, Stephen was intelligent enough to see that no merely human system or philosophy or creed could ever effectually relieve that gloom; not the best intention of a Buddha, or a Mohammed, a Luther or a Kant, or a Huxley or a Talmud-reading Maimonides—all of them only thickened the confusion of tongues, none could say the decisive word. And then there arose before his mind the luminous and all-merciful figure of Christ, saying what no other could say without seeming ridiculous: "I am the light of the world." Not even Moses could say that and be taken seriously by millions of men for nineteen centuries. And so, stumbling out of the darkness of his mind into the darkness of the confessional, Stephen had come upon that light, and had found himself saying, like Thomas the Doubter in the Upper Room, "My Lord and my God!"

(From the novel *Out of the Whirlwind*)

CONFESSION OF GREATER

BENEFIT

THAN PSYCHOANALYSIS

THE REV. JOHN A. O'BRIEN

PSYCHOANALYSIS may be said to be but the confessional technique developed by the psychiatrist in the probing of psychic disturbances and in effecting their removal.

. . . It is evident that the ideal agency for obtaining such disclosures with complete candor is the confessional of the Catholic Church. Here the patient is conscious that his revelation is protected by an inviolable secrecy. He knows that the confessor would gladly sacrifice his life rather than disclose one single word whispered in the confessional.

Furthermore, he is free to enjoy a complete anonymity by going to a confessional where both confessor and penitent are perfect strangers. Every human consideration calculated to prove helpful to the penitent in unbosoming himself of his troubles, sins and disturbances will be found in the regulations governing the administration of the sacrament of confession.

In addition, there are spiritual considerations which no psychoanalyst can provide. There is the religious faith which reminds the penitent that he is confessing to God, and that the confessor is acting merely as the human ambassador of the Most High, extending mercy and forgiveness in His name. He realizes that the concealment of a grievous misdeed would not only nullify the confession but would add to the penitent's soul the guilt of sacrilege. That is why the confessional in the humblest Catholic Church in the world is a more efficacious agency for a complete catharsis than the office of any psychoanalyst, no matter how many technicians it may have and no matter how persuasive they may be in pleading for a frank dislodgment of the disagreeable and painful out of the buried past.

While the mere disclosure of sin to a sympathetic friend has a therapeutic value, confession in the Catholic Church has a far greater and more beneficial effect because it not only permits the confession of sins but gives to the penitent that which he craves above all else—the assurance of God's pardon. It is this latter element which, far more than the former, restores peace and tranquility to the troubled soul. Why should he worry, when because of his sorrow and purpose of amendment he has received through the ambassador of God the pardon of the Most High? There is a craving, it is true, to confess one's guilt. But the far deeper and more insistent craving is for the *remission* of the guilt. This is the real reason why the confessional exercises such a marvelous influence upon the mental health of the hundreds of millions of people who use it.

XI

Hitherto you have not asked any thing in my name. Ask, and you shall receive, that your joy may be full.

St. John 16:24

THE ESSENCE OF PRAYER

THE MOST REV. ALBAN GOODIER, S.J.

ABOVE and before all else it is the raising of the mind and heart to God that matters, and my prayer is then best when I do this most effectually, leaving earth alone, leaving myself alone, realizing God and even a very little of that which He means, and letting my tiny soul prattle to the Lord in whatever feeble way it may, once it has come in contact with Him. This is of the essence of prayer; without it prayer is not. . . . He who raises mind and heart to God cannot but be and become a better man. . . .

The Jesuit Father was himself an experienced man of prayer who used regularly to advise his clients: "Pray the way you like best." Indeed, this is the one way to learn, the one way to make progress. Prayer is not a philosophy;

it is not an abstract science; it cannot be learnt from books; it cannot be taught by theory. To know about prayer and to be a man of prayer are by no means always the same thing. Prayer is a life, an activity, and to make progress in it we need to practice it according as we know it. This alone keeps prayer true; and prayer that is not true is futile vanity; if not worse. This alone keeps prayer real, part of ourselves; and prayer that is not that is sheer imitation. Let us learn to take our poor little souls as we find them. Some of us, a very few, may possibly begin high; the majority of us, who are none the less "called to be Saints," will find perfection on a lower gradient. But whether high or low, our best will be according to our powers; and only by using the powers we actually possess can we learn to do more. For some prayer will be the constant repetition of a word, or a phrase, or a form; for others the concentration upon a single thought or idea; for others, again, who aspire to meditation, a sequence of thoughts leading from one definite point to another; but all—be it never forgotten—raising the mind and heart to God. If I do that I succeed in prayer, from whatever starting point I set out, in whatever way I proceed, at whatever goal I arrive.

LOOK at the incredible ease of prayer. Every time, place, posture is fitting; for there is no time, place, or posture, in and by which we cannot reverently confess the Presence of God. Talent is not needed. Eloquence is out of place. Dignity is no recommendation. Our want is our eloquence, our misery our recommendation. Thought is quick as lightning, and quick as lightning can it multiply effectual prayer. Actions can pray; sufferings can pray. There need be no ceremonies; there are no rubrics to keep. The whole function is expressed in a word, it is simply this—the child at his father's knee, his words stumbling over each other from very earnestness, and his wistful face pleading better than his hardly intelligible prayer.

THE REV. FREDERICK WILLIAM
FABER

SPIRITUAL joy arises from purity of the heart and perseverance in prayer!

ST. FRANCIS OF ASSISI

THE SOURCE OF PRAYER

FATHER JAMES, O.F.M. CAP.

WE THINK of prayer wrongly if we seek its source in men. Nothing begins in man, least of all the life of prayer. His soul is just the little lake that is filled by God. The impulse to pray, the ultimate impulse, is the inrush of the divine waters, waters that must return to the ocean of the Godhead and in their return bear along with them the soul of man. Else, why did Christ bequeath to us His Spirit, the living Spirit of Prayer Who helpeth our infirmity?

The perfect form of prayer is also reflected in the curving jet of water. If we regard the prayers that we know, the prayers with the seal of the Spirit on them, the prayers of the Church, we see how they rise on wings of poetry to address the all-holy God, an upward movement of praise and adoration, and the downward curve of blessings for humanity. . . . "Glory to God in the Highest . . . and on earth peace to men of Good Will." And we know that they spring from the Spirit of prayer in the Church, coming down from God, like life itself, and endeavoring to return to Him like the humble jet of water that seeks the sky. The rainbow spray of water teaches the perfect grace and perfect rhythm of true prayer that ascends on high and then returns to make the music of peace upon the earth.

WE MUST have a lively faith and firm confidence that God will not refuse us the assistance necessary for serving him faithfully, and working out our salvation. A soul replenished with this holy confidence, is like a sacred vessel, into which the divine mercy pours the treasures of his grace, and the more capacious this vessel is, the greater abundance of heavenly blessings will it receive through prayer. For how can God, whose goodness cannot deceive, ever refuse His gifts to those whom He so earnestly presses to demand them, and to whom he has promised His holy Spirit, if we sue for it with faith and perseverance?

Our motive for prayer must be the divine will, not our own; applying ourselves to this great duty, because God commands it, and desiring to be heard no further than what is agreeable to Him; thus our intention will be to conform entirely our will to His, and not to make the divine will subservient to our own.

D. LAURENCE SCUPOLI

WHAT I have learned is this: that the entire foundation of prayer must be established in humility, and that, the more a soul abases itself in prayer, the higher God raises it.

ST. TERESA OF ÁVILA

BE TRUE TO YOURSELF WHEN PRAYING

DOM HUBERT VAN ZELLER, O.S.B.

IF YOU have nothing to say, say so. God in any case has seen into your mind before you have, and if there is really nothing there for the time being He won't in the least resent your being honest about it. This is to be true, to be humble; it is what He wants. Certainly it would be a mistake under such circumstances to fall back upon a sentiment which looks for the sort of thing one ought to feel, merely for the sake of finding something—incidentally something not quite true—to talk about. The object is not to keep up a constant flow. We are not asked to be raconteurs. One mouth, God has given us, to two ears. Yet the moment we start listening in our prayer for what God may have to say we begin to worry lest we should become illuminates, quietists, presumptionists and heaven knows what besides. The truth of it is that this waiting upon God in prayer, this prayer of simple regard which more often than not sees nothing but mist and blankness, both bores us and makes us uneasy. So we abandon it. We discard the fruits of prayer, and continue, with an industry not altogether free of self-esteem, to chew upon the pips. "At least you can get your tooth into a pip . . . pips can be chewed upon for ages." Quite so, but they are not very nourishing. . . .

Sincerity is one of the absolute essentials to prayer. Be true to the self which God has given you. Whatever your mood, your habit, your desire, give Him that. If you are drawn to ask for things, ask. Don't feel that the prayer of petition is a grasping sort of prayer, and that the only thing to do is to put up a prayer which looks very well on paper but which answers nothing in your mind at the moment. Ask on, and give thanks to God for the grace to be praying about it. Whether He answers by giving or refusing what you want doesn't matter much: the main object has already taken place—He has got you into the frame of mind which sends you directly to Him about something which directly concerns you. This is the real achievement, this is you at your truest. This is praise of God as well as petition. It is taking Him at His word.

THE soul has needs as urgent as the body's. They are not a luxury for a chosen few. The soul needs to pray in the same way as we need to eat and breathe and sleep. The more we are weighed down with toil the more we need to be relieved (the Gospel text says *re-made*).

PAUL CLAUDEL

A DAILY ACT OF CONSECRATION

THE REV. JOSEPH MC SORLEY, C.S.P.

THE devotion known as the Apostleship of Prayer has now made it a fairly general custom among Catholic people to offer themselves to God as the first conscious act of the day. Thus to orientate the soul by taking one's proper place at the very moment of rising is to make a good beginning. It means that we have definitely committed ourselves to a Christ-like course of conduct for the day; and already one good blow has been delivered "on the side of the angels."

A profitable prayer may be made by merely dwelling on the implications of the morning offering, by deliberately repeating, with new conviction and fresh emphasis, the consecration of self in all the various ways that love suggests. . . .

At its best, this self-offering, this act of consecration, is an ideal prayer. It begins to tend toward that high perfection as soon as I fix my attention on God and try to adjust myself to His will. It grows and expands when, in the succeeding moments, I ratify and endorse my choice of His will as mine, resolving at all costs to do whatever He shall wish, and to give myself to Him in whatever way He shall suggest. If I succeed in opening my soul widely enough, He will enter and take complete possession. It is as if I stand upon the pinnacle of all the world and then, looking into His eyes, I make the leap; and, for one splendid instant, I am a saint, caring for nothing in the universe but the fulfilling of His will, believing in Him wholeheartedly, trusting Him absolutely, loving Him with all my soul.

This act of consecration suggests itself as in peculiarly perfect harmony with the act of assisting at the Mass; for the Mass is essentially Christ's offering of Himself to the Father, continued and renewed day by day upon all the altars of the world, in order that we, members of His Mystical Body, may enjoy unending opportunities to unite ourselves with Him in the only Perfect Sacrifice that ever has been, or ever will be, in human history. Preparing for this by a confession of sin at the beginning of Mass, the Confiteor, we go on gradually deepening and strengthening the sentiment of oneness with our Lord, until at the Elevation we too are consecrated, transformed, lifted up and given to God without reserve. *"Consummatum est":* It is consummated. I have been given to God with a finality attainable in no other way. Simply then, as if inevitably, I go on to Communion and to Thanksgiving.

Now, when we are gathered together in the church, we praise God; but when we depart each to his own business, it is as if we cease to praise Him. Let a man not cease from right living, and then he is ever praising God. Thou dost cease from praising God when thou turnest aside from justice and from all that pleaseth Him. For, if thou never turn aside from a good life, though thy tongue be silent, yet thy life crieth out, and the ear of God is open to thy heart.

ST. AUGUSTINE

THE "GRAND MANNER" OF THE SPIRITUAL LIFE

RT. REV. ROMANO GUARDINI

WHEN we pray on our own behalf only we approach God from an entirely personal standpoint, precisely as we feel inclined or impelled to do according to our feelings and circumstances. That is our right, and the Church would be the last to wish to deprive us of it. Here we live our own life, and are as it were face to face with God. His Face is turned towards us, as to no one else; He belongs to each one of us. It is this power of being a personal God, ever fresh to each of us, equally patient and attentive to each one's wants, which constitutes the inexhaustible wealth of God. The language which we speak on these occasions suits us entirely, and much of it apparently is suited to us alone. We can use it with confidence because God understands it, and there is no one else who needs to do so.

We are, however, not only individuals, but members of a community as well; we are not merely transitory, but something of us belongs to eternity, and the liturgy takes these elements of us into account. In the liturgy we pray as members of the Church; by it we rise to the sphere which transcends the individual order and is therefore accessible to people of every condition, time and place. . . .

Both methods of prayer must co-operate. They stand together in a vital and reciprocal relationship. The one derives its light and fruitfulness from the other. In the liturgy the soul learns to move about the wider and more spacious spiritual world. . . . The soul acquires in the liturgy, the "grand manner" of the spiritual life—and that is a thing that cannot be too highly prized. On the other hand, as the Church herself reminds us—and the example of the Orders who live by the liturgy is a proof of this—side by side with the liturgy there must continue to exist that private devotion which provides for the personal requirements of the individual, and to which the soul surrenders itself according to its particular circumstances. For the latter liturgical prayer in turn derives warmth and local color.

HE PRAYS in the temple of God who prays in the peace of the Church, in the unity of Christ's body; which body of Christ consists of the many in the whole world who believe. And therefore he who prays in the temple is heard. For he prays in spirit and in truth who prays in the peace of the Church.

ST. AUGUSTINE

FASTING DISPOSES US TO PRAYER

THE MOST REV. W. BERNARD ULLATHORNE

PRAYER is good with fasting. We fast that we may draw nearer unto God, and Lent is therefore the season of prayer. By fasting we recover possession of our soul;

by prayer we recover possession of God. By fasting we mortify the deeds of the flesh; by prayer we lift up our hearts to God. Prayer gives courage and force of will to deny ourselves; fasting disposes us for prayer. . . . Happy are they who learn to direct the attention of their soul to God, instead of suffering it to relapse into the desire of comforting the animal man, instead of returning to the complete indulgence of its appetites. This is the work of prayer. By the exercise of prayer we gain a better foundation, a more spiritual support, a diviner foundation for our life. By prayer we lean on the Arm of God, by prayer we obtain the strength of Christ, by prayer we receive the gift of endurance. Fasting puts us on the Cross; prayer lifts up our hearts above the Cross. Fasting tries the patience, which prayer strengthens. Fasting teaches us our weakness, and prayer seeks out the strength of God.

MEDITATION teaches us what it is that we lack, and prayer obtains it.

Meditation shows us the way, and prayer makes us walk therein. Finally, meditation lets us know the dangers which threaten us, and prayer makes us avoid them by the grace of Our Lord Jesus Christ.

ST. BERNARD OF CLAIRVAUX

THE LORD'S PRAYER

FRANÇOIS DE CHATEAUBRIAND

THE common prayers of the Church are admirable; it is only the habit of repeating them from our infancy that renders us insensible to their beauty. The world would resound with the praises of Plato or Seneca if their works contained a profession of faith so simple, so pure, so luminous, as that article of the creed—

"I believe in one God, the Father Almighty, Maker of heaven and earth, and of all things visible and invisible."

The Lord's prayer is the production of a God who understood all our wants. Let us duly consider its words:—

Our Father who art in heaven:— Here is an acknowledgement of one only God.

Hallowed be thy name:— These words indicate the duty of worshipping God; the vanity of earthly things; God alone is worthy of being hallowed.

Thy kingdom come:— The immortality of the soul is pointed out.

Thy will be done on earth as it is in heaven:— This expression of pious resignation, while it implies the attributes of the Deity, embraces the whole moral and physical order of the universe.

Give us this day our daily bread:— How impressive and philosophical! What is the only real want of man? a little bread; and that he only requires for this day; for, will he be alive tomorrow?

And forgive us our trespasses as we forgive them that

trespass against us:— A code of morality and charity comprised in the smallest compass.

And lead us not into temptation, but deliver us from evil:— Behold the human heart exposed without reserve! behold man and all his weakness! Let him not ask for strength to overcome; let him pray only that he may not be attacked and may not suffer.

For me, prayer is an uplifting of the heart, a glance towards Heaven, a cry of gratitude and of love in times of sorrow as well as of joy. It is something noble, something supernatural, which expands the soul and unites it to God. When my state of spiritual aridity is such that not a single good thought will come, I repeat very slowly the "Our Father" and the "Hail Mary," which suffice to console me, and provide divine food for my soul.

ST. THÉRÈSE OF LISIEUX

THE INFINITE MEANING OF
OUR PRAYERS

THE REV. JAMES M. GILLIS, C.S.P.

When we pray we use words and phrases that would stop us dead in our tracks if their full meaning were suddenly to dawn upon us. We say, for example, "O my God I love Thee above all things with my whole heart and soul." Some day, half way through that prayer, we shall be struck dumb with amazement that any such astounding declaration could have come from our lips. . . .

It need not be a profoundly mystical expression that suddenly stuns us. The most matter of fact prayers are fraught with infinite meaning. "I believe in God," is a simple, declarative sentence, and seemingly a modest affirmation, but it is in reality a world-shaking manifesto, a challenge to Satan "the spirit who denies," an act of defiance of the forces of atheism, and at certain times and in certain places, as now over half the world, an enormous blasphemy against the Omnipotent State. Since Michael the Archangel drew sword against the apostate angels, there has been no such tremendous war-cry as "I believe in God." All the conflict between heaven and hell is in these four words which in our morning and night prayers we speak with so little advertence. . . .

So perhaps, after all, it is best that we see the truths of religion "darkly." God has placed between us and the sun a buffer of many miles of atmosphere. Otherwise the cosmic rays would pierce our flesh and bone and destroy us. Likewise the merciful Lord tolerates our dull senses and our blunt intellect. "To see Thee in Thine own brightness, mine eyes could not endure," says the Imitation.

As with God so with God's revelation. "No man can see God and live." No man can see God's truth and live. We catch sudden glimpses of truth now and again. The sight startles us. It may prostrate us, or at least incapacitate us for our daily tasks.

THE more time you can reasonably give to being alone with God, the easier it becomes to enjoy it (I don't mean pleasure, but the feeling that it is worth doing—that you are not simply lazy and wasting time). The test is not whether you feel anything at the time, but whether *afterwards* you feel better, and more determined to serve God. The one thing you should gain by quiet prayer (just remaining with God and making a number of aspirations to keep your imagination from wandering) is to feel the rest of the day that you want God's Will and nothing else.

DOM JOHN CHAPMAN, O.S.B.

"WE GO AWAY WONDERING"

THE REV. J. P. LE BUFFE, S.J.

And they both ran together, and that other disciple did outrun Peter and came first to the sepulchre.

St. John 20:4

LIKE St. Peter and St. John, we, too, hurry each morning of our lives to the sepulchre, yet not like them to a sepulchre emptied of its dead treasure, but to the sepulchre of the tabernacle, the altar prison of our living God. Like St. Peter, we too, go away wondering in ourselves at that which has come to pass. It may be we have received Holy Communion and Christ Our Lord has been true to His name "Emmanuel," for He has been "God-with-us" in a way that staggers our "thin minds that creep from thought to thought." He whom all space cannot contain has made His home within our breasts, and falling down we have adored Him. Then we go away wondering! If the Sacred Heart has opened out its riches to us and filled our poor, tired souls with sweetness and consolation, then we are wondering at the goodness of a God who stinted not in His gifts, at the power of a God, "who turned the rock into pools of water and the stony hill into fountains of water." We go away wondering, too, when our hearts have been dry and our minds have fared far afield into the crowded markets of the world at a time when they should have been cloistered with their God. We wonder at the patience of Him who stands all the slights and rebuffs of our waywardness. Or, again, on a morning when prayer has been more or less colorless, when we have sounded neither the depths of desolation nor the heights of God-sent joy, when we have just "prayed as usual," then we are set wondering at the unwavering, undiminishing love for our commonplace souls of a God to whom the music of the spheres is ever new, to whom the songs of Angels are always an oasis amid the dissonant jarring of rational creation.

Again we come to Our Lord during the heat and press of the long day. Footsore and weary with pilgrimage of life, our minds dark with forebodings for those we love, and our hearts fearful for their good, we cast ourselves before our King, waiting for the "light that shineth in a dark place until the day dawn and the day-star arise in our hearts" and lo! when we depart and slowly close the door behind us, we are "a-wondering" whence it is that our spirits are so light, whence it is that the day is so bright and the music of the birds so sweet. "Surely,"

248

a faint voice tells us, "He hath borne our infirmities and carried our sorrows." "Our God is our refuge and strength; a helper in troubles which have found us exceedingly. . . . The Lord of Armies is with us; the God of Jacob is our protector." "O the depth of the riches of the wisdom and of the knowledge of God!" Who can fathom the mind of God, who from the unbeginning days has been plotting to win the love of our wayward hearts?

CONSIDER to what degree of happiness you are raised by prayer, and how great prerogatives are attributed to it. You thereby speak to God Himself, you entertain yourself and converse with Jesus Christ; you therein desire what pleases you, and you ask whatsoever you desire.

ST. JOHN CHRYSOSTOM

WORK AND SUFFERING CAN
BE PRAYERS

ANONYMOUS

PRAYER is an offering to God, rising like clouds of incense before His throne above. And that offering goes by the path of words and thoughts, by the path of toil, and also by the path of pain and weariness. One is as good as another, provided it be pointed out by the finger of God as *the* path by which He desires *your* offering to ascend. The blind fiddler earning coppers by the road-side, the poor patient on a bed of pain; these may be leading lives of continued and beautiful prayer, as truly as the cloistered religious who remains on bended knee for hours day by day. Believe this and act upon it; take it deeply to heart at this time; let it console and encourage you. *Qui laborat orat*—"he that works also prays"—is an old and true maxim. "He that suffers with patience and resignation prays continually and well."

Probably no period of your life has been more full of merit and given more glory to God, or been so full of true prayer and done so much for sinners, as the days of your sickness. It is a penitential prayer that indeed arises from your bed to the hands of God, but remember that the lips of our Lord, whence came His sacred words, are applied to your pain, and thence, as from some delicious fruit, He draws reparation and joy. Thus your prayer of pain is every moment bringing down graces on this poor world, by which souls are helped and saved, and all the while is registering a hundred-fold reward for you hereafter.

THINK of a little child trying to get at the handle of a door to open it, when it is too small to reach it. Any one would of course help it, by opening the door for the little thing. No more can God help opening the door for us, when we pray for high graces. God is more touched at our trying to reach that handle than words can say.

THE REV. FREDERICK WILLIAM FABER

A VILLAGE AT VESPERS

HILAIRE BELLOC

As I was watching that stream against those old stones, my cigar now being half smoked, a bell began tolling, and it seemed as if the whole village were pouring into the church. At this I was very much surprised, not having been used at any time of my life to the unanimous devotion of an entire population, but having always thought of the Faith as something fighting odds, and having seen unanimity only in places where some sham religion or other glozed over our tragedies and excused our sins. Certainly to see all the men, women, and children of a place taking Catholicism for granted was a new sight, and so I put my cigar carefully down under a stone on the top of the wall and went in with them. I then saw that what they were at was Vespers.

All the village sang, knowing the psalms very well, and I noticed that their Latin was nearer German than French; but what was most pleasing of all was to hear from all the men and women together that very noble good-night and salutation to God, which begins—

"Te, lucis ante terminum."

My whole mind was taken up and transfigured by this collective act, and I saw for a moment the Catholic Church quite plain, and I remembered Europe and the centuries. Then there left me altogether that attitude of difficulty and combat which, for us others, is always associated with the Faith. The cities dwindled in my imagination, and I took less heed of the modern noise.

I went out with them into the clear evening and the cool. I found my cigar, and lit it again, and musing much more deeply than before, not without tears, I considered the nature of Belief.

LET us be mutually mindful of each other, of one heart and one mind, let us ever on either side pray for one another, by mutual love lighten our burdens and difficulties. And if one of us shall, by the speediness of the divine command, depart hence the first, let our love continue in the presence of the Lord; let not prayer for our brethren and sisters cease in the presence of the mercy of the Father.

ST. CYPRIAN, TO CORNELIUS

"THE MOTHER OF FAITH"

THE REV. JEAN BAPTISTE LACORDAIRE

IF FORCE met not somewhere a barrier to arrest it, if there were here below but force against force, there would be no hope for the lonely and wretched. God vouchsafed to feebleness and to misery an arm which causes the sword to fall, calms anger, turns aside insult, makes amends for the inequality of conditions; He gave them prayer. Prayer is the queen of the world. Clothed in humble garments, with bowed head, with outstretched hands, it protects the universe by its supplicant majesty; it passes ceaselessly from the heart of the weak to the heart of the strong; and the lower the place whence its plaint ascends, and the greater the throne which it reaches, the more its empire is assured. If an insect could pray to us when we are about to tread upon it, its prayer could move us to great compassion; and as nothing is higher than God, no prayer is more meritorious than that which ascends to Him. It is prayer which re-establishes our relations with God, reminds us of His action, does Him violence without affecting His liberty, and is, consequently, the mother of faith.

WHAT a spectacle for heaven and earth is not the Church at prayer! For centuries without interruption, from midnight to midnight, the divine psalmody of the inspired canticles is repeated on earth; there is no hour of the day that is not hallowed by its special liturgy; there is no stage of human life that has not its part in the thanksgiving, praise, supplication and reparation of this common prayer of the Mystical Body of Christ which is His Church!

PIUS XI (May, 1932)

MATERIAL AIDS TO PRAYER

DOM HUBERT VAN ZELLER, O.S.B.

OBJECTS of piety stir the soul to prayer. Relics, ceremonies, pictures, the sacramentals are found to be an enormous help to prayer. That is what they are for. The material element here is obvious. From these helps that can be seen or performed, the soul goes on higher and makes use of helps that operate more interiorly: it meditates while doing the Stations of the Cross or while saying the rosary. The material element is still there, but the spiritual is beginning to take its place. The images which are formed in the mind are suggested by outward physical things, but it is the mind that is doing the work. It is the beginning of mental prayer. Imagination is painting the pictures, memory is framing them and hanging them up. But there is still too much of sense in this for the requirements of really interior prayer, so the soul goes on to the next stage where there is hardly anything of sense at all. This is where the intellect and will come into their own. This is spiritual prayer. This is the proper correspondence between the soul and God.

PICTURE God as saying to you, "My son, why is it that day by day you rise and pray, and genuflect, and even strike the ground with your forehead, nay, sometimes even shed tears, while you say to me: 'My Father, my God, give me wealth!' If I were to give it to you, you would think yourself of some importance, you would fancy you had gained something very great. Because you asked for it, you have it. But take care to make good use of it. Before you had it you were humble; now that you have begun to be rich you despise the poor. What kind of good is that which only makes you worse? For worse you are, since you were bad already. And that it would make you worse you know not; hence you asked it of Me. I gave it to you and I proved you; you have found—and you are found out! Ask of Me better things than these, greater things than these— Ask of Me spiritual things. Ask of Me Myself."

ST. AUGUSTINE

THE NATURE AND MEANING
OF THE ROSARY

THE REV. VINCENT MC NABB, O.P.

LET me explain a simple thing in a simple way. It is sometimes urged against the Rosary that it is a simple thing. Non-Catholics who don't know what it is and Catholics who don't know what it might become to them, think lightly of it because it is a simple thing. They see the beads. . . . It looks for all the world like a child's toy. . . .

If anyone complains to you that the Rosary is too simple you can always reply: "The simplest thing of all things is God." Now the Rosary is first of all a prayer, then it is a vocal and mental prayer, and finally it is a prayer full of the life, death and resurrection of Jesus Christ. . . .

The Rosary is vocal and mental prayer.

It is vocal prayer. We say it with our lips, and more than that, with our fingers. Deaf mutes speak with their fingers; you and I can pray with our fingers. When death comes to us we shall no longer be able to pray with our brains. It is our thought that is first attacked. When life is driven out and remains only in the extremities, God grant that we may pray with our finger-tips and clasp in our hands the image of Christ crucified. When anyone is praying, do not for God's sake criticize his way of prayer, but commend yourself to his prayers. I would almost beseech you not to criticize your *own* way of praying. It is a mustard-seed and may grow into something better.

The Rosary is mental prayer. Today the words "mental prayer" are almost unknown outside the Church. The old puritans used to say long prayers, but that has gone out of practice. Yet mental prayer flourishes with us. A man may pray anyhow, walking along the street, doing his daily work; his thoughts, wishes, love, hate, all may be turned to prayer. Even horrible imaginations may become prayer if they stir up revolt, if he flashes upon the screen of his imagination the beautiful mysteries of the life and death of Christ.

The Incarnation is the center of all our spiritual life. One of the means by which it is made so is the holy Rosary. There is hardly any way of arriving at some realization of this great mystery equal to that of saying the Rosary. Nothing will impress it so much on your mind as going apart to dwell in thought a little space each day on Bethlehem, Golgotha, on the Mount of Ascension.

SOME people do not like to take the medicine that would heal them, and call it nonsense. The Rosary is exactly that nonsense, which cures an amazing deal of nonsense. Call it spiritual homeopathy if you like. Many a proud spirit has been brought down by it—many a faddy spirit has been made patient by it. Many a queasy spirit has been made strong by it. Many a distracted spirit has become recollected by it. "The weak things of this world hath God chosen to confound the strong."

THE MOST REV. W. BERNARD
ULLATHORNE

WE HAVE all heard some evening in a country church the grave voices of the peasants reciting in two choirs the Angelical Salutation. Who has not met with processions of pilgrims passing through their fingers the beads of the rosary, and beguiling the tedium of the road by the alternative repetition of the name of Mary? When anything attains to perpetuity and universality, it must of necessity be in harmony with the wants and the destiny of man.

THE REV. JEAN BAPTISTE LACORDAIRE

XII

And the angel being come in, said unto her: Hail, full of grace, the Lord is with thee; blessed art thou among women.
                        St. Luke 1:28

"OUR LADY SAID YES FOR US ALL"

CARYLL HOUSELANDER

THE Church keeps the Feast of the Annunciation on the twenty-fifth of March. There is still a touch of austerity upon the earth, there is still a silver emptiness in the skies, but expectation of spring is already stirring the human heart, the bud is beginning to break on the tree, the promise of blossom has quickened the spirit of man.

This is the season when we celebrate the wedding of the Holy Spirit with humanity, the wedding of the Spirit of Wisdom and Love with the dust of the earth.

I think the most moving fact in the whole history of mankind is that wherever the Holy Spirit has desired to renew the face of the earth He has chosen to do so through communion with some humble little human creature.

In the instance we know of, it has not been to great and powerful people that the Spirit has come but to the little or the frightened, and we have seen them made new, and known that the subsequent flowering of their lives was nothing else but Christ given to them by that sweet impact.

It is always a love story, a culmination of love between the Spirit of Light and the Bride of the Spirit.

This is something which can happen to everyone now, but it could not have happened to anyone but for the *fiat* of the peasant girl in Nazareth whom the whole world calls Our Lady.

It is in Our Lady that God fell in love with Humanity.

It is upon her that the Dove descended, and the love of God for Humanity culminated in the conception of Christ in the human race.

When she surrendered herself to God, there was indeed a miraculous New Heaven and New Earth. The Spirit entered the world—light and wisdom and love, patience, fortitude, and joy entered the human heart and mind, and in the sight of God a springtime of loveliness woke in the world.

In the virginal emptiness of the girl, Mary of Nazareth, Christ was conceived; it was the wedding of God to a human child, and the wonder of it filled the earth for all time. . . .

It was so tremendous, yet so passive.

She was not asked to do anything herself, but to let something be done to her.

She was not asked to renounce anything, but to receive an incredible gift.

She was not asked to lead a special kind of life, to retire to the temple and live as a nun, to cultivate suitable virtues or to claim special privileges.

She was simply to remain in the world, to go forward with her marriage to Joseph, to live the life of an artisan's wife, just what she had planned to do when she had no idea that anything out of the ordinary would ever happen to her. . . .

The one thing that He did ask of her was the gift of her humanity. She was to give Him her body and soul unconditionally, and—what in this new light would have seemed absurdly trivial to anyone but the Child Bride of Wisdom—she was to give Him her daily life. . . .

It certainly seemed that God wanted to give the world the impression that it is ordinary for Him to be born of a human creature.

Well, that is a fact. God did mean it to be the ordinary thing, for it is His will that Christ shall be born in every human being's life and not, as a rule, through extraordinary things, but through the ordinary daily life and the human love that people give to one another.

Our Lady said yes.

She said yes for us all.

It was as if the human race were a little dark house, without light or air, locked and latched.

The wind of the Spirit had beaten on the door, rattled the windows, tapped on the dark glass with the tiny hands of flowers, flung golden seed against it, even, in hours of storm, lashed it with the boughs of a great tree —the prophecy of the Cross—and yet the Spirit was outside. But one day, a girl opened the door, and the little house was swept pure and sweet by the wind. Seas of light swept through it, and the light remained in it; and in that little house a Child was born and the Child was God.

Our Lady said yes for the human race. Each one of us must echo that yes for our own lives.

We are all asked if we will surrender what we are, our humanity, our flesh and blood, to the Holy Spirit and allow Christ to fill the emptiness formed by the particular shape of our life.

The surrender that is asked of us includes complete and absolute trust; it must be like Our Lady's surrender, without condition and without reservation. . . .

Our Lady has made this possible. Her *fiat* was for herself and for us, but if we want God's will to be completed in us as it is in her, we must echo her *fiat*.

IT IS impossible to think of any individual who has ever contributed or ever will contribute as much service toward the reconciliation of men with God as has Mary. It was she, surely, who brought the Savior to men when they were rushing on to their eternal destruction, at the very time, that is, when, "in the place of the whole human race," she received and wondrously consented to the message which the Angel brought to earth announcing the mystery of reconciliation. She it is "of whom was born Jesus" (Mt. 1:16), she who is His true Mother and for this reason is justly regarded as *Mediatrix to the Mediator.*

LEO XIII (1896)

THE MARY WE KNOW AND HONOR

THE MOST REV. ALBAN GOODIER, S.J.

THE name of Mary tells us all she has been and is to us; and the recollection fills us full of gratitude and fire. The name of Mary reminds us of what we are to her; and surely there is nothing that gives us a stronger sense of hope. "Sweet is thy name, O Mary, to the poor exile's heart," says the hymn, and it is true of each one of us, no matter who we may be—strong men who are not given much to sentiment, or weak women, who are sated with its excess; great sinners, whose consciousness of guilt, or whose reckless use of life has all but stifled all they had of affection, or innocent souls, still open to deep feeling; rich or poor, young or old,—for all of us the name of Mary is one that makes us raise our eyes. "In the name of Jesus every knee shall bow"; in the name of Mary every head shall be lifted up. . . .

Mary, the simple maid of Nazareth, yet declared "Blessed among women"; Mary, the outcast Mother of an outcast Child, and yet the very Mother of God; Mary, the silent wonderer, who spoke but little, and passed through life little noticed, who "understood not" all her Son said and did, but kept it and pondered it in her heart, while the rest of men forgot it; Mary, the secluded looker-on, while her Son went out to save mankind; Mary, the faithful companion, who stood there while her Son was hanged before her; Mary, triumphant now in Heaven, but with her mother's nature unchanged— this is the Mary of the Gospels, the Mary whom we know, the Mary whom God and men delight to honor.

Never have men been more dearly shown that notoriety is not greatness; nowhere does hiddenness more closely appear as identical with heroism; in no other case is sanctity, perfection seen more emphatically to consist in truth of life whose very evenness is its concealment.

GOD so created Mary that no one can fear her. Not justice, but mercy alone belongs to her. The Lord has endowed her with goodness and compassion so great that she can despise no one fleeing to her for help; she can deny assistance to no one pleading for it. God gave us Mary for a support in our weakness, a consolation in our sufferings, a help in our dangers, and a refuge in our sinfulness. Even crime cannot prevent our having recourse to this Mother so full of tenderness. When in danger of losing peace, let us flee at once to Mary.

THE REV. FATHER DE LEHEN, S.J.

PIUS XII PLEADS FOR
DEVOTION TO MARY

IN ALL cities, towns and villages, wherever the Christian religion thrives, there is a sanctuary, or at least an altar, in which the sacred image of the Blessed Virgin Mary is enshrined for the devotion of the Christian People. We desire that the faithful should throng thither in great numbers and should offer to our Most Sweet Mother not only private but also public supplications with one voice and with one mind. . . .

There are many things, indeed, which all, in the present circumstances, should petition from the protection, patronage and intercessory power of the Blessed Virgin. In the first place, let them ask that, with the assistance of Divine grace, the way of life of each one may be daily made more conformable to the Christian Commandments. . . .

Let them also ask with supplication that there may grow up a generous and promising youth, pure and unblemished, and that the beautiful flower of youth may not suffer itself to be infected by the corrupt breath of this world and grow up in vice: that their unbridled zeal and bursting ardor may be governed with even moderation, and that, abhorring all deception, they may not turn toward what is harmful and evil, but raise themselves up to whatever is beautiful, whatever holy, lovable and elevating.

United in prayer, let all implore that both in manhood and in old age men may shine by their Christian probity and fortitude; that domestic life may be conspicuous for inviolate faithfulness, that it may flourish through proper and saintly education of its children and be strengthened by true concord and mutual help.

Let them finally ask that the aged may so rejoice over the fruits of a well-spent life, that, as the end of their mortal course approaches, they may have nothing to fear, no pricks or anxieties of conscience, no cause for shame, but rather firmly trust that they will soon receive the reward of their long labors.

Let them, besides, supplicate the Divine Mother, asking bread for the hungry, and justice for the oppressed; return to the fatherland for those banished and exiled; a hospitable roof for the homeless; due liberty for those unjustly cast into prison or custody; for those, who, after so many years have elapsed since the last war, still silently languish and sigh in captivity, the long-desired homecoming; for those blind in body or soul, the joy of refulgent light. And for all those separated from each other by hatred, envy and discord, let them implore reconciliation through fraternal charity and through that harmony and peaceful industriousness which is founded on truth, justice and mutual friendship.

(September, 1953)

THERE is no surer or easier way to unite all men to Christ and to obtain through Him that perfect adoption of sons, by which we become holy and immaculate in the sight of God, than through Mary.

ST. PIUS X (1904)

CONSOLATIONS FROM MARY

JOHN HENRY CARDINAL NEWMAN

WHAT shall bring you forward in the narrow way, if you live in the world, but the thought and patronage of Mary? What shall seal your senses, what shall tranquilize your heart, when sights and sounds of danger are around you, but Mary? What shall give you patience and endurance when you are wearied out with the length of the conflict with evil, with the unceasing necessity of precaution, with the irksomeness of observing them, with the tediousness of their repetition, with the strain upon your mind, with your forlorn and cheerless condition, but a loving communion with her! She will comfort you in your fatigues, raise you after your falls, reward you for your successes. She will show you her Son, Your God and Your All. When your spirit within you is excited, or relaxed, or depressed, when it loses its balance, when it is restless and wayward, when it is sick of what it has not, when your eye is solicited with evil and your mortal frame trembles under the shadow of the tempter, what will bring you to yourselves, to peace and to health, but the cool breath of the Immaculate, and the fragrance of the Rose of Sharon?

I DID not greatly like the idea of prayers for my cure, when I myself had not prayed in a disinterested way since I lost the faith of my childhood. You lack simplicity when you are far from God.

One day when my illness was at its worst and I was suffering terribly, Madame Bloy came to see me and sat down at my bedside. She told me to pray, and said that she was going to give me a medal of the Blessed Virgin. I could not speak, but I felt extremely vexed at what seemed to me a great indiscretion. As Jeanne Bloy heard no answer, she placed the medal around my neck. In a moment, and without truly realizing what I was doing, I was confidently appealing to the Blessed Virgin, and then fell into a gentle and healing sleep.

RAÏSSA MARITAIN

"SHE IS OUR GUIDE"

PIUS IX

LET all the children of the Catholic Church . . . cherish, invoke, and beseech the Blessed Virgin Mary, Mother of God, conceived without original sin, and let them with entire confidence have recourse to this sweetest Mother of grace and mercy in all dangers, difficulties, necessities, doubts and fears. For nothing need be feared, and nothing need be despaired of, so long as she is our guide, our patroness, so long as she is propitious, she our protectress. Surely, she who bears toward us the affection of a mother, and who through her interest in the affairs of all mankind is solicitous for our salvation, and who has been appointed by the Lord as Queen of heaven and earth, and has been exalted above all the choirs of the angels and the ranks of the saints, surely, she, standing at the right hand of her only-begotten Son, our Lord Jesus Christ, and with a mother's prayer, is most influential in her intercession, and obtains what she asks and cannot be denied.

(1854)

POOR sinners! do not despair; raise your eyes to Mary, and trust in the mercy of this good mother.

ST. BONAVENTURE

MARY, MOTHER OF MANKIND

FRANCIS CARDINAL SPELLMAN

Within the twilit arch and window frame,
Beneath the mantle reverence wraps 'round stone,
Where thousands pause to leave a whispered prayer,
Or candle flame symbolic of their needs,
There stands a mother's image, marble-hued,
Her hands down-turned to claim each suppliant,
Strangers as well as friends, who here implore
In common need a Queen's uncommon love—
Nor are they strangers at this Mother's feet.

What is a mother? Who shall answer this?
A mother is a font and spring of life,
A mother is a forest in whose heart
Lies hid a secret ancient as the hills,
For men to claim and take its wealth away;
And like the forest shall her wealth renew
And give, and give again, that men may live.
A mother is a forest in whose trees
The breath of God makes melodies all day,
While in the night she shelters in her breast
The weak, the timid, the oppressed of earth.
A mother is a song begun in spring,
Deep'ning in summer and in autumn filled
With life's rich meaning and exalted truth.
A mother is a song flung from God's lips
When all the world was joyous at its dawn,
And echoes still His love across time's vale.
A mother is God's image here recast
And fairer now in Mary than in Eve—

The second casting has a flawless grace,
The second flowering a whiter rose.

We turn to Mary in her motherhood,
And ask of her that which her love concedes,
A mother's ceaseless care for one and all,
That men may take Christ's hand before too late,
May touch with Thomas His faith-giving wounds,
May know with Magdalen conversion's joy,
And come at last into that holy place,
The kingdom builded by a Father's love,
And sealed with the dear blood of His own Son,
And graced by Mary for her children's rest
When, in good time, this night shall be no more.
And kneeling humbly there before her shrine,
"O Mary Mother of Mankind," we pray,
"Unto thy Son our intercessor be,
Lift us to Him, bring down God's peace to us."

LET us be drawn to her [Mary] by a certain very power-ful impulse and let us trust to her confidently all that is ours—joys, if we rejoice; woes, if we are in trial; hopes, if we endeavor to rise to better things. If the Church falls on difficult times, if faith wanes and charity grows cold, if morals, private and public, grow worse, if any danger threatens the Catholic cause or civil society, let us have recourse to her begging help from heaven; in the supreme trial of death, when all hope, all help, is gone, let us lift up our eyes in tears and trembling, imploring through her pardon from her Son and eternal joy in heaven.

PIUS XI (1931)

"STAR OF THE SEA"

ST. BERNARD OF CLAIRVAUX

O THOU who findest thyself tossed by the tempests in the midst of the shoals of this world, turn not away thine eyes from the star of the sea if thou wouldst avoid shipwreck. If the winds of temptation blow, if tribulations rise up like rocks before thee, a look at the star, a sigh to Mary, will be thy aid. If waves of pride, ambition, calumny, jealousy threaten to swallow up thy soul, look towards the star, pray to Mary. If anger, avarice, or love of pleasure shiver thy frail vessel, seek the eyes of Mary. If horror of thy sins, trouble of conscience, dread of the judgments of God, commence to plunge thee into the gulf of sadness and the abyss of despair, attach thy heart to Mary. In thy perils, thy anguish, thy doubts, think of Mary, call on Mary. Let the name of Mary be on thy lips, in thy heart; and in taking refuge with her in petition lose not sight of the example of her virtues. Following her thou canst not wander. While thou prayest to her thou canst not be without hope. As long as thou thinkest of her thou wilt be in the right path. Thou canst not fall while she sustains thee; thou hast nothing to fear while she protects thee. If she favor thy voyage, thou shalt reach thy port of safety without weariness.

WHAT special consolation will the just man receive at the hour of death from the devotions performed in honor of the Mother of God, from the Rosaries he has recited, from his visits to her image, from his fasts on Saturdays, from his frequent attendance at her Confraternities! Mary is called the faithful Virgin. Oh, how great is her fidelity in consoling her faithful servants at the hour of death! A certain person devoted to the Most Holy Virgin said in his last moment to Father Binetti: "You cannot conceive the consolation which the thought of having served Mary infuses at the hour of death. If you knew the happiness I feel on account of having served this Mother. I am not able to express it."

ST. ALPHONSUS DE' LIGUORI

"OUR ADVOCATE"

THE MOST REV. FULTON J. SHEEN

WHEN the wine of your life is failing and your faith is weak, and your charity growing cold, go to her who at Cana's feast interceded to her Divine Son for the replenishing of the wine of gladness. When your whole frame racks beneath the tempter fly to the patronage of her Immaculate Heart, whose heel crushes the head of the serpent. When the cold hand of death is laid upon those whom you love, and your heart seems torn in twain, climb to the Hill of Calvary to be consoled by the Mother of Sorrows who is also the Cause of Our Joy. When sin corrodes your soul and rusts your heart and you are weary without God, then have recourse to Mary the Refuge of Sinners, for she, the Sinless One, knows what sin is—for she too lost her God. When the sweet inspirations of the Holy Spirit call you away from the passing tin and tinsel of earthly joys to the life of sanctity, then pray to her that you may follow her dictates to love Her Divine Son: "Whatsoever he shall say to you, do ye." Never was it known that anyone who fled to her protection, or asked her help, was left unaided. She is our advocate before the Father. Until Eternity dawns you who live in the hope of that eternal union with the Daughter of the Father, the Mother of the Son, and the Spouse of the Holy Ghost, pray from the bottom of your hearts that prayer which is the counterpart of the Our Father, the prayer of the children of Mary, and say to her:—

"Hail Mary, full of grace, the Lord is with thee. Blessed art thou amongst women, and blessed is the fruit of thy womb, Jesus.

"Holy Mary, Mother of God, pray for us sinners, now and at the hour of our death. Amen."

"THE MOTHER OF EACH INDIVIDUALLY"

RT. REV. MSGR. RONALD KNOX

IF THE Church, rich in the merits of so many saints, still has recourse first of all to her [Mary], still prefixes her name to every solemn invocation, what of ourselves, so unventuresome in our faith, so conscious of weakness and of past failure? Shall we not too call her in as an advocate for our private needs, however little their importance? The Queen of Heaven, yet she is a woman, of the same fashioning as ourselves. We say to her, as Mardochaeus said to Esther, "Remember the days of thy low estate; and do thou speak to the king for us, and deliver us from death." We have all of us this instinct about our Blessed Lady, that she is not merely the Mother of all our fallen race, but the Mother of each individually, not *our* Mother, but *my* Mother. Protestants sometimes laugh at us because we address ourselves, now to our Lady of Perpetual Succour, now to our Lady of Good Counsel, now to our Lady of Lourdes, and so on, as if they were so many different people. But the case is much worse than that, if they only knew; every individual Catholic has a separate our Lady to pray to, his Mother, the one who seems to care for him individually, has won him so many favors, has stood by him in so many difficulties, as if she had no other thought or business in heaven but to watch over him.

"ALL GRACE OF THE WAY"

MAISIE WARD

St. Philip at the Last Supper asked Our Lord how they were to find the way to follow Him to heaven, and Our Lord replied, "I am the Way." And now the Church tells us that in Our Lady is all grace of the way. It must be so because she bore Christ and brought Him into the world. It must be so because she is the Mother of the Mystical Body, the Mother of each one of us.

While with heart and mind we seek always to find Christ, our Way to heaven, we have to walk daily the ways of this world: of our life from morning till night and from night till morning.

We often need grace of the way when it is hard to

273

walk. We need hope of life and of virtue when our hope fails in the maze of this world. In the Rosary we rejoice, sorrow and triumph with Our Lady as she walks the same path we have to walk. But now she has reached the end: and we can think of her, too, restfully, as a "fair flower by the water brooks," giving to us the Water of Life. So the Church, telling us to rejoice on all Our Lady's feasts, gives us on this feast [Rosary Sunday] this thought in particular—grace of the way:

> Maria regnans in Patria
> Ora pro nobis in via.
> (Mary reigning in our Fatherland, pray for us
> who are still upon the way.)

For in thee is all Grace of the Way, and we shall find thee at our journey's end.

XIII

*Peace I leave with you; my peace I give
unto you; not as the world giveth, do I
give unto you.*

St. John 14:27

THE HIGHER ORDER OF
CHRISTIAN HAPPINESS

THE REV. JOSEPH RICKABY, S.J.

GIVE yourself over to God: ever put Him first in your
desires; and then, come what may, ever be cheerful. You
will have temptations against cheerfulness, plenty of
them, as also against purity. St. John Chrysostom says that
you should resist the one temptation as you resist the
other.

They then deserve ill of religion, and do the Church
great disservice, who bring on over the minds of good
people clouds of gloomy and distressing thoughts of God
and the ways of God. . . .

The world is full of troubles: Religion is not meant to
add to your troubles, but to lighten them. Religion is to
give rest to our souls (Matt. xi. 29,30). Oh, how many

more souls we should win to Christ if this doctrine of cheerfulness were more resolutely preached! Those preachers and spiritual writers who set the gospel in an unamiable light will have much to answer for.

Christ our Saviour's permanent offer to mankind through His Church is an offer, not only of eternal, but of temporal happiness also. It is an offer to the individual and an offer to society. . . .

Of course there is the doctrine of the Cross, the fundamental doctrine of Christianity. The Cross does not abolish suffering, but transforms it, sanctifies it, makes it fruitful, bearable, even joyful, and finally victorious. The happiness of the Christian is of a higher order than pleasure and enjoyment and comfort and ease. The cheerfulness of the Christian is the cheerfulness of the soldier in action in a Cause that he is enthusiastic for, and under a Leader in whom he is fully confident.

FOUR general reasons can be brought forward to show that perfect happiness consists neither in riches, nor in honour or fame, nor in power. Of which the first is that perfect happiness is not compatible with any evil. The second is that happiness is self-sufficient; once obtained no other human prize is wanting, such as good health and wisdom. The third is that no harm results from happiness, whereas sometimes *riches are kept to the hurt of the owner,* and this may also be the case with the other goods we have mentioned. The fourth reason is this; happiness wells up from within, but the goods we have mentioned come from external causes and often from good luck.

ST. THOMAS AQUINAS

276

STAND fast in peace and nourish your soul with the sweetness of heavenly love, for without it the heart has no life and life no blessedness. Yield not at all to sadness, for it is an enemy of piety. Why should anything trouble the servant of Him who will be our everlasting joy? Nothing should be capable of annoying or angering you, except sin. And even sorrow for sin must finally give way to holy consolation and sweet joy.

ST. FRANCIS DE SALES

"THE GREATEST JOY"

POPE ST. GREGORY THE GREAT

THERE is this difference, dearly beloved brethren, between spiritual and earthly pleasures. So long as we do not yet enjoy them, earthly pleasures are greatly desired; but when they are partaken to the full our liking for them soon begins to pall. Spiritual joys, on the other hand, are a matter of indifference to us when we do not possess them, but once we begin to experience them, we are filled with desire; the more we enjoy them, the more we desire them. With pleasures of the body, it is desire that delights us, realization which disappoints; with pleasures of the soul, desire is weak but spiritual experience is a source of the greatest joy. . . . When our souls are full of spiritual joy we long for more, since by tasting it we learn to desire it more eagerly. We cannot love what we do not possess, because we do not know its savor. For who can love what he does not know? Therefore the Psalmist admonishes us, "Taste and see that the Lord is sweet." As if he were to say more explicitly, "You know not His sweetness if you have never tasted it; let then your heart but taste the Bread of Life, that coming to know its sweetness you may be able to love it." Adam lost these delights when he sinned in Paradise; he went out from thence when he no longer opened his mouth to the heavenly food which filled him with spiritual joy. And so it comes to pass that we too, born into the miseries of this exile, find ourselves here below indifferent to our true good and not knowing what we should desire. This indifference is a malady which progresses as the soul withdraws itself from partaking of that heavenly food. . . . As we do not wish to taste interiorly the spiritual sweetness which is offered us, wretched as we are we love our own hunger.

OUR joy is to breathe deeply not the hot air of generalization but what is precise and straightforward, practical and life-giving. Our need is to have something within reach to cling to, something durable and solid with a recognizable shape and figure, a permanent mooring-stake, a wretched acknowledgement of something greater than ourselves to embody some kind of answer to our call for help; this is what idolatry tried to satisfy with its poor puppets. But instead of marble and wood, instead of those mannequins, impassive in the face of uncertainty, escaping reality in contortion, faith comes forward to bring us this living, active thing we need only breathe to have pass inside us, to be kindled by it and to be made all burning and alight by this meaningful and creative fire. . . . It lies entirely with you to be full of what made the

world and conquers the world, this elucidating Spirit
which nothing can withstand. Drink long and deep of this
proof of your own existence.

PAUL CLAUDEL

"JOY IS THE GIFT OF
THE CHURCH"

GEORGES BERNANOS

PAGANISM was no enemy of nature, but Christianity alone
can exalt it, can raise it to man's own height, to the peak
of his dreams. If I could get hold of one of these learned
gents who say I obscure the truth, I'd tell him! I'd say:
I can't help wearing an outfit like an undertaker's man.
After all, the Pope rigs himself up in white and the
cardinals in red, so what's the odds? But I'd have the
right to go around adorned like the Queen of Sheba because I'm bringing you joy. I'll give it to you for nothing, you have only to ask. Joy is the gift of the Church,
whatever joy is possible, for this sad world to share. Whatever you did against the Church, has been done against
joy. I'm not stopping you from calculating the procession
of the equinoxes or splitting the atom. But what would
it profit you even to create life itself, when you lost all
sense of what life really is? Might as well blow your brains
out among your test tubes. Manufacture "life" as much
as you like, I'd say! It's the vision you give us of death
that poisons the thoughts of poor devils, bit by bit, that
gradually clouds and dulls their last happiness.

THE Church and the spirit of worship it fosters probably does more to lift the spirit of man above the dreads of existence than anything else in the world. What surprised the pagan world when Christianity was introduced, was the gaiety of heart and light-heartedness of disposition, even in the face of the hard things of life, or it might even be death itself, that characterized these Christians. Their faith made them believe that they were in the hands of God and that His will would be done, and as they prayed every day in the prayer the Lord Himself gave them, "Thy will be done," they were ready to accept whatever happened as coming from His hand. No wonder they had the freedom of spirit of the children of God.

JAMES J. WALSH

LET the Brothers take care that they do not present the appearance of hypocrites, with dark and castdown mien, but that they show themselves glad in the Lord, cheerful and worthy of love, and agreeable.

ST. FRANCIS OF ASSISI

CATHOLICISM, A JOYOUS RELIGION

THE REV. B. W. MATURIN

THE Catholic faith unquestionably develops in the soul that is true to its teaching a sense of sin and the need of penitence and self-sacrifice such as is known in no other form of Christianity. She holds up in her great religious orders the highest standard of virtue and consecration, and in her doctrine of Purgatory and Indulgences she keeps before the minds of her children the consequences of sin even to the penitent. Forgiveness does not restore the penitent to the same position as the innocent; the temporal consequences of sin must be endured either in this life or the next before the soul can be admitted to the vision of God. The life of man on earth must be the life of penitence. And yet there is no religion so full of joyousness and brightness as the Catholic Church. All who witness its effects upon her children feel this; many wonder at, many are even disedified by it. It is one of the first things that strikes those who have entered it after experiencing some other imperfect form of Christianity. . . . Life is dark enough and hard enough as it is; the Catholic faith floods it with light and joy and hope. It impresses at once to the full the sterner side of religion, and its power of bringing joyousness and peace.

No ONE can live without joy, not even the Christian soul following the path of perfection. Indeed, a cheerful, happy, friendly spirit is more often encountered among believers and Christians than among unbelieving and irreligious men. Among the saints the proportion of joyous souls is particularly great. It is not the "moderns" in arts and letters, but the religious writers and poets and artists, that have most carefully cultivated, most warmly befriended, and most sincerely championed the cause of joy. In the history of modern literature we find a shocking number of famous names listed as foes of joy and prophets of pessimism, from Leopardim "the black swan of Recanati," to Schopenhauer, Nietzsche and their lugubrious disciples.

RT. REV. PAUL WILHELM VON
KEPPLER

LET those who belong to the devil hang their heads—we ought to be glad and rejoice in the Lord.

ST. FRANCIS OF ASSISI

PEACE WHICH THE WORLD CANNOT GIVE

THE MOST REV. JOHN CUTHBERT
HEDLEY, O.S.B.

TO THE Catholic believer there is, in this world, a Sacramental influence which, like the interposition of angelic powers in an earthly battle, is divinely connected with the establishment of peace. I use the word Sacramental in a wide sense—not merely for the Sacraments proper, but for all that visible dispensation of word and rite, of sacrifice and sacrament, which is the work of the Spirit of Jesus. . . . The priest at the altar prays that you may have peace. The giver of a Sacrament invokes peace upon you. When your sins are confessed, you are told to go in peace. Peace, joy, patience, tranquillity are the gifts the Church prays for throughout her liturgy. It is as if Christ, Who Said, "Peace be to you," when He appeared on the day of His Resurrection, were still saying it in the multiplied ordinances of that visible kingdom which thinly veils His hand and majesty from our sight. He seems to tell us how He feels for our life-long struggle; to remind us that He, and He alone, can calm our passions and kill our evil inclinations. For this purpose has He sought the earth; for this has He lived, died, and risen again. For this does the Church exist, for this the altar is erected; for this the sacred ministry is established. True, His fortifying and illuminating grace can visit us in any way He pleases. But the wide Sacramental ordinance, as it is established by Him in fact, so also is certainly grounded on wisdom; and it is to men the ordinary means of the peace which the world cannot give.

It is no stern and gloomy religion that our Lord teaches, but one full of present consolations and capable of kindling the noblest enthusiasm. The Christian whose life is all sadness, and whose only hopes lie beyond the grave, may then be sure that there is something amiss in his life or in his method. We know upon the highest authority that though the demands upon the soul are great and ever increasing, yet that the blessings even in this life are still greater. Indeed we may go further, we may test the reality of the virtue by the reality of the blessing.

THE REV. B. W. MATURIN

The characteristic of all those who have attained to perfect love of God, is an exceptional and imperturbable happiness, a cheerfulness so surprising, so permanent, so frank and childlike, that the prejudiced children of this world are tempted to get vexed at it. . . . Whoever encounters souls of this kind, perceives from their very appearance that their condition does not depend on the world around them but originates in their own spiritual depths. Their minds are not easily upset by storms, for their lives are built upon God who is inaccessible to the disturbing influence of the elements. They have naught to fear from God; they are at peace with themselves. Why then, should they not be happy?

THE REV. A. M. WEISS, O.P.

THE BEST USE OF OUR LIVES

THE MOST REV. ALBAN GOODIER, S.J.

OUR Lord said, at the conclusion of the Sermon on the Mount: "Sufficient for the day is the evil thereof"; and He went on to explain the potential application of His words: "Be not therefore solicitous for tomorrow; for the morrow will be solicitous for itself." By this He does not encourage callousness or want of foresight; He does not condemn thrift and prudence; He only warns us against the commonest source of all our vainest anxieties, the imaginary fear of what may be. Of all the many kindnesses of God to man, is there any kindness greater than the permission to live each day as a life apart, to make of each day a perfect thing, unspoiled by what may have been, still more by what may not be? And yet is there any kindness of God more commonly neglected, more recklessly thrown away?

The present alone is ours, and we are letting life slip through our fingers. The past is gone, whether for good or evil, to be stored up in better hands than ours. The future still belongs to God and love; and it is not the least of His wonderful mercies that He keeps it entirely to Himself. It is what I am now, not what I have been or shall be; what I do now, not what I have done or shall do; that here and now matters most, to me, and to God and to all the world besides. Those who face that which is actually before them, unburdened by the past, undistracted by the future, these are they who live, who make the best use of their lives; these are those who have found the secret of contentment. For such there is no day but it can be lived through, no matter what it may bring; there is no circumstance but it can be put to the best advantage, no matter how contrary and galling. "Now is the acceptable time, now is the day of salvation," cried out St. Paul, and he pushed on from day to day, saying every morning with the Psalmist: "Now I have begun," until he discovered that his many beginnings had enabled him to fight the good fight and to complete his course. To be ready for each day's duty, as it comes, that will make us ready, when it comes, for the duty of the last day of all.

THERE can be no better proof of a healthy soul than habitual cheerfulness. Christian cheerfulness is that modest, hopeful, and peaceful joy which springs from charity and is protected from the bacchic outbursts of sensual joy and the egotistical thrills and self-applauding laughter, as from melancholy gloom of self-absorbing sadness; of all which disorderly excesses true cheerfulness is the gentle but most decided adversary. It is the well-regulated vigor of spiritual life that throws off all morbid humors and depressing influences, refusing them a lodgment in the soul devoted to God.

THE MOST REV. W. BERNARD
ULLATHORNE

CHRISTIAN JOY

GILBERT K. CHESTERTON

IT IS said that Paganism is a religion of joy and Christianity of sorrow; it would be just as easy to prove that Paganism is pure sorrow and Christianity pure joy. Such conflicts mean nothing and lead nowhere. Everything human must have in it both joy and sorrow; the only matter of interest is the manner in which the two things are balanced or divided. And the really interesting thing is this, that the pagan was (in the main) happier and happier as he approached the earth, but sadder and sadder as he approached the heavens. The gaiety of the best pagans, as in the playfulness of Catullus or Theocritus is, indeed, an eternal gaiety never to be forgotten by a grateful humanity. But it is all a gaiety about the facts of life, not about its origin. To the pagan the small things are as sweet as the usual brooks breaking out of the mountain; but the broad things are as bitter as the sea. When the pagan looks at the very core of the cosmos he is struck cold. Behind the gods, who are merely despotic, sit the fates, who are deadly. Nay, the fates are worse than deadly; they are dead. And when rationalists say that the ancient world was more enlightened than the Christian, from their point of view they are right. For when they say "enlightened" they mean darkened with incurable despair. . . .

The mass of men have been forced to be gay about the little things, but sad about the big ones. Nevertheless (I offer my last dogma defiantly) it is not native to man to be so. Man is more himself, man is more manlike, when joy is the fundamental thing in him, and grief the superficial. Melancholy should be an innocent interlude, a tender and fugitive frame of mind; praise should be the permanent pulsation of the soul. Pessimism is at best an emotional half-holiday; joy is the uproarious labour by which all things live. Yet according to the apparent estate of man as seen by the pagan or the agnostic, this primary need of human nature can never be fulfilled. Joy ought to be expansive; but for the agnostic it must be contracted, it must cling to one corner of the world. Grief ought to be a concentration; but for the agnostic its desolation is special through an unthinkable eternity. This is what I call being born upside-down. The skeptic may truly be said to be topsy-turvy; for his feet are dancing upward in idle ecstasies, while his brain is in the abyss. To the modern man the heavens are actually below the earth. The explanation is simple: he is standing on his head; which is a weak pedestal to stand on. But when he has found his feet again he knows it. Christianity satisfies suddenly and perfectly man's ancestral instinct for being the right way up; satisfies it supremely in this; that by its creed joy becomes something gigantic and sadness something special and small. The vault above us is not deaf because the universe is an idiot; the silence is not the heartless silence of an endless and aimless world. Rather the silence around us is a small and pitiful stillness like the prompt stillness in a sick-room. We are perhaps permitted tragedy as a sort of merciless comedy: because the frantic energy of divine things would knock us down like a drunken farce. We can take our own tears more lightly than we could take the tremendous levities of the angels. So we sit perhaps in a starry chamber of silence, while the laughter of the heavens is too loud for us to hear.

IT IS not the purpose of Christ's religion to make men rich and comfortable; it is the purpose and end to lift them to worlds where riches and comforts cease to have value or meaning. They who turn from the things the vulgar crave, and seek the source of true life in the spheres to which the senses do not lead, alone know the infinite sweetness and joy there is in serving Him. They must learn to be cruel to themselves; to withstand even their lawful desires, if they would drink the living waters of the fountain of peace and bliss.

THE MOST REV. JOHN LANCASTER
SPALDING

XIV

*Let not your heart be troubled. You be-
lieve in God; believe also in me.*

St. John 14:1

SURRENDER BRINGS SERENITY

THE MOST REV. FRANÇOIS FÉNELON

HAPPY he who gives himself to God! he is set free from
the bondage of his own passions, from the judgment of
worldly men, from the malignity and tyranny of their
maxims; from their chilling, heartless mockery; from the
sorrows which the world ascribes to fortune, the inconstancy of friends, the snares of enemies; from his own
weaknesses; from the uncertainty of life, the terror of
an unholy death, the bitter remorse following on crimi-
nal pleasure; and, finally, from God's eternal condemnation. From all these countless evils he is delivered, inasmuch as committing his will into God's Hands, he only
desires whatever God wills, and thus finds comfort in
faith, and hopes amid all his fears. Surely it is great folly
to be afraid to give yourself to God, and to commit yourself to so enviable a condition!

Happy they who cast themselves blindfold and head

foremost into the Arms of the Father of Mercies and God of all comfort, as St. Paul says! Then the prominent wish is to know what is owing to God, and the greatest fear not to see clearly enough what He requires. A new light in the path of faith is as welcome as treasure-trove to a miser! The true Christian, come what may, accepts whatever befalls him, and wishes for nought withheld; the more he loves God the happier he is, and the highest perfection, so far from oppressing him, lightens his yoke.

What folly it is to be afraid of giving too much to God! It is to be afraid of being too happy, afraid of loving God's Will always, afraid of having overmuch courage to bear up under inevitable crosses, overmuch comfort in God.

IF ALL the sorrows and calamities of these stormy times, by which the countless multitudes are being sorely tried, are accepted from God's hands with calm submission, they naturally lift souls above the passing things of earth to those of heaven that abide forever, and arouse a certain secret thirst and intense desire for spiritual things. Thus, urged by the Holy Spirit, men are moved, and, as it were, impelled to seek the Kingdom of God with greater diligence; for the more they are detached from the vanities of this world and from inordinate love of temporal things, the more apt they will be to perceive the light of heavenly mysteries.

PIUS XII (1943)

To SUFFER God to work his will in us is a form of soul activity.

ABBÉ HUVELIN

"FIDELITY TO THE ORDER OF GOD"

THE REV. J.P. DE CAUSSADE, S.J.

SANCTITY consists in but one thing—fidelity to the order of God; and this fidelity is equally within the reach of all, whether in its active or in its passive part.

The active part of fidelity consists in fulfilling the duties imposed upon us either by the general commandments of God and the Church, or by the particular state we have embraced.

Its passive part consists in lovingly accepting all that God sends us each moment. . . .

Is there anything easier or more reasonable? What excuse can be urged against it? Yet this is all the cooperation God requires of the soul in the work of its sanctification.

He requires it of great and small, of strong and weak; in a word of all, at all times, in all places.

Therefore He only requires of us what is easy, since to attain eminent sanctity requires but a simple goodwill.
. . . He sends us the attractions and graces which facilitate the practice of them. He urges no one but in proportion to his strength and according to his attainments. . . .

Observe your life; of what does it consist? Of a mul-

titude of unimportant actions. Yet with these same unimportant actions God deigns to be content. This is the
cooperation required of the soul in the work of its perfection. God Himself expresses it too clearly to admit of
doubt: "Fear God, and keep His commandments: for this
is all man" (Eccles. xii. 13). That is to say, this is all that
is required on man's part; in this consists his active fidelity. Let him fulfil his part; God will do the rest. Grace,
working by itself, effects marvels which surpass the intelligence of man. For ear has not heard, eye has not seen,
heart has not felt, what God conceives in His mind, re-
solves in His will, executes by His power in souls wholly
abandoned to Him.

The passive part of sanctity is still easier, since it consists in accepting what very often we cannot avoid, and
bearing with love, that is, with consolation and sweetness,
what we too frequently endure with weariness and ir-
ritation. Again let me repeat, herein lies all sanctity. It is
the grain of mustard seed the fruits of which we do not
gather, because we fail to recognize it in its littleness.

WE ARE always in touch with God; everything that happens is His arrangement, His Providence, and a means
of grace, a push on to Heaven, only most people try to
go their own way, and thus put obstacles to God's action.
Once give yourself wholly to Him, and you realize that
He is always working outside you by circumstances, and
inside you by your thoughts and distractions,—unless you
resist. This is the way of pure love. It is very dark and
painful on the surface; but there is something behind
which is really strength and peace, only those are not

the right words,—there are no words—when you think of it there is nothing at all. But don't think,—and it carries you on.

DOM JOHN CHAPMAN, O.S.B.

HUMAN frailty is allowed sometimes to have some personal wish in which God wills otherwise. It would be difficult for you never to have any personal wish; but lift up your eyes at once to Him Who is over you. You are subject to Him and He is above you; He is the Creator and you are a creature; He is the Lord and you are the servant; He is the Almighty and you are a weak man. He corrects you and unites you to His will by the words, *Not what I will, but what Thou wilt, Father.* How are you separated from God when you will what He wills? Therefore you will be righteous, and praise will become you, because praise becomes the righteous.

ST. AUGUSTINE

THE REWARDS OF SURRENDER
TO GOD

THE REV. ALFRED H. DOLAN,
O. CARM.

OUR Lord said: "My yoke is sweet and My burden light," but He called it both a yoke and a burden. Let us not forget as we continue that He spoke of a burden and of a yoke.

The human heart, until it knows by actual experience, that His yoke is sweet, does ordinarily shrink from the yoke of God. Such a feeling comes to us all at times. We wonder and we fear what God will do with us if we give ourselves to Him. The poet Francis Thompson expresses that thought when he says: "Although I knew His love, yet was I sore adread lest having Him I must have naught beside." He is afraid that the surrender of self to God would mean loss not gain—afraid that having God, life would be hard and lonely. We have all felt or will feel that dread at times as we go through life.

Such a fear is experienced only by those who have not surrendered to God. Those who have surrendered to Him have no such fears, for they know by valid, genuine experience that He fills the soul, satisfies it; that life with Him as a Friend is not dull or lonely but rich and peaceful. They know that His burden is light and His yoke sweet. But that is a conviction that springs from experience.

HE WHO is united with the divine will, enjoys, even in this life, a perpetual peace. Whatsoever shall befall the just man, it shall not make him sad. Yes, for a man cannot enjoy greater happiness than that which arises from the accomplishment of all his wishes. He who wills only what God wills, possesses all that he desires; for whatever happens to him, happens by the will of God.

ST. ALPHONSUS DE' LIGUORI

You are the block, God is the sculptor. You cannot know what He is cutting you for, and you *never will* in this life. All you want is patience, trust, confidence, and He does it all.

DOM JOHN CHAPMAN, O.S.B.

SURRENDER BRINGS FREEDOM

RT. REV. ROMANO GUARDINI

IF MAN obeys and accepts the fundamental sacrifice of self-surrender and trusts himself to the Church; if he extends his ideas to the universal scope of Catholic dogma, enriches his religious sentiment and life by the wealth of the Church's prayer, strives to bring his conduct into conformity with the lofty, complete pattern of perfection, a pattern, moreover, which moulds the private life of the spirit presented by her communal life and her constitution, then he grows in freedom. He grows into the whole, without abandoning what is distinctly his own. On the contrary, for the first time he sees his individuality clearly when it is confronted with all the other human possibilities to be found in the Church. He sees its true significance to be a member of the whole. He perceives it as a vocation, a God-given task, the contribution made possible by his unique character as an individual, which he has to make towards the great common task of life and production.

THE soul that is not united solely to the will of God will find neither rest nor sanctification in any self-chosen means—not even in the most excellent exercises of piety. If that which God Himself chooses for you does not suffice, what other hand can minister to your desires? If you turn from the food the divine will has prepared for you, what viands will not prove insipid to a taste so depraved? A soul cannot be truly nourished, strengthened, purified, enriched, sanctified, except by the fulness of the present moment.

THE REV. J. P. DE CAUSSADE, S.J.

CONFIDENCE IN GOD

DOM JOHN CHAPMAN, O.S.B.

WE HAVE to become like little children. We have just the feelings which God gives us; we thank Him for them, whether they are joys or temptations. We must not worry about our souls. We can't do much. We must remove obstacles (chiefly by continually humbling ourselves and being little) and God does the rest.

Therefore have *absolute confidence* in God, and none in yourself. Also *pray,* quite definitely and absolutely, for whatever you think God wishes you to pray for, whether for yourself or for others; and make up your mind that you will get it not because you deserve it, but because God is good.

You are on the look out for "consolation"; merely because you still imagine that you are not serving God properly, when you are in dryness. Make up your mind once for all that dryness is best, and you will find that you are frightened at having anything else! Embrace aridities and distractions and temptations, and you will find you love to be in darkness, and that there is a super-sensible light that is simply extinguished by consolation.

Do you know when people really become spiritual? It is when they become the slaves of God and are branded with His sign, which is the sign of the Cross, in token that they have given Him their freedom.

ST. TERESA OF ÁVILA

XV

*And calling the multitude together with
his disciples, he said to them: If any man
will follow me, let him deny himself and
take up his cross and follow me.*

St. Mark 8:34

THE JOY OF RENUNCIATION

THE REV. BENEDICT WILLIAMSON

RENUNCIATION, that is the *way*, if you want a joyous,
happy life; then you can be happy under any conditions,
and even, if some of the very few wants you have retained
as necessary are, on occasion, missing, you can still "keep
smiling." Why religion and long faces should always be
associated I really cannot think; joy full and complete,
that is the note of the Catholic religion; it is because
people have got hold of the wrong religion in England
that long faces and piety are supposed to be identical.
Nothing will give you so much joy as renunciation. Every
sacrifice you make will increase it; there is no joy like the
joy of sacrifice. . . .

At every turn we are in conflict with the world-spirit,
at every turn, as a consequence, we must be renouncing
and sacrificing ourselves and our own interests. . . .

It is because religion has been presented to the people

of today in this washed-out, milk-and-water way that they feel no desire for it; they see it as quite useless in face of the stern reality of life. The Catholic religion is a sacrificing religion, it demands sacrifice, unflinching service, utter loyalty. There is no watering down, no softening of the hard sayings of Eternal Truth; there they are, *you must take the whole or leave the whole.* . . .

"If any man will come after Me, let him deny himself daily, take up his cross, and follow Me." That means renunciation. It is in the most austere and severe religious orders that you find joy, happiness and laughter. Renunciation and self-sacrifice, that is the way to perfect joy.

ONE thing, and one thing alone, thoroughly redeems life and makes it worthwhile; to learn to suffer in patience, in humility, in confidence—in confidence that suffering has a meaning and purpose; not the only meaning and purpose, but the supreme meaning and purpose of life. In learning to suffer so, there is peace, and more than peace; just in proportion as the lesson is deeply and thoroughly learned, there is positively joy. This paradox is the central fact of existence so far as the human race is concerned, and it constitutes the mystery which lies in the heart, or rather in the root of Catholicism, and which the Church "gets over" somehow, into the minds, or at any rate into the lives, of all her children, even the most ignorant, stupid, or superstitious, provided they are sincere and earnest. This is fact Number One about Catholicism, and outweighs in its importance all other facts. Catholicism is the Religion of the Crucifix, the Way of the Cross.

THE REV. RUSSELL WILBUR

THE CROSS AS A SYMBOL OF
ULTIMATE JOY

THE REV. PAUL WILHELM
VON KEPPLER

THE cross with its stern lines,—a cold, bare, branchless
tree with its rough-hewn stumps for arms,—is indeed at
first sight a sad and joyless thing to look at, so true an
image is it of harsh contradiction, so good a symbol of
bitter pain. Yet men find that the cross possesses a certain
beauty. In its sturdy clear-cut, well-proportioned form
they see a picture of steadfastness, of aspiring effort, of
opposition conquered and contradictories reconciled.
The sight of a man hanging in agony upon the cross
arouses, at first, no sense of joy, it is true. Yet there is a
wellspring of joy in the sure faith, that the Divine Hero
bleeding on the cross is dying in battle against the fiercest
foe of joy and of salvation, and conquering as He dies.
The cross becomes the symbol of victory and thereby
the symbol of joy. Darkness and gloom are dispelled and
everywhere is shed the glory of the resurrection. In its
light, the tree of the cross becomes the tree of life, of
resistless power; the dried trunk is clothed with blossoms
and fruit; and out of the crown of thorns spring forth
roses.

Thus also it is with the cross and the crucifixion in the
life of each individual Christian. That a man should take
up his cross daily; that he should not only bear his cross,
but crucify the flesh, the old man—these are not forced
figures of speech, but stern demands which certainly do
seem likely to lead far away from joy. Yet the battle to

which they summon is waged not against joy, but against joy's worst enemies. The cross obliges us to renounce the apples of Sodom, the wild cherries of sin, which are really no joys at all, but it does not demand a total renunciation of legitimate natural joys; it only insists that they be used in moderation and with a good intention. This much would be required not by Christian morality alone, but by reason and health as well. Excessive enjoyment always begets disgust. Unrestricted activity and gratification of the sensual instincts does not add to the sum of joy, but ruins both joy and the man.

UNDER the influence of fear we support the cross of Christ with patience; under the more inspiring influence of hope we carry the cross with a firm and valiant heart; but under the consuming power of love we embrace the cross with ardor.

ST. AUGUSTINE

THE LESSON OF THE CROSS

THE REV. FIDELIS RICE, C.P.

THE first lesson of the Cross is to show us what matters most. All the confusion in the world results from not knowing the proper order of things, or from not following that order. Indeed, peace has been defined as the "tranquility of *order*." The supreme lesson of the Cross is that the things of God come first. Nothing—absolutely nothing—can be permitted to interfere with the things of God. "Seek ye therefore first the kingdom of God and His justice" (Matt. 6:33). The Cross has etched that truth forever in the sky against the crest of time. This is the great primal Wisdom that the Cross proclaims; the first great key to human happiness. The centuries that have passed since that great proclamation of Wisdom was first lifted against a lowering sky upon a Judean hilltop have only proved that all the darkness that has fallen since has come because that Wisdom was forgotten.

The second great lesson of Wisdom that the Cross teaches is that sin is an utter abomination. It is because the things of God come first that sin is such a hideous evil, for it seeks to invert God's order and God's scheme of things. It says, in effect: "God is not as important as this pleasure, or these riches, or this honor." It turns existence upside down and puts heaven in things of earth. And so the Cross is raised.

If men had to resort only to abstract principles in solving life's problems, they might easily convince themselves that there are circumstances and times when sin is quite legitimate and quite justified. They cannot take refuge in the weak excuse when they are confronted with the Cross. It is too stark a challenge to admit of subterfuge. It shuts off all the avenues of escape. Neither above nor below, neither to right nor to left, shall we find an outlet for sin, for the Cross reaches out to embrace all directions. It is as all-embracing as the air we breathe. It permits no compromise with sin. It is as incisive as a surgeon's scalpel cutting out the roots of malignancy. This dynamic challenge looms up always on the horizon of life. You cannot have the Cross and sin. And so the Cross speaks with a trumpet blast, when even the noblest philosophy only lisps. Henceforth men need not guess as to what constitutes evil; because of the Cross, we know. This basic wisdom is fastened to the rough-hewn Cross: in sin there is only destruction; that way madness lies.

A third great lesson of Wisdom which the Cross teaches us is the mysterious value of suffering. All the great minds of all ages had grappled with the problem of suffering, sorrow, and frustration. They had never found the answer. For them, suffering was always evil, always degrading, always abhorrent. The Cross of Christ changed all that. It became a guidepost at the crossroads of time, wherein there was suspended a message penned in crimson on the thin parchment of the body of Christ, that all who passed might read. Suffering is the mysterious transforming power hidden within the heart of the universe. It is only this power that can make life over again. "Unless the grain of wheat fall into the ground and die, it remains alone. But if it die, it brings forth much fruit." (John 12:24, 25) The Cross proves that teaching right.

The Cross of Christ unlocks the great mystery of suffering. No one need grope blindly again to learn why suffering must be. We tread the wine press of sorrow that we may make wine to gladden the hearts of men. The wheat of life is crushed, that the bread of life may be made. Sorrow is only a process—the agonizing process—of being reborn and remade. It is not frustration, but achievement. It is not failure, but triumph. It is not the end of everything, but the beginning. It is not death, but life.

THE Catholic point of view is not to be identified with some vague variety of "Consolation"—a kind of pulling down the blinds so as not to see the storm. It is basically a heroic manifesto, a decision to follow and serve, though earth "spin like a fretful midge." . . . Our banners are not to be kept stainless, intact, in their cases, but to be carried onward, through conflict and surrender, to the victory. The whole will be in the shred we retain; the rest is to be accounted for by the fighting.

And what is the fighting for? Not to win God, certainly, in whose service we are, but with His help to become triumphant over the rest of reality, to understand it, to subject it to the great plan according to which our bastions are to be builded, in a word to "domesticate" it.

GEORGE N. SHUSTER

COMFORT FROM CALVARY

THE REV. VINCENT MCNABB, O.P.

If we, who are children of the Church, have given ourselves up to her teaching during the last few weeks and especially during the last few days, we shall be in a state to receive the impressions of Good Friday. For the Church has gradually been shorn of things that appeal to us. The color of the vestments has changed to purple and even to black. The music of the Church has somewhat changed its character. Even to hear you singing the "Stabat Mater" without accompaniment would strike an outsider as strange. They would say: "What is the matter? What has gone wrong?" And then this church, which is so much to us, has become now simply a meeting-place.

You know what I mean. The tabernacle doors are flung open. The Blessed Sacrament has been taken away. Our church, which is unique, has become like other things. The King is not there. There is a strange and unwonted chill. And a man must be very dead to Catholic sentiment if Good Friday doesn't make a great difference to his train of thought.

Today a most unusual thing has taken place; we are keeping a day of death. This is one of the days when the Church fearlessly confronts the thought of death. It is a day taken from the heart of spring, when, in spite of sunshine, we face death and eat bread covered with the ashes of the tomb. Death, though an angel from the side of God, comes first to make us fear. . . .

The whole world is putting something to death and for the rest of time will bear on its brow the blood of the great crucifixion. And then we suddenly realize that we who have been criticizing are ourselves a part of the group. In ten thousand different ways and by ten thousand subtleties of treason we have put Him to death again and again. We have put Him to death in our own soul; we have been here with this crowd, here with that, round the Cross. . . .

There is one last thought and it is one of comfort— not, indeed, comfort from ourselves, cold-blooded executioners that we are, who slew Him by our lust or pride —but comfort from the one slain, the superb miracle worker, Who wrought His greatest miracle when men thought Him all undone. . . . The last thought is of God's overwhelming mercy and love. He who came to pursue us and catch us in the tissues of mercy, turns and rends us with love. . . .

Have we ever heard the word of consolation uttered in our souls when we have reached out to something beyond ourselves, when we have done a good thing and blushed to find a new strength and new courage in our hearts? There was a flame within us, a new incendiarism. Has it left us just as before, or has it burnt down the old bad walls of sin and made us a new kingdom unto God?

There are then great truths that only enter into a soul by tearing it up by the roots and imposing their jurisdiction on the whole being. Henceforth the world is new to us. . . .

Such a word is the word of crucifixion. "Indeed, this Man was the Son of God." [St. Mark xv:39] That is the word. Everything hinges about that. If it is true everything is new, fateful, tremendous, almost infinite. The earth becomes a risen sepulchre. The dead rise up and walk. If He is the Son of God, every trifle connected with His death becomes tremendous in its issues. . . .

Is the Crucifixion a mere tragedy of death? "Indeed, this Man was the Son of God." God could not call us from the thought of mere bloodshed and death better than by reminding us Who it was that suffered. It is God's great effort to speak in terms of human suffering, God's pathetic moan: "I thirst." From henceforth the world is new to us. It has heard its sermon. The Preacher has preached. And in the same way that there is no new Sacrifice in the Church but only the re-echo of the old, so there is no new sermon, but the old sermon preached again and again, Christ crucified. Every sermon is a Good Friday sermon. Whether we pipe to those who dance or sing to those who mourn, we must ever speak of Golgotha, and the sermon from this pulpit untouched by note of crucifixion and suffering would be as the murmur of a distant drum or as nothing.

WHEN everything is rosy in life then the Catholic Church may fail in its appeal, but when trials come into life, when money and health and friends fail, then the Church is a very alluring mother to come to in order to find consolation. There would be no need of religion if life were one long sweet song and if there were no such things as suffering and disappointment. But the only solution for the mystery of suffering is that there is another life and that the Church must guide us along the path that leads to that other life.

JAMES J. WALSH

"THE CONSOLING TRUTH"

THE REV. JOSEPH MC SORLEY, C.S.P.

THE lesson we most need to learn is that which teaches us how to bear trials and endure suffering. Inevitably nature will protest against what is unpleasant, nature will argue, nature will rebel.

How many good people, even apparently spiritual people, complain when trial comes, almost as if they thought our Lord had promised that no disciple of His should ever have to bear a cross. How many times temporal prosperity is expected, even demanded, as if it were the fixed reward of a virtuous life. How often, alas, do we not find people alienated from religion because church-going or the keeping of the Commandments has not protected them from material misfortune!

But after the warning given by Christ's own lips, who can reasonably persist in so gross a distortion of our Lord's teaching? Has He not told us beforehand to anticipate trials, injustice, pain, even death? Did He not bid us remember His Word, when these things should come to pass—and remembering it be comforted by the knowledge that His Spirit is with us?

Yet this is precisely what we most commonly forget— the consoling truth that despite all hardships, and amid every hardship, the heart of the faithful disciple is the abode of the Spirit of God. If we could but remember that fact constantly, then, like the martyrs of old, we should be invulnerable of soul. Nothing could hurt us; nothing could defeat us; out of every loss and every pain we should draw occasion of new sanctity to ourselves.

BEYOND all the gifts of grace which God grants to His friends through the Holy Spirit is that of conquest of self, of willingly accepting sufferings, injuries, insults, and discomforts for His love. We cannot glory in all the other gifts of God, since they are not ours, but His. And for this reason the Apostle says: "What have you that you did not receive from God? And if you did receive it from Him, wherefore do you glory therein as if you had it of yourself?" But we may glory under the weight of sorrow and affliction, since this is our own; hence the Apostle says: "I would not glory save in the cross of our Lord Jesus Christ."

ST. FRANCIS OF ASSISI

SUFFERING AS A CONDITION TO SPIRITUAL HAPPINESS

E. I. WATKIN

IF THE Christian doctrine be true . . . there is no reason to expect an excess of happiness in this life. On the contrary Christ has promised His followers suffering in this world, joy in eternity; the cross here, the crown hereafter. Indeed, the Church teaches, and with the Church is the unanimous consent of all mystics and deeply religious souls, sinful man cannot in the very nature of things attain to the spiritual happiness for which he was created, without suffering. Purgatorial suffering, whether in this world or in the next, is the inevitable passage and entrance into the Divine Joy. There is, moreover, so the experience of the noblest and holiest souls bears it consentient witness, a peculiar and a sovereign joy in the suffering itself when rightly borne, "a joy which surpasses all other joys attainable on earth, and renders the suffering as desirable to them as it is hateful to those who have not shared their secret." . . .

There is in suffering a value which happiness does not possess. Not only my faith but my reason, compels me to affirm this, notwithstanding all my loathing of pain and my thirst for pleasure. Some one I once knew said there could be no good God who allowed suffering of the innocent. That same person in another context told me that no one was really understanding and sympathetic who had not suffered.

This does not prove that all suffering possesses this goodness. If it could, there would be no problem of suffering. Nor is it to say that suffering is ultimately better than happiness. Even the saints look forward to an eternity of happiness beyond the suffering of this life. . . . But the experiences of the saints, and the deepest if occasional experience of the average man, does prove in suffering a value for which we can conceive no other equivalent. Hence the existence in the world of suffering, pre-eminently of that personally undeserved or vicarious suffering which alone possesses in its fulness this peculiar worth, is a good and not an evil. . . .

To the objection that evil is a denial of God's providence in the world, I would ask: Which, even to our feeble vision, is better and worthier of God—to permit no suffering or to reveal Himself in a suffering humanity? To remove the possibility of defeat and failure or to give the possibility of conquest and attainment? To obtain external mechanical perfection by quick but mechanical methods productive only of machines, or in the patience of humanity's slow travail to bring about a living and therefore free organism? To make of man a slave who knows not his master's purpose, or a son who by the very means of suffering and sin has come to a son's free service in communion and free self-identification with his Father's purpose and life. . . .

If we in our human ignorance can dimly perceive the supreme and unique value of free will and victory, and the love which involves struggle and victory, we can surely believe that it was in infinite wisdom and love that God willed their existence even at the cost of all the evil, alike of suffering and of sin, involved in their attainment. The problem of evil remains, and must remain unsolved. But in the divine revelation given to us in Christ and His Church of the divine purpose in the world, we have at least an indication of the nature of that solution. A ray of light emerging from rain clouds on the faint orange dawn in the eastern sky, reveals to us the presence of a hidden sun and the quarter from whence to expect its appearance. Such is the light of Christ to the evil in the world.

Ask and you shall receive. He came only for that, to ask us to ask and not to cease asking, nor to cease towards Him our attitude of desire and aspiration. To this end none of the powers He gave us and none of the absence of powers, none is useless or despicable, none but is worth trying out wholeheartedly. Intelligence, study, mourning, joy, penance, humility, the spirit of indignation and justice, the constriction and dilation of the heart, all is to the good! But so is dryness, so is tediousness, when we have to take ourselves by the scruff of the neck to get ourselves along to the end of our *Via Crucis.*

PAUL CLAUDEL

THE COSTS AND COMPENSATIONS
OF CHRISTIANITY

THE REV. IGNATIUS SMITH, O.P.

THE costs of genuine Christianity were anticipated by Christ Himself and He told His followers the truth. He did not paint for them an alluring picture of earthly happiness as a reward for their loyalty. He did not deceive them with roseate promises of heaven on earth for their fidelity. He sought no followers under misrepresentation. He told them the truth. He said that His religion would be a yoke and a burden—a yoke that was sweet and a burden that was light—nevertheless a yoke and a burden. He told them that to follow Him meant to take up a cross that must be carried up the Calvary of life, that Christian life was to be a life of sacrifice. . . .

The definite costs that Christians must pay for their membership with Christ were indicated by the Master in that incomparable sermon on the mount. There, in pointing out to them how to find happiness He mentioned the costs they would pay for their loyalty to Him. To live with Him would bring them poverty, in comparison with the riches of those who lived without conscience. In the midst of violent aggression and pride they would have to stand by meek and submissive. In a sea of unrestrained pleasure and laughter they would have to shed tears of sorrow and loneliness. In the epidemics of irreligion and spiritual indifference they would have to be unlike the rest of men. In pandemics of rage and fraternal hatred they would have to keep alive in the world universal love and peace. In the contagions of lust and immorality they would have to stand unsullied for the sake of purity of heart and life. When other men would spread sedition and misunderstanding they would have to stand, even alone, in their efforts for peace. Even if the rest of the world should lose its appreciation of suffering and the motives for suffering, they, His followers, were to look at the blood-stained Cross on Calvary, and to suffer with Christ. . . .

But genuine Christianity has many compensations. I

do not emphasize the delayed pleasure and enjoyment that it holds out until the future life. I do not stress the happiness of future existence. There is not time. I refer to the compensations which genuine Christianity provides here.

Christianity gives sacredness to human personality, to both body and soul. It saves souls. It sanctifies the home. It ennobles Womanhood and motherhood. It gives certainty,—certain and uplifting answers to the great problems of origin and destiny. It gives me Christ for imitation and this is a compensation when I realize that so many persons have gone wrong and are unhappy because they have had no one uplifting to imitate. Christianity gives me a wider world in which to live. One that reaches out to my loved ones departed. Christianity gives peace of mind and conscience by giving release from the torturous tauntings of past misdeeds. Christianity gives me confidence in myself by placing me in direct and immediate contact with Jesus Christ. Christianity gives me pride,— pride in the Founder of my religion, pride in the divinity of His teaching, pride in the civilization created by His doctrine, pride in its culture, charity, learning, architecture, music, art, sculpture, and literature, pride in an institution endowed by the Omnipotent God with imperishable and uncrushable life. These,—all of them, —are compensations that can not be purchased by wealth or irreligion; and they are enjoyments without which men can not be happy.

The happiness of Christian life is shut against no one. The gates of mercy are open to all. A woman taken in adultery and about to be stoned to death by the men who had probably sinned with her is rescued by the merciful Jesus. She is forgiven and consoled. A Magdalene, of tempestuous beauty and of many sins, is forgiven much because she loved much. She is welcomed into the circle of the Master's friends. A dying thief on Calvary calls for happiness, confesses his sins, asks for pardon, and is rewarded by a dying Christ with life eternal with Jesus. That same invitation is repeated by Christ today to live with Him and for Him. "Come to me, all you that labour and are burdened, and I will refresh you."

IT IS commonly said that the Catholic faith is a good religion to die in, but a hard religion to live by. Certainly it affords no promise of immunity from suffering for the life that now is. But who *is* immune from suffering. The world is not divided into men who suffer and men who do not suffer, but into men who carry the cross and men who do not and will not carry the cross. To carry the cross means, whatever one suffers, to offer it up in union with the sufferings of Christ and in accordance with the will of God. Also to dare and do what involves suffering, when it is *better for me to do it*. Querulous, cowardly, self-indulgent people refuse the cross: are they the happier for their self-indulgence? Sometimes we see them sink into becoming the most miserable of mankind.

THE REV. JOSEPH RICKABY, S.J.

"A DEATH WHICH LEADS
TO A LIFE"

DÉSIRÉ JOSEPH CARDINAL MERCIER

THE Christian is not isolated, lost in the wood, in a fleeting moment of time. He lives in the immortal life of the Church, to which he belongs, and in which he shares all the phases of birth, growth, struggle, death and resurrection. The work of the Church, the joint work of Christ and of His Members, is the redemption of the world. And because institutions, established by the providence of God prosper in proportion as they are in accord with the spirit of their Founder, we have to take the spirit of Christ, to open our hearts wide to the action of the Holy Spirit, to accept our share in the Passion of our divine Savior, before having any pretension to the honor of sharing the triumph of His Resurrection, of His Ascendancy, of His reign at the right hand of the Father Eternal. Listen to the sentence from the author of *The Imitation of Christ:* "If you do not give up your soul to suffering without reservation; if you cannot await with firmness all the will of our God of love, do not say, and do not allow it to be said, that you love Him." . . .

Christianity is essentially a death which leads to a life; the death of the old man which gives birth to the new; the decomposition in the earth of the grain of wheat from which is germinated a more plenteous life. Christianity is the work of Christ Who acquired, by His death, the right to unite our souls to Him, to pour His own life into them, by means of the effusion of His Holy Spirit in us. It is, therefore, the sacrifice of Christ that our

315

lives ought, above all, to show forth. This is the price of our personal sanctification and of the success of our apostleship.

WHY dost thou dread to take the cross, sith it is the very way to the kingdom of heaven, and none but that? In the cross is health, in the cross is life, in the cross is defense from our enemies, in the cross is the infusion of heavenly sweetness, in the cross is the strength of mind, the joy of spirit, the highness of virtue, and the full perfection of all holiness; and there is no health of soul nor hope of everlasting life but through virtue of the cross. Take the cross, therefore, and follow Jesus, and thou shalt go into life everlasting. . . . If thou die with Him, thou shalt live with Him; and if thou be fellow with Him in pain, thou shalt be with Him in glory. . . .

If thou wilt gladly bear the cross, it shall bear thee, and bring thee to the end that thou desirest, where thou shalt never have anything to suffer.

THOMAS À KEMPIS

XVI

Jesus said to her: I am the resurrection and the life; he that believeth in me, although he be dead, shall live.

St. John 11:25

LIFE'S INTIMATIONS OF ETERNITY

JOHN HENRY CARDINAL NEWMAN

OUR earthly life . . . gives promise of what it does not accomplish. It promises immortality, yet it is mortal; it contains life in death and eternity in time; and it attracts us by beginnings which faith alone brings to an end. I mean, when we take into account the powers with which our souls are gifted as Christians, the very consciousness of these fills us with a certainty that they must last beyond this life. . . .

Over and above our positive belief in this great truth, we are actually driven to a belief, we attain a sort of sensible conviction of that life to come, a certainty striking home to our hearts and piercing them, by this imperfection in what is present. The very greatness of our powers makes this life look pitiful; the very pitifulness of this life forces on our thoughts to another; and the prospect of another gives a dignity and value to this life which promises it; and thus this life is at once great and little, and we rightly contemn it while we exalt its importance. . . .

To those who live by faith, every thing they see speaks of that future world; the very glories of nature, the sun, moon, stars, and the richness and the beauty of the earth, are as types and figures witnessing and teaching the invisible things of God. All that we see is destined one day to burst forth into a heavenly bloom, and to be transfigured into immortal glory. Heaven at present is out of sight, but in due time, as snow melts and discovers what it lay upon, so will this visible creation fade away before those greater splendors which are behind it, and on which at present it depends. In that day shadows will retire, and the substance show itself. The sun will grow pale and be lost in the sky, but it will be before the radiance of Him whom it does but image, the Sun of Righteousness, with healing on His wings, who will come forth in visible form. . . . For this glorious manifestation the whole creation is in travail, earnestly desiring that it may be accomplished in its season.

By LEADING a good life you may be hopeful about seeing Him by whom you are seen when leading a bad one. For in doing this you are seen, and cannot see; but in leading a good life, you are both seen and you see. . . . Nathaniel said to God, whom he did not yet know, "How didst Thou know me?" And our Lord replied, "Whilst thou was under the fig tree, I saw thee." Christ sees you in these shadows; shall He not see you in His eternal light? . . . Prepare yourself to see Him in glory by whom you were seen in mercy.

ST. AUGUSTINE

"I AM THE RESURRECTION"

FATHER JAMES, O.F.M. CAP.

THE Thing stressed by Christ is a Resurrection. "I am the resurrection and the life; he that believeth in Me, although he be dead, shall live. And everyone that liveth, and believeth in Me, shall not die for ever." This implies a survival not of soul and spirit only, but the vital restitution of human nature, soul and body, and a future world, "a new earth and sky" which, as has been beautifully said, may be no less different from the world of our sensible experience than is a symphony of Beethoven from the complicated mechanism which has been formed to transmit it. . . .

Jesus Christ addressed His message to *all* men; He put a premium on neither race nor aristocracy; to every man, to slaves and freemen, to Gentile and Jew, He offered a goal of life that was beyond all knowing, and a present life that could be like His, divine. . . .

What is hidden beneath the offer made by Jesus Christ to men is what we need to see. Christ was a revelation of God. This revelation was nothing short of revolutionary; it burst upon the world like some new sun or planet. No human mind had ever clearly seen the possibility of this stooping down of Godhead, this love of God for man. In itself the Incarnation is the most astounding proof of the value of human nature. Of all possible natures, God selected that of man for espousal. Had His predilection stopped at that, no other proof were needed. But the downward descent of God's love was not exhausted by the Incarnation; Redemption was the end and aim of Christ's appearance on earth. On Calvary Christ becomes the intermediary between the distant Divinity and man's nothingness aggravated by his sinfulness. . . .

Christianity does not shut its eyes to the reality of human life, its inner tension, the conflict of good and evil, of flesh and spirit, of self and others, the intermeddling of fate and fortune, the cruelty of pain and suffering, but that Christ should have died for men, that for all eternity He will be a God-Man bearing upon Him the marks of His victory, that finally He will gather His elect around Him, must embolden us to meet life with an optimism that accepts the Cross as the power and wisdom of God.

THE Catholic doctrine of Merit, laid down by the Council of Trent, is that every good work, done in the state of grace, is rewarded by God with a title to an increase of happiness in heaven. God is the Great Employer, and He pays for every human deed of goodness, done by any servant and child of His in grace.

THE REV. JOSEPH RICKABY, S.J.

EVERY STEP IN GOD'S PATH
LEADS TO HEAVEN

THE REV. EDWARD F. GARESCHÉ, S.J.

THERE is not a step we take along the paths of God's service in our life journey, but brings us nearer to heaven. There is no single little act of goodness, but sets us just so much forward in the road of supernatural merit that leads to the gates of that dwelling of delight. Time, so relentless in his flight, carrying us forward so swiftly, is only hurrying us toward eternal joy and peace and glory. If God permits us sometimes to be severely tried, tempted, cast down, beset with sorrows, it is because these hard paths lead to heaven.

Courage and strength and cheer will come to us if we learn the secret of the saints, looking forward, with humble confidence to our unending home.

Incomparably greater than the passing solace of looking forward to better days in this world, is the deep consolation of anticipating that peace which will never end. . . .

There is an immense consolation, amid the sufferings and anxieties of this life, in the thought of eternity. The swift stroke of death brings to those who are friends of God a sudden peace. From the whirling shadow of time, from the weariness of body and the vexation of soul that plague them here, they come suddenly into a bath of peace and rest.

O ETERNITY towards which we go! We do not walk towards thee, ordinarily, by leaps or by heroic strides, but
rather by tiny steps, made longer by our hopes.

THE REV. ANTONIN SERTILLANGES,
O.P.

"THE ROAD IS CLEAR"

THE REV. WILLIAM LAWSON, S.J.

WHAT you notice about all the great men and women in
the Church—apostles, missionaries, the founders of religious orders, the builders of churches and parishes, the
makers of Catholic families—is that they all know where
they are going. . . . Every member of the Church has
the knowledge, included in his knowledge of God and
of his own nature, that his life must go from the point
of time and space where it begins to eternal life. There
are many Catholics who seem to be off their course, but
at least they know that they have a course, and they know
when they are off it. . . .

What is the difference in equipment between the
apostles and ourselves? Essentially, there is no difference.
At the end of our road, Our Lord is waiting. But from
where we are now in space and time we have to reach
him. The road is clear, however difficult it may be: and
the one requirement for keeping to the road is that we
should have in us the goodness which Our Lord has given
us in baptism and through the Sacraments and the Mass.
Prudence then, for us, is to have the purpose of our
life clear in mind and decided upon in will, and to be

322

supernatural strategists and tacticians in achieving our purpose.

WE MUST not think of death as a great gulf fixed between earth and eternity, between life here and life hereafter. For the Christian, death is but a passage, the passing from an imperfect supernatural life to its full perfection. . . . Death is not then a break, a rough and complex rupture, separating two forms of existence which no ties can ever bind together again; it is an open door, opening on to a wider, fuller and more perfect life.

THE REV. Y. E. MASSON, O.P.

"GOD'S MOST BEAUTIFUL ANGEL"

CANON P. A. SHEEHAN

GOD's greatest and most beautiful angel, who comes to us so softly, and so gently unweaves the bands of flesh, and touches so quietly that wound that the very touch is an anaesthetic; and gradually weakens and uncoils the springs of existence, so that when at last he touches the last frail thread, it snaps without pain, and the soul sinks into a languor that is a sweet prelude to the eternal rest. Why do men fear it? Is it the inertia of life that will not bear transmission? Or the habit of life that will not bear being broken? Or the dread of

The undiscovered country, from whose bourn
No traveler returns?

Or a foolish fear, as of children who see spectres everywhere, and will not walk on unknown land, lest unseen terrors should leap forth to paralyze or appal? . . .

Reason argues against the fear of death and discountenances it. Religion laughs at it: "O death, where is thy sting? O grave, where is thy victory?" And yet, there seems to be but little use in arguing against it. Foolish men, who know so little, and do so much evil with that little knowledge, call it the "King of Terrors," as if we did not know . . . that there is no passion that cannot conquer Death. "Revenge triumphs over it; love slights it; honor aspireth to it; grief flieth to it; fear preoccupateth it; nay, Seneca adds niceness and satiety. Think how often thou has done the self-same things. It is not the strong man, and the miserable man, but, even the weary man can wish to die"—that is, weary of doing the same thing over and over again.

Perhaps, outside the magnificent hopes and promises of religion, there is no greater, there is no sweeter anodyne of Death than the reflection: It is the Law! Birth, Reproduction, Death,—this is the programme of all things, sentient and insensible, spiritual and material; it is the unalterable decree in every kingdom, animal, vegetable, mineral. It is even the necessary law, if the universe is to continue. Tithonus was wretched, because immortal. He was placed outside the pale of law, and hence, he craved Death. All must go. The type and species alone remain; and these too must change in form in order to be permanent in reality. . . .

And whither all things go, we too are tending. Borne

along on the river of Life, now fast, now slow, now glid-
ing smoothly, and anon tossed hither and thither on the
surface of ruffled and angry waters, there is no pause, no
stay, no hiding under shady banks, no retreating to forgotten and darkened coverts. The stream of humanity
moves ever onward to the great gulf, and we are borne
with it. Let us not repine, nor fret at the inevitable. We
are going the way of emperors and conquerors.

IN THE perfect happiness of heaven nothing more will remain to be desired; in the full enjoyment of God man will
obtain whatever he has desired in other things. *Who fills
thy desire with good things.* (Ps. cii. 5, Vulgate.) The desire is stilled: the desire not only for God, but also what
lies at the heart of all other desires. Therefore the joy of
the blessed is perfectly complete, and more than complete,
indeed over-full, for there they find more than is enough
for desire. *It has not entered into the heart of man what
God hath prepared for those that love him.* (I Cor. ii. 9.)
Good measure, and flowing over. (Luke vi. 38.) Nevertheless, because no creature is capable of joy such as God's,
the text says, not that man grasps this joy, but that he
enters into it: *Enter thou into the joy of the Lord.* (Matt.
xxv. 21.)

ST. THOMAS AQUINAS

SPIRITUAL SECURITY

THE REV. VINCENT P. MC CORRY, S. J.

CHRIST our Lord . . . spoke of entry into heaven as the beginning of a true and vigorous life, as the possession of a kingdom, as a sharing in the infinite, divine joy, as a paradise of happiness, as an intimate union with Himself, as a final and ecstatic coming home. All these make rich and stirring images. He wanted us to *want* heaven, which is another way of saying that God wants to be wanted and loves to be loved. Heaven must be something far more exciting and soul-satisfying than a gray alternative to the everlasting bonfire.

Assuming for a moment that heaven implies some sort of happiness, let us rather begin by noting that eternal happiness, being eternal, means permanence. Permanence in joy represents, of course, one of the deepest desires of the human heart. We are all haunted by a very real dread of endings. Every human joy is flawed and streaked by the fear, which becomes a suspicion which swells into a monstrous certainty, that this cannot last, that a change must ensue, that present happiness waxes only to wane. . . . Stand as we will in the flashing sunlight of human joy, we always cast a shadow. That shadow is the deep, human sense of impermanence. When, however, we shall stand in the full noonday blaze of Eternal Light, there will be no shadow. For the first time our joy will be absolutely permanent and immutable. It will be exactly as our Savior promised: "Your hearts will be glad; and your gladness will be one which nobody can take away from you" (John 16:22). Our Lord knew the human heart: He knew that our joy, in order to be full, must be permanent. Heaven is joy without end or alteration.

Eternal salvation imparts something even broader and deeper than permanence in joy. It means absolute security, and so answers another profound yearning of the heart. . . . Heaven implies something else which many people need very badly. Heaven means rest. . . . Finally, and as we might have said at the outset, heaven means happiness. It means positive happiness, total happiness, unmarred happiness. That is to say, heaven means the perfect satisfaction of the ultimate craving of the human heart.

Come to Me all you who labor. Why do we all labor if it is not because we are mortal men, weak and infirm, carrying earthen vessels, with which our fellow-men come into painful collision? . . . What then do the words signify, *Come to Me all you who labor,* if not, "Come to Me that you may not labor?"

ST. AUGUSTINE

THE LAST RITES

THE REV. J. P. LE BUFFE, S. J.

THOUGH through most of our life in this passing world the sweet obligation of visiting falls on us, the day comes when Christ must return the call. The deadening weight of unremitting work, or the sharp frictioning of anxious care, or the noiseless rub of the fleeting years has laid us captive on our bed of pain. No longer may we hurry down the street and enter, without knocking, the home of our Friend. Those portals are still open as they were yesterday and the day before, but not for us to pass through them, only to let our Friend hasten thence to us.

Quickly will the good Lord Jesus come, if we but call Him to us; yes, and unbidden, too, will He hurry to our side when He knows we need His presence. Borne on the breast of His consecrated priest, through the crowded thoroughfares and silent streets, in sunshine or in rain, in the darkness or in the light, He will seek us in our homes, and no earthly friend will whisper such words of cheer as will fall from the lips of our gentle Master.

That sickness may be one from which we shall rise again, and then our good Master, while cheering our weakened hearts, will take us back over the years, and teach us the lessons that none know too well. He will tell us the old, old truths, that the world is but a passing show, and the loudest praise of men is but "a dying echo from a falling wall"; that the things of time cannot be balanced against eternity. Thus will He speak, that, when we are well once more, we may not stray far from His side, or lose full sight of the eternal shore.

But if that sickness be our last and the hand of death lie tighteningly on our own, who can tell the music of His voice when He comes to call us home? In the years of long ago our child's heart beat fast and tears jeweled our happy cheeks, as we rushed to mother's arms, welcoming us home. But was the best of mother's accents like to His? The voices of the world may have been loud before He came, and the calls of earthly friends to stay with them may have wrung our soul, but all is stilled now He is here. Our best Friend is come to take us home.

THE sacrament of communion is given me for the purpose of strength that springs from the nearness of His presence, and never is that Presence more required than when I go out alone from life into the doors of death. For me, then, the vision of faith will light up that valley, that I may see upon the hill the crowded forms of those who come to bid me enter into joy. I die, indeed, alone, but only that I may pass into the company of the elect of God. The prayers that are said about the bed of death repeat the thought that there is a welcome beyond, and that I shall not be left lonely in the dread moment when most I need the assistance of others, their comradeship, their supporting affection. Freely, then, I shall face whatever befalls, conscious of that hand held in mine, trusting in His own blessed words that I shall not be left forsaken, but that to the end of the world He shall be with me always.

THE REV. BEDE JARRETT, O.P.

GOD SEARCHES FOR THE GOOD IN US

THE REV. R. H. J. STEUART, S.J.

GOD does not judge me that He may punish but that He may reward me: He is not looking for the evil in me but for the good: and if it terrifies me to think that in that hour I shall find myself to be so much worse than ever I thought, it should comfort me by a far better title to think instead how much better, perhaps, I shall find myself to have been than ever I had dared to imagine. For I shall see myself then as God sees me—that is, I shall look at myself in the manner that God looks at me, in a light enkindled of His love of me which will throw first into the foreground of all that love desires to see in me, my good, His good, Himself.

I shall make far less mistake about it and run far less risk of affecting the true balance of my vision of the Judge if I think of Him as delving, so to say, into my life in eager search of whatever He can commend and reward, be it ever so little gold among a very great deal of dross. . . .

God's judgment about me, therefore, will be the truth about me: and the measure of the truth about me will be the measure of the good that is found in me: and not until the Judgment, when I shall know "even as I am known," shall I know what that is. But in the meantime I have warrant for it that I shall know my Judge the better the more I think of Him as my Advocate.

DEATH does no more than alter the conditions under which our spirit is called to enjoy the eternal; linked to this we have nothing to fear. Heaven opens to receive our soul long before the tomb opens to receive our body. When death is spoken of as a tearing asunder, we forget that it tears especially the veil of appearances and of deceptions which conceal from our view the depth of reality and of others and ourselves. Beyond that, it tears only what would tear even without it; it touches only what time destroys. On the other hand, it binds us to what is enduring; it even renders us independent of its own fleeting power.

THE REV. ANTONIN SERTILLANGES, O.P.

THE SOLACE OF THE SOULS
IN PURGATORY

ABBÉ ALBERT MICHEL

THE souls in Purgatory . . . together with their unspeakable suffering . . . experience an indescribable joy.

They rejoice in the certainty of salvation, and as the prayer of the Mass expresses it, sleep the sleep of peace. Their time of waiting is not shadowed by any uncertainty or fear. . . .

Another of their joys arises from their impeccability, for, with that unchangeableness that characterizes the soul's action in the next life, they now cleave to their last true end, God. He is the only object of their desires and their aspirations. Their attachment to Him is so strong, that they detest whatever could separate them from Him, and cling to everything that can increase their knowledge and love of Him. And, therefore, they welcome and love their sufferings because they know that through them they are purified and brought nearer to God. . . .

The joys of Purgatory have their source in the love of God that burns in the holy souls. As soon as they enter Purgatory they are set on fire by so great a love that, in St. Thomas' opinion, any venial sin is instantly washed away. . . . The love of God gives to the soul a contentment beyond expression.

WHEN we pray, *Our Father who art in Heaven,* we do not intend to say that God is not on earth, but rather that we, as His children, belong with Him to Heaven, that we are a heavenly race, whose Father thrones in the heavens, that a heavenly seed has been sown in us, which is to spring up into a heavenly life.

ST. PETER CHRYSOLOGUS

THE BEATIFIC VISION

DOM ANSCAR VONIER, O.S.B.

THE vision of God is the central joy of Heaven. It is not merely a theological opinion that the spirit of the saved will see God for ever, it is a matter of Catholic Faith. . . .

The main idea conveyed by the term vision is this: it is God, as He is in Himself, Who is seen by the mind; it is not a mere image of Him, a mere idea of Him, however clear; it is Himself. It is a direct, unintercepted gazing on God's beauty. . . .

In Beatific Vision, according to the profound doctrine of St. Thomas, God Himself becomes the idea which is in the mind of the elect. All our cognitions are ideas, of more or less extent and clearness, that come to our mind through a hundred channels. We see clearly that the idea of a thing is not the thing itself; for the thing is outside me, whilst the idea is in my mind, and makes of my mind, from an unknowing mind, a knowing mind.

Now, says our great master, in Beatific Vision there is no such idea of God, as distinct from God, to stand for God in my mind. God's very nature is the idea. In fact God has to be the idea, for nothing could ever do duty for God Himself in my mind. . . .

The eternal hills rise higher and higher, and the

332

thoughts of God on their summits are getting purer and purer; but they are mere thoughts of God, they are not God yet. They are mere ideas of God. These thoughts are so high indeed that if one of them were communicated to us mortals, we should feel as if we have been lifted bodily to the Throne of God; yet even on those high summits, the created mind has not met with God yet. In Beatific Vision, God Himself is the idea, God Himself is in the mind; and here we have the radical difference between Beatific Vision and every other kind of divine knowledge, however sublime. . . .

The vision of God, enjoyed by the Blessed, is the vision of the totality of God. . . .

By this we mean that the Blessed behold intellectually not only all and every one of God's attributes, but also behold the Trinity of God: in one word, every elect beholds the infinity of God, though he does not behold that infinity with infinite intellectual keenness.

HAVE pity upon every man, Lord, in that hour when he has finished his tasks and stands before Thee like a child whose hands are being examined.

PAUL CLAUDEL

AT THE day of judgment it shall not be asked of us what we have read, but what we have done; nor how well we have said, but how religiously we have lived.

THOMAS À KEMPIS

Index of Authors

WITH SOURCES

Adam, Karl (1876–), *The Spirit of Catholicism*, trans. by Dom Justin McCann, O.S.B., *120*

Alphonsus de' Liguori, St. (1696–1787), *Preparation for Death*, ed. by Rev. Eugene Grimm, *7, 147, 211, 270, 294*

Ambrose, St. (340?–397), *On Penance*, *128*

Anonymous, *The Treasures of the Mass*, compiled from various sources by Benedictine Convent of Perpetual Adoration, Clyde, Mo., *185, 189, 192*

Anonymous, *A Hundred Readings*, compiled for and published by Catholic Truth Society, London, England, 1908, *21, 36, 37, 42, 249*

Aquinas, St. Thomas (ca. 1225–1274), *Philosophical Texts of*, sel. and ed. by Thomas Gilby, O.P.:

Summa Theologica, 1a–2 ae. ii.4, *276*

Summa Theologica, 2a–2ae. XXI, iii.3, *325*

Quoted in Y. E. Masson's, O.P., *The Christian Life and the Spiritual Life*, from *Summa*

Theologica, 11a, I 11a1. qu. 24, a.3, ad. 2 m., *140*

Arintero, John Gonzalez (1860–1928), *The Mystical Evolution in the Development and Vitality of the Church*, trans. by Jordan Aumann, O.P., 2 vols., Vol. 1, *147*

Augustine, St. (354–430), In *Library of Nicene Letters*, ed. by E. B. Pusey:

Ennaration on Psalms, Serm. 1, 6, *11*

Ennaration on Psalms, CXXX-VII, 13, *14*

Ennaration on Psalms, LX, 4, *44*

Ennaration on Psalms, XCVII, 3, *177*

Ennaration on Psalms, CXLVIII, 2, *240*

Ennaration on Psalms, CXXX, I, *242*

In Joannis Evangelium tractatus, XXIII, 6, *35*

Sermones (de Scripturio Novi Testamenti), LXXXI, 6, *36*

In *Leaves From St. Augustine*, sel. and trans. by Mary H. Allies:

(1)